GRAMMAR In Plain English

Third Edition

by
Harriet Diamond, M.A.
President
DIAMOND ASSOCIATES
Multi-Faceted Training and Development
Westfield, New Jersey

and

Phyllis Dutwin, M.A.
President
DUTWIN ASSOCIATES
Training and Development Programs
Wickford, Rhode Island

BARRON'S EDUCATIONAL SERIES, INC.

This book is dedicated to the many GED students who were our very personal inspiration.

Pertinent directions are reprinted from *The Official Teacher's Guide to the Tests of General Educational Development,* with permission from the American Council on Education.

Portion of material adapted from Russell Baker's "Backwards Wheels the Mind," *The New York Times,* July 1, 1973.

Quote from Richard Bach's *Jonathan Livingston Seagull.*

Portions of material throughout this book adapted from DIAMOND ASSOCIATES' *Business Writing Worth Reading.*

Portions of material throughout this book adapted from *English the Easy Way* by Harriet Diamond and Phyllis Dutwin.

All inquiries should be addressed to:
Barron's Educational Series, Inc.
250 Wireless Boulevard
Hauppauge, New York 11788

Library of Congress Catalog Card No. 96-41601
International Standard Book No. 0-8120-9648-7

Library of Congress Cataloging-in-Publication Data

Diamond, Harriet.
Grammar in Plain English / by Harriet Diamond and Phyllis Dutwin. — 3rd ed.
p. cm.
ISBN 0-8120-9648-7
1. English language—Grammar. 2. English language—Problems, exercises, etc. I. Dutwin, Phyllis. II. Title.
PE1112.D48 1996
428.2—dc20 96-41601
CIP

PRINTED IN THE UNITED STATES OF AMERICA

10 9

TABLE OF CONTENTS

Acknowledgments

We wish to express our appreciation to Walter Hauck, former director of the New Jersey State Department of Education's Office of High School Completion, for his encouragement and assistance.

Thanks to Harry Linkin, former director of Adult and Continuing Education at the Union County Regional Adult School, to Wayne Hemingway, former director of the High School Equivalency Program, and to Ted Gnagey, former director of Adult Education at the South Orange-Maplewood Adult School, for providing the teaching atmospheres that allowed us to work creatively and develop our material.

Finally, we would like to thank our families for their patience and encouragement with special thanks to Ellen Diamond for her excellent contributions to the second and third editions.

Introduction

In traditional grammar programs, students are often baffled by the necessity of memorizing numerous definitions of grammatical terminology, none of which has any practical meaning in terms of day-to-day speech and writing. The confusion that results is often detrimental; the student's frustration ultimately overcomes his or her desire to learn.

Grammar—In Plain English is designed to encourage, not frustrate, the student. Written specifically for students who are preparing for the Writing Skills test, Parts I and II, of the Tests of General Educational Development (GED), *Grammar—In Plain English* also serves as an invaluable tool for all English language improvement programs.

The book's main feature is a common-sense approach to language study. Recognizing that traditional grammar is not included in the GED test, *Grammar—In Plain English* emphasizes language structure. This approach is based on the belief that adult students have a fund of knowledge regarding the structure of the English language. *Grammar—In Plain English* builds upon this structure. Thus, the main purpose of this format is to motivate by showing how much the student already knows about the language.

Grammar—In Plain English builds upon the student's basic understanding in an organized way. Beginning with the basic sentence pattern (performer-action) the book continues until all essential elements are introduced. Ample practice material follows each newly introduced concept. Because of the manner of presentation of the instructional material, *Grammar—In Plain English* lends itself easily either to group or individualized classroom instruction or to independent study.

Since not all learners have the same needs, the authors have included in this new edition a reference section called *Guide to Grammatical Terms*. The addition recognizes that some students are ready to tackle more traditional terminology and grammatical concepts. The *Guide* is divided into sections that follow the sequence of the book and provides additional terms and concepts, as needed, plus examples of their use.

This publication covers all areas of the GED Writing Skills test, Parts I and II, an examination that tests the following skills:

Part I		*Percentage of Questions*
	Sentence Structure	35
	Usage	35
	Mechanics (spelling, punctuation, capitalization)	30
	Total	100

As you will note, formal grammatical terminology is not tested on the GED. Rather, understanding of word functions and relationships is stressed.

Part II

Part II of the GED Writing Skills test assesses examinees' actual writing ability. The test provides a single topic on which examinees must write an opinion or explanation. Topics will identify an issue or situation about which adults would have general knowledge; specialized knowledge is not required.

During the 45 minutes permitted for this section of the test, examinees are encouraged first to plan their responses. Either space in the answer booklet or scrap paper will be available for relevant notes and outlines. Writing must demonstrate organization, support, clarity, and correctness of expression.

Effective Use of This Book

Because *Grammar—In Plain English* is a cumulative study, we recommend beginning with Chapter 1 and continuing consecutively. Two chapters, "Spelling" and "Word Usage," do not fit into the consecutive pattern of the book. Spelling rules can be summarized in one chapter, but they cannot be learned in one lesson. The same is true of word usage. The authors, therefore, recommend that students begin studying these chapters early in their program and continue on a regular basis.

Guard against skimming over instructional material. Skipping instructional material in order to complete practices quickly results in unnecessary errors and time lost. Before you attempt a Cumulative Review, the authors recommend reviewing the major concepts presented in the chapters that precede it.

The Writing Skills, Part I section of the GED test consists of paragraphs with numbered sentences and questions that refer to these sentences. The following items represent the types of questions you will encounter on the test.

1. Sentence 3: **Domestic violence is an issue of major concern of women and their families because women and children are the victims.**

   Which of the following is the best way to write the underlined portion of this sentence? If you think the original is the best way, choose option (1).

   (1) their families because
   (2) their families, it is because
   (3) their families. Because
   (4) their families; because
   (5) their families, and

2. Sentence 1: **My brother, he changes jobs at least twice a year.**

   What correction should be made to this sentence?

(1) remove the comma after brother
(2) remove , he
(3) change changes to change
(4) move at least to the end of the sentence
(5) replace a with each

3. Sentence 4: **Telephone technology is changing rapidly and with it the way we live our lives.**

If you rewrote sentence 4 beginning with

Our lives are being changed rapidly

the next word should be

(1) so
(2) and
(3) by
(4) that
(5) since

4. Sentences 6 and 7: **When you present your proposal to Mr. Powers, be firm and forceful. Remember to listen carefully and respond to his concerns.**

The most effective combination of sentences 6 and 7 would include which of the following groups of words?

(1) forceful, so remember
(2) forceful. Always remembering
(3) forceful, but remember
(4) forceful, remember
(5) forcefull, but remember

ANSWER KEY

1. (1)	3.(3)
2. (4)	4.(3)

Consistent use of the *Answer Key* is essential to proper study. The authors recommend that students check each practice exercise with the *Answer Key* before going on to the next section. By checking answers after each exercise, students can avoid repeating errors. Cumulative Reviews should be considered tests and should be taken in their entirety before checking answers. Students should note the kinds of errors made in Cumulative Reviews (these answers have been keyed to the applicable review chapters) and return to these appropriate chapters for reinforcement of the correct concepts.

Test-Taking Tips

1. **FOLLOW DIRECTIONS.** Read directions carefully and completely before beginning each section. Although directions may seem the same, they do vary for different types of questions.

2. **ANSWER ALL QUESTIONS.** Take a guess even if you don't know the answer.

3. **READ THE ENTIRE QUESTION AND ALL THE CHOICES** before selecting an answer.

4. **MARK THE ANSWER CAREFULLY ON THE ANSWER SHEET.** The GED answer sheet requires you to mark a numbered space. Be sure you are blackening the correct space. A marked answer sheet would look like this:

   ① ● ③ ④ ⑤

5. **SELECT THE BEST ANSWER FROM THE ANSWERS GIVEN.** You may think that the correct answer has not been included among the choices, but you are limited to those choices given.

6. **RECORD ONLY ONE ANSWER FOR EACH QUESTION.** If you blacken two spaces for one question, your answer will be marked wrong.

7. **PLAN YOUR ESSAY BEFORE STARTING TO WRITE IT.**
   - Jot down main ideas.
   - Follow with supporting details.
   - Develop strong opening and concluding sentences.

8. **EDIT YOUR ESSAY.**
   - Read through for good organization.
   - Check sentence structure.
   - Check grammar, spelling, punctuation.

1.

The Simplest Complete Thought

"Twas brillig and the slithy toves
 Did gyre and gimble in the wabe;
All mimsy were the borogroves,
 And the mome raths outgrabe.

"Beware the Jabberwock, my son!
 The jaws that bite, the claws that catch!
Beware the Jubjub bird, and shun
 The frumious Bandersnatch!"

—Lewis Carroll
"Jabberwocky"

A Word With You . . .

"Jabberwocky," the most famous nonsense poem ever written, can be enjoyed on several levels. Literary detectives have tried to find hidden meanings in the made up words, while others have been amused by the poet's cleverness with sounds and rhythms.

Although Lewis Carroll never heard of "the flink glopped," it is a phrase he might have approved of—especially in the way it is used in the chapter you are about to read.

What You've Always Known . . .

The flink glopped.

What is the above sentence about? What action is taking place in this sentence? Who is performing this action? You are able to understand the nonsense sentence because you are familiar with that sentence pattern: a person or thing performing an action.

PERFORMER ACTION

(The) flink glopped.

You frequently see it written, and you hear it spoken.

Another clue in this sentence is a clue to time. Is the action past, present, or future? What was the clue? Yes, the *-ed* ending is the clue to time. The action occurred in the past.

Notice the word endings in the following sentences:

> The flink glops.
>
> Two flinks glop.

When the performer *(flink)* is *singular*, an s is added to the present action. When the performer *(flinks)* is *plural* (more than one), no s is added to the present action.

This simple pattern may have *more than one performer:*

> The *flink and his brother glop.*

There may be one performer and *more than one action:*

> The *flink glops and glarks.*

There may also be *more than one performer and more than one action:*

> The *flink and his brother glop and glark.*

Now, let's examine some real sentences that use the same pattern: a person or thing performing an action and the action. As you read the following sentences, think about who or what is performing the action, what the action is, and when the action occurs (present, past, or future). Next, write in the spaces provided the performer, the action, and the time. The first sentence is done for you.

	PERFORMER	ACTION	*present past future* TIME
1. The law student completed the difficult exam.	student	completed	past
2. Mrs. Smith sings in the church choir each Sunday.			
3. The plane raced across the sky.			
4. They will speak at the November meeting.			
5. The interviewer listened attentively.			

	PERFORMER	ACTION	TIME (*present / past / future*)
6. A cashier always counts the change.			
7. Star Cleaners picks up and delivers cleaning.			
8. The woman and her children crossed the street.			
9. The gardener rakes the leaves and cuts the grass.			
10. Diane and Joe dined at the tavern and attended the theater.			

PRACTICE I

Directions: Complete the pattern in each of the following sentences by adding either the person or thing performing the action or the action.

1. The children ______________ into the street.
2. ______________ barked at the mailman.
3. ______________ will signal at the light.
4. The choir ______________ last Sunday.
5. ______________ hesitated in the doorway.

PRACTICE II

Directions: Draw a line from the people or things in the left column to the actions in the right column to make complete sentences.

PERFORMERS	ACTIONS
The jury	travel.
An accident	will attend.
A salesman and his assistant	occurred.
A motorcycle	convened and concurred.
We	backfires.

PRACTICE III

Directions: Write three sentences of your own using the sentence pattern you have just studied: a person or thing performing an action.

PERFORMER ACTION

1. Susan walked her Dog
2. The mail man Drove up the Street
3. The Choir Sang in Church on Sunday

PRACTICE IV

Directions: In each of the following sentences one word is underlined. If the underlined word is the person or thing performing the action, blacken circle 1. If the underlined word is the action word, blacken circle 2.

1. The *manager* shouted at the salesman. ① ②
2. A large delivery *truck* approached the intersection. ① ②
3. We *celebrated* her graduation. ① ②
4. The *mayor* proclaimed a clean-up week. ① ②
5. The members *contributed* large sums of money. ① ②
6. The huge *machine* sputtered menacingly. ① ②
7. A committee *will convene* within the week. ① ②
8. The *union* struck after much negotiation. ① ②
9. The checkbook *balances* for the first time. ① ②
10. A soprano *will sing* this part of the opera. ① ②

PRACTICE V

Directions: Blacken circle 1 if a sentence has one performer and one action; blacken circle 2 if a sentence has more than one performer and one action; blacken circle 3 if a sentence has one performer and two actions; blacken circle 4 if a sentence has more than one performer and two actions.

1. This candidate addresses the issues. ① ② ③ ④
2. His opponent evades difficult questions. ① ② ③ ④

3. Meditation relaxes many people. ❶ ② ③ ④
4. Mr. Valdez proposed several good ideas. ❶ ② ③ ④
5. Six team members shouted at the coach. ① ❷ ③ ④
6. Maria and Julia sold their pottery. ① ❷ ③ ④
7. The electrician and his assistant stopped and rested. ① ② ③ ❹
8. The audience cheered and applauded. ① ② ❸ ④
9. Batman always wins. ❶ ② ③ ④
10. I asked a searching question. ❶ ② ③ ④

Recognizing Complete and Incomplete Thoughts

You are ready now to add another element to your understanding of complete thoughts.

Example: When you arrive.

The above sentence has a performer *(you)* and an action *(arrive)*; yet, it is not a complete thought. Because the sentence begins with the word *when*, the thought is not complete as it stands.

Any sentence that begins with words such as *when, after, because, as soon as, before,* or *since* needs to have a completing thought.

Possible thought completions for *When you arrive* are:

a. When you arrive, *relax*.
b. When you arrive, *call me*.
c. When you arrive, *I will leave*.

Example: The tall figure walking hurriedly through the park.

The above sentence has a performer *(figure)*, but the action *(walking)* is incomplete. It would be correct to say the figure *was walking* or the figure *is walking*.

Possible thought completions for *The tall figure walking hurriedly through the park* are:

a. The tall figure *is walking hurriedly through the park*.

b. The tall figure *was walking hurriedly through the park.*

c. The tall figure *walked hurriedly through the park.*

PRACTICE VI

Directions: Blacken the circle containing the number that corresponds to the number of the incomplete sentence in each group. If there is no error, blacken circle number 5.

1. (1) After McCarthy's defeat, he retired from public office. ① ② ③ ④ ⑤
   (2) Bring me a cup of coffee, please.
   (3) When Richard called his office.
   (4) The two truckers arrived at the delivery depot at the same time.
   (5) No error

2. (1) The man in the blue suit and the lady in the tan coat walking. ① ② ③ ④ ⑤
   (2) The legislature meets daily.
   (3) I did not buy enough yarn for the sweater.
   (4) A large delivery truck reached the intersection.
   (5) No error

3. (1) The nervous waitress spilled the coffee in the celebrity's lap. ① ② ③ ④ ⑤
   (2) The fumbling, bumbling clown dancing.
   (3) The county official faced the angry crowd.
   (4) The women in the community organized a boycott against Sam's Market.
   (5) No error

4. (1) A favorite history question involves the causative factors of the Civil War. ① ② ③ ④ ⑤
   (2) Federal spending cuts will cause much discussion.
   (3) The winning pitcher threw a fast ball.

(4) Her considerate husband brought a dozen roses for their anniversary.
(5) No error

5. (1) The students studied and reviewed. ① ② ③ ④ ⑤
(2) Flour, sugar, and three eggs blending.
(3) The book fell suddenly from the shelf.
(4) The mayor proclaimed a clean-up week.
(5) No error

6. (1) Leona working harder than any other lawyer in the firm. ① ② ③ ④ ⑤
(2) A soprano will sing this part in the opera.
(3) Robert and Chico prepare the finest paella.
(4) The candidate spoke the truth.
(5) No error

7. (1) The man threw away the garbage. ① ② ③ ④ ⑤
(2) The soldiers walked quietly.
(3) When I have finished dusting and vacuuming and washing, I will relax.
(4) The mayor commended the members of the local rescue squad.
(5) No error

PRACTICE VII

Directions: The following items are based on paragraphs that contain numbered sentences. Some of these sentences are incomplete. Read the paragraph and answer the items based on it. Choose the one best answer to each item.

Items 1 and 2 refer to the following paragraph.

(1) Jan's specialty item business has outgrown her home-based office. (2) She is looking to rent office space. (3) Not on the second floor. (4) Room to expand. (5) Jan hopes to move into an office in March.

1. Sentence 3: **Not on the second floor.**

Which of the following is the best way to write this sentence?

(1) Only on the first floor. ① ② ③ ④ ⑤

(2) Jan does not want to climb stairs so not on the second floor.

(3) Not on the second floor because of stairs.

(4) Jan does not want a second-floor office.

(5) Not an office on the second floor.

2. Sentence 4: **Room to expand.**

Which of the following is the best way to write this sentence?

(1) Needs room to expand. ① ② ③ ④ ⑤

(2) Plans to expand.

(3) She wants an office with room to expand.

(4) She wants an expanding room.

(5) If she needs to expand.

<u>Items 3 and 4</u> refer to the following paragraph.

(1) Many supermarket chains throughout the country now use plastic instead of paper bags. (2) A definite problem here. (3) While plastic bags may be easier to store and to carry. (4) Plastic is not usually biodegradable or recyclable. (5) Paper bags are more environmentally sound.

3. Sentence 2: **A definite problem here.**

Which of the following is the best way to write this sentence?

(1) Which is a definite problem here. ① ② ③ ④ ⑤

(2) This change is causing problems.

(3) Serious problems here.

(4) Causing problems here.

(5) A problem here because of this change.

4. Sentence 3: **While plastic bags may be easier to store and to carry.**

Which of the following is the best way to write this sentence?

(1) While plastic bags may be easier to store, and to carry. ① ② ③ ④ ⑤

(2) While plastic bags may be easier to store and carry, they are not easier to discard.

(3) While plastic bags are not easier to discard.

(4) While plastic bags may be easier to store and carry so are paper bags.

(5) While plastic bags may be easier to store and carry environmentalists claim they are a major problem when it comes to disposing of them since they are not like paper in the way they break down so easy isn't best.

Action Words: Special Problems

Many action words undergo simple changes to show changes in time. *For example:*

PRESENT	PAST	ACTION WORDS USED WITH HELPING WORDS SUCH AS HAS, HAD, HAVE, IS, ETC.
kick	kicked	kicked
plan	planned	planned
cheer	cheered	cheered

The simplest change is the addition of an *-ed* ending.

1. I *kick* the ball 200 yards each time.
2. The tenants' association *planned* a victory party.
3. The overzealous Viking fans *had cheered* before they realized that the Eagle quarterback was really injured.

Many action words use entirely different forms to show these same time changes. *For example:*

PRESENT	PAST	ACTION WORDS USED WITH HELPING WORDS SUCH AS HAS, HAD, HAVE, IS, ETC.
break	broke	broken

1. Anna never *breaks* a promise.
2. Rosemary *broke* several promises to Anna.
3. Rosemary *has broken* her last promise.

Following is a list of commonly used action words that change their forms to show time changes.

PRESENT	PAST	ACTION WORDS USED WITH HELPING WORDS SUCH AS HAS, HAD, HAVE, IS, ETC.
begin	began	begun
blow	blew	blown
break	broke	broken
bring	brought	brought
build	built	built
burst	burst	burst
choose	chose	chosen
dive	dived or dove	dived
do	did	done
draw	drew	drawn
drink	drank	drunk
drive	drove	driven
eat	ate	eaten
fall	fell	fallen
flee	fled	fled
fly	flew	flown
forbid	forbade	forbidden
freeze	froze	frozen
get	got	gotten or got
give	gave	given
go	went	gone
grow	grew	grown
have, has	had	had
know	knew	known
lay (place)	laid	laid
lead	led	led
leave (depart)	left	left
lie (recline)	lay	lain
pay	paid	paid
raise (elevate)	raised	raised
ride	rode	ridden
ring	rang	rung
rise (ascend)	rose	risen
run	ran	run
see	saw	seen
shake	shook	shaken
shine	shone, shined	shone, shined

PRESENT	PAST	ACTION WORDS USED WITH HELPING WORDS SUCH AS HAS, HAD, HAVE, IS, ETC.
shoot	shot	shot
shrink	shrank, shrunk	shrunk
sing	sang	sung
sit	sat	sat
slay	slew	slain
speak	spoke	spoken
spring	sprang	sprung
steal	stole	stolen
sting	stung	stung
swear	swore	sworn
swim	swam	swum
swing	swung	swung
take	took	taken
tear	tore	torn
throw	threw	thrown
wake	waked *or* woke	waked
wear	wore	worn
write	wrote	written

PRACTICE VIII

Directions: Choose one of the action words in the parentheses to finish each sentence. Find the correct form of the word in the list above.

1. The employee entered the correct code and the gate (rose, rise). (Hint: Choose the word that means *goes up,* or *ascends*.)
2. I bought new running shoes because the heels had (worn, wore) down in the old ones.
3. If we had (knew, known) how long the movie was, we wouldn't have rented it.
4. The laundry had (shrinked, shrunk) my only good shirt just before the awards dinner.
5. The children always have (lain, laid) the money on the counter when they arrived, but today it was not there. (Hint: Choose the word that means *to place*.)

PRACTICE IX

Directions: Which is the best way to write the underlined portion of each sentence? If you think the original is the best way, choose option (1).

1. I have rang her doorbell several times today.
   (1) have rang ① ② ③ ④ ⑤
   (2) have rung
   (3) am ringing
   (4) rung
   (5) ring

2. Last year, Marlene lead the church choir.
   (1) lead ① ② ③ ④ ⑤
   (2) had lead
   (3) had led
   (4) led
   (5) has led

3. The plaintiff swore to tell the truth.
   (1) swore ① ② ③ ④ ⑤
   (2) sweared
   (3) had sweared
   (4) has sweared
   (5) sworn

4. The opinionated Mr. Dobbs never had ran for office himself.
   (1) never had ran ① ② ③ ④ ⑤
   (2) never has ran
   (3) never had run
   (4) never run
   (5) has never ran

5. Mother had threw out my favorite old sneakers before I could stop her.
   (1) had threw ① ② ③ ④ ⑤

(2) throwed
(3) had thrown
(4) thrown
(5) throws

6. I had not wrote before the summer ended.
(1) had not wrote ① ② ③ ④ ⑤
(2) have not wrote
(3) did not written
(4) had not written
(5) have not written

PRACTICE X

Directions: Blacken the circle that corresponds to the number of the sentence with the incorrect action word in each group. If there is no error, blacken number 5.

1. (1) Tulips reappear and grow well in that spot each year. ① ② ③ ④ ⑤
(2) I have ran into her at the water cooler more than once.
(3) After we had set the new furniture in place, the room looked complete.
(4) Having ridden for hours, the sightseers were ready to check into a motel.
(5) No error

2. (1) Angela led the tour of the plant. ① ② ③ ④ ⑤
(2) Last year, Marlene choose our vacation week.
(3) I never have chosen the week.
(4) Have you ever led a pony with a screaming child on it?
(5) No error

3. (1) I gave that to Carlo. ① ② ③ ④ ⑤
(2) The defendant gave her statement.
(3) Her grandparents have given her gifts very often.
(4) All of the witnesses have been given instructions.
(5) No error

4. (1) Martina Navratilova has swung many tennis rackets in her time. ① ② ③ ④ ⑤
(2) I, on the other hand, have never swung a tennis racket quite like she did during that decisive game.
(3) I wonder if Joani swings a golf club correctly.
(4) He swinged a tennis racket fairly well.
(5) No error

5. (1) The employee bringed a sick child to daycare. ① ② ③ ④ ⑤
(2) Colonel Adams has run five miles daily for many years.
(3) I have done aerobics for three years.
(4) Mrs. Diaz plans to begin next year.
(5) No error

6. (1) Did you pay Mattie? ① ② ③ ④ ⑤
(2) Arthur paid her twice last month.
(3) I had not been payed before the summer ended.
(4) Mrs. Scott has always written excellent business letters.
(5) No error

7. (1) The cleaning crew had threw out my notes before I returned for them. ① ② ③ ④ ⑤
(2) I wouldn't throw out someone else's notebook without asking first.
(3) I saved those notes from being thrown out several times.
(4) This time, they were thrown out for the last time.
(5) No error

PRACTICE
XI

Directions: The following items are based on a paragraph that contains numbered sentences. Some of the sentences may contain errors in tense. Other sentences are correct as they appear in the paragraph. Read the paragraph and answer the items based on it. Choose the one best answer to each item.

(1) Joe and I place bets on the Superbowl every year. (2) We sat in front of the T.V. with potato chips and soda. (3) Joe never agrees with the referees, who he insisted are blind. (4) I usually think that they are right. (5) Sometimes we argue about a call through the next play.

1. Sentence 2: **We sat in front of the t.v. with potato chips and soda.**

Which of the following is the best way to write this sentence? If you think the original is the best way, choose option (1).

(1) We sat in front of the t.v. with potato chips and soda. ① ② ③ ④ ⑤
(2) We did sit in front of the t.v. with potato chips and soda.
(3) We set in front of the t.v. with potato chips and soda.
(4) We sit in front of the t.v. with potato chips and soda.
(5) We don't sit in front of the t.v. with potato chips and soda.

2. Sentence 3: **Joe never agrees with the referees, who he insisted are blind.**

Which of the following is the best way to write this sentence? If you think the original is the best way, choose option (1).

(1) Joe never agrees with the referees, who he insisted are blind. ① ② ③ ④ ⑤
(2) Joe never agreed with the referees, who he insisted are blind.
(3) Joe never agrees with the referees, who are blind he insists.
(4) Joe never agrees with the referees, who he insists are blind.
(5) Joe never agreed with the referees, who he insists are blind.

REVIEW EXERCISES

PRACTICE XII

Directions: The following items are based on a paragraph that contains numbered sentences. Some of the sentences may contain errors in tense. Some sentences may be incomplete. Other sentences are correct as they appear in the paragraph. Read the paragraph and answer the items based on it. Choose the one best answer to each item.

(1) The guest lecturer nervously approached the microphone. (2) Pausing for a moment after clearing his throat. (3) An eloquent gesture sends his notes

flying. (4) While retrieving his notes, the reddened speaker overturned a water pitcher onto some wiring. (5) He disappears during the resulting blackout.

1. Sentence 2: **Pausing for a moment after clearing his throat.**

   Which of the following is the best way to write this sentence? If you think the original is the best way, choose option (1).

   (1) Pausing for a moment after clearing his throat. ① ② ③ ④ ⑤
   (2) Pausing for a moment after clearing his throat, he then began to speak.
   (3) Pausing for a moment after clearing his throat and beginning to speak.
   (4) Pausing for a moment after clearing his throat and speaking.
   (5) Clearing his throat and pausing for a moment.

2. Sentence 3: **An eloquent gesture sends his notes flying.**

   Which of the following is the best way to write this sentence? If you think the original is the best way, choose option (1).

   (1) An eloquent gesture sends his notes flying. ① ② ③ ④ ⑤
   (2) An eloquent gesture will send his notes flying.
   (3) An eloquent gesture has sent his notes flying.
   (4) An eloquent gesture sent his notes flying.
   (5) An eloquent gesture sending his notes flying.

3. Sentence 5: **He disappears during the resulting blackout.**

   Which of the following is the best way to write this sentence? If you think the original is the best way, choose option (1).

   (1) He disappears during the resulting blackout. ① ② ③ ④ ⑤
   (2) He disappears as a blackout results.
   (3) During the resulting blackout, he disappears.
   (4) He had disappeared during the resulting blackout.
   (5) He disappeared during the resulting blackout.

PRACTICE XIII

Directions: For each topic sentence below, write a four- or five-sentence paragraph. Remember, your first sentence sets the tense; be consistent. All sentences must express complete thoughts. Include details to support your topic sentence. End with a closing sentence.

1. Tina exercises every week.

____
____
____
____
____

2. When he gets a raise, Lester will buy a new car.

____
____
____
____
____

ANSWER KEY

Chapter 1

The Simplest Complete Thought

Page 2.

	PERFORMER	ACTION	TIME
1.	student	completed	past
2.	Mrs. Smith	sings	present
3.	plane	raced	past
4.	they	will speak	future
5.	interviewer	listened	past
6.	cashier	counts	present
7.	Star Cleaners	picks up, delivers	present
8.	woman, children	crossed	past
9.	gardener	rakes, cuts	present
10.	Diane, Joe	dined, attended	past

Practice I *Page 3.*

Answers will vary. *Sample* answers:

1. The children *ran* into the street.
2. *The dog* barked at the mailman.
3. *Henry* will signal at the light.
4. The choir *sang* last Sunday.
5. *Susan* hesitated in the doorway.

Practice II *Page 3.*

1. The jury convened and concurred.
2. An accident occurred.
3. A salesman and his assistant travel.
4. A motorcycle backfires.
5. We will attend.

Practice III *Page 4.*

Answers will vary. *Sample* answers:

1. *John cashed* a check at the bank.
2. The *roses bloomed* early this year.
3. My *mother-in-law calls* every Friday.

Practice IV *Page 4.*

		PERFORMER	ACTION
1.	(1)	manager	
2.	(1)	truck	
3.	(2)		celebrated
4.	(1)	mayor	
5.	(2)		contributed
6.	(1)	machine	
7.	(2)		will convene
8.	(1)	union	
9.	(2)		balances
10.	(2)		will sing

Practice V *Page 4.*

		PERFORMER	ACTION
1.	(1)	candidate	addresses
2.	(1)	opponent	evades
3.	(1)	meditation	relaxes
4.	(1)	Mr. Valdez	proposed
5.	(2)	members	shouted
6.	(2)	Maria and Julia	sold
7.	(4)	electrician and assistant	stopped and rested
8.	(3)	audience	cheered and applauded
9.	(1)	Batman	wins
10.	(1)	I	asked

Practice VI *Page 6.*

Possible Corrections:

1. (3) a. When Richard called his office, the phone rang unanswered.
   b. Richard called his office.
2. (1) a. The man in the blue suit and the lady in the tan coat walk.
   b. The man in the blue suit and the lady in the tan coat, walking along the street, were stopped by a stranger.
3. (2) a. The fumbling, bumbling clown danced.
   b. The fumbling, bumbling clown dancing makes the children laugh.
4. (5) No error

5. (2) a. Flour, sugar, and three eggs are blended.
   b. Blend flour, sugar, and three eggs.
6. (1) Leona worked harder than any other lawyer in the firm
7. (5) No error

Practice VII *Page 7.*

1. (4) Jan does not want a second office.
2. (3) She wants an office with room to expand.
3. (2) This change is causing problems.
4. (2) While plastic bags may be easier to store and carry, they are not easier to discard.

Practice VIII *Page 11.*

For additional study, review the list of action words on pages 9–11.

1. rose — *Entered* is in the past time; therefore, use *rose* also in its past form.
2. worn — With the helping word *had*, use *worn*.
3. known — With the helping word *had*, use *known*.
4. shrunk — With the helping word *had*, use *shrunk*.
5. laid — With the helping word *have*, use *laid*.

Practice IX *Page 12.*

1. (2) I *have rung* her doorbell several times today.
2. (4) Last year, Marlene *led* the church choir.
3. (1) The plaintiff *swore* to tell the truth.
4. (3) The opinionated Mr. Dobbs never *had run* for office himself.
5. (3) Mother *had thrown* out my favorite old sneakers before I could stop her.
6. (4) I *had not written* before the summer ended.

Practice X *Page 13.*

1. (2) run — Use this form with the helping word, *have*.
2. (2) chose — Use *chose* to show that the action took place in the past.
3. (5) No error
4. (4) swings or swung — The action could be in the present or in the past. There is no such word as *swinged*.
5. (1) brought — There is no such word as *bringed*.
6. (3) paid — *Payed* is an incorrect spelling of the action word.
7. (1) thrown — Use *thrown* with the helping word, *had*.

Practice XI *Page 14.*

1. (4) We sit in front of the t.v. with potato chips and soda.
2. (4) Joe never agrees with the referees, who he insists are blind.

Practice XII *Page 15.*

1. (2) Pausing for a moment after clearing his throat, he then began to speak.
2. (4) An eloquent gesture sent his notes flying.
3. (5) He disappeared during the resulting blackout.

Practice XIII *Page 17.*

Answers will vary, of course.

1. Tina exercises every week. She does aerobics, swims, and lifts weights. Tina's figure is improving. She does not smoke any more. Everyone comments on how wonderful she looks. Sometimes, however, she yearns for a pizza with the works, a hot fudge sundae, and a pack of cigarettes.
2. When he gets a raise, Lester will buy a new car. He will read *Consumers Report* and research the manufacturers thoroughly. When he finds the perfect car, he will install as many options as possible. Then, Lester will drive around with the sun roof open and the radio playing. If Lester is not careful, however, his toupee may fly through the sun roof.

2.

Performer and Action: Understanding Time and Number

Every so often, Mr. Spector called on Vinnie to answer, and that was when English 117 really came to life.

"So I says to Angie . . ."

"No, Vinnie," interjected Mr. Spector, "you didn't '*says*' to Angie, you 'said' to him."

"That's right," continued Vinnie, "I *says* to Angie . . ."

"Go on," Mr. Spector replied wearily; "You *says* to Angie . . ."

"That's what I *said*, man" snorted Vinnie. "Can't a guy tell a story without bein' interrupted?"

Roger Talifiero
Our Little Red Schoolhouse

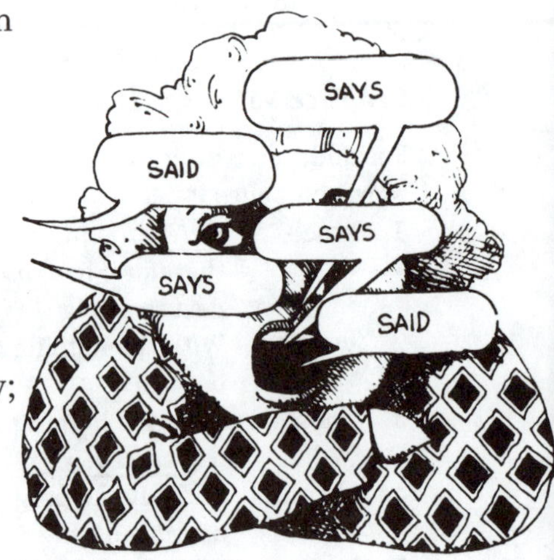

A Word With You . . .

Mr. Spector's English class was a lively place because the teacher encouraged free and open discussion. At times, however, Mr. Spector's classical training set his teeth on edge when he saw a misspelling or a failure to capitalize, etc.

In this excerpt, his student, Vinnie, was confused about different forms of the action word *to say*. After you read Chapter 2, you should know why Mr. Spector often needed an aspirin after English 117.

Understanding Time

As you learned in Chapter 1, actions occur at different times. *For example:*

John walks. *(present)*

John walked. *(past)*
John will walk. *(future)*

PRACTICE I

Directions: Use *work*, *worked*, or *will work* in each of the following sentences.

1. Willie Farris __________ overtime last week.
2. We must __________ a certain number of hours each day.
3. Four employees __________ overtime next week.

It is easy to determine the time of the action word in a single sentence. When sentences appear in paragraph form, however, the time of each action is more difficult to determine. *The time of all action words in a paragraph must be the same.* The action word in the first sentence sets the time for the paragraph. *For example:*

INCORRECT: John *entered* the library. He *speaks* to the librarian. Finally, John *chooses* a book.

CORRECT: John *entered* the library. He *spoke* to the librarian. Finally, John *chose* a book.

Because *entered* is in the *past*, *spoke* and *chose* must be in the *past*, too.

PRACTICE II

Directions: The following items are based on a paragraph that contains numbered sentences. Some of the sentences may contian errors in the time of the action word. Other sentences are correct as they appear in the paragraph. Read the paragraph and answer the items based on it. Choose the one best answer to each item.

(1) The crowd filed into the meeting room. (2) The chairman raps his gavel. (3) An angry murmur continued in the room. (4) The chairman rapped his gavel a second time. (5) Quiet finally settles over the room. (6) The chairman has begun his report.

1. Sentence 2: **The chairman raps his gavel.**

What correction should be made to this sentence?

(1) change chairman to chairmen ① ② ③ ④ ⑤
(2) insert a comma after chairman
(3) change raps to rapped
(4) change raps to will rap
(5) no correction is necessary

2. Sentence 5: **Quiet finally settles over the room.**

Which of the following is the best way to write the underlined portion of this sentence? If you think the original is the best way, choose option (1).

(1) settles ① ② ③ ④ ⑤
(2) is settling
(3) settling
(4) settled
(5) has settled

3. Sentence 6: **The chairman has begun his report.**

What correction should be made to this sentence?

(1) replace has begun with is beginning ① ② ③ ④ ⑤
(2) replace has begun with began
(3) replace has begun with will begin
(4) change has begun to had begun
(5) no correction is necessary

Understanding Number

The performer in a sentence may be singular (one) or plural (more than one). A plural performer may be expressed in one word (girls) or in more than one word (Mary, Sue, and Jane). When we talk about a performer's number, we are talking about whether it is singular or plural.

PERFORMER-Singular

Example: Sometimes the *computer* works.

PERFORMER-Plural

Example: Sometimes the *computers* work.

A plural performer may be expressed in one word that ends in s (girls) or in one word that does not end in s (children). A plural performer also may be expressed in more than one word (a chair, a desk, and a personal computer), none of which ends in s.

PERFORMER-Plural

Example: Fresh *fruits* add substance to your diet.

PERFORMER-Plural

Example: An *apple and an orange* add substance to your diet.

PERFORMER-Plural

Example: The *children* take a bus to after-school activities.

PRACTICE III

Directions: In each of the following sentences, underline the performer or performers. Write an *S* over the word if the performer is singular or *P* if the performer is plural.

S

Example: *Mr. Warner* knows everyone in town.

1. The women work well together.
2. Mr. Smith and his son address the Cub Scouts.
3. Flour, sugar, and milk complete this recipe.
4. Connie Martine understands community relations.
5. Mr. Luchner's grandchildren often visit him.

As you are beginning to see, the performer and action words *work together* (grammarians say they *agree*—see the *Guide*) to show that they are singular or plural.

SINGULAR Performer SINGULAR Action Word

Example: That *car travels* at top speed.

PLURAL Performer PLURAL Action Word

Example: Those *cars travel* at top speed.

Did you notice anything surprising? You are probably saying to yourself, as you did in Chapter 1, "Why is there an s at the end of a singular action word (travels)? An s means the word is plural, doesn't it?" Well, sometimes. Here we see that an s at the end of an action word (comes) shows that the action word is singular and should be used with a singular performer.

SINGULAR Performer SINGULAR Action Word

Example: Our *relative comes* to dinner every Sunday.

PLURAL Performer PLURAL Action Word

Example: Our *relatives come* to dinner every Sunday.

SINGULAR Performer SINGULAR Action Word

Example: The *house stands* on a hill.

PLURAL Performer PLURAL Action Word

Example: The *houses stand* on a hill.

PRACTICE IV

Directions: Correct the number error in each underlined action word.

1. In the 1990s, a company want employees who work well on teams.
2. More people owns a fax machine than ever before.
3. My thoroughly cleaned car do not stay clean for very long.
4. That kind of test stump me every time.
5. Some friends listens very well.

You have been working with performers in the present time: *comes*, *travels*, *stands*, etc. Now we've come to the easier part: performers in past time. Why easier? You will see that although the performer changes in number, the action word remains the same. For example, we can select the action word *ride* and use it in its past form, *rode*. Now when we change the performer in every sentence below so that there are both singular and plural performers, what happens to the word *rode*? Nothing. *Rode* remains the same. *For example:*

	I *rode* the subway.
	You *rode* the subway.
(He)	David *rode* the subway.
(She)	Pam *rode* the subway.
	Who *rode* the subway?
(We)	David and I *rode* the subway.
	You and Pam *rode* the subway.
(They)	Ellen and Linda *rode* the subway.

In the following sentences, the time is present. Notice that the form of the action word changes for singular and plural performers. You see that an *s* is added to the action word when the performer is *singular*—except when the performer is *I* or *you*.

Example: The lady rides the subway.
The ladies ride the subway.

	I *ride* the subway.
	You *ride* the subway.
(He)	David *rides* the subway.
(She)	Pam *rides* the Subway.
	Who *rides* the subway?
(We)	David and I *ride* the subway.
	You and Pam *ride* the subway.
(They)	Ellen and Linda *ride* the subway.

PRACTICE V

Directions: The following items are based on paragraphs that contain numbered sentences. Some of these sentences may contain errors in the number (singular or plural) of the action words. Other sentences are correct as they appear in the paragraphs. Read the paragraphs and answer the items based on them. Choose the one best answer to each item.

Items 1 and 2 refer to the following paragraph.

(1) A shopping trip makes me angry. (2) Prices soar each week. (3) Meat prices changes almost daily. (4) Oranges, apples, and bananas cost more than ever. (5) A shopper needs more and more money each week.

1. Sentence 1: **A shopping trip *makes* me angry.**

   Which of the following is the best way to write the underlined portion of this sentence? If you think the original is the best way, choose option (1).

   (1) makes ① ② ③ ④ ⑤
   (2) is making
   (3) made
   (4) has made
   (5) make

2. Sentence 3: **Meat prices changes almost daily.**

   What correction should be made to this sentence?

   (1) insert a comma before almost ① ② ③ ④ ⑤
   (2) change changes to change
   (3) replace changes with has changed
   (4) remove the word almost
   (5) replace changes with is going to change

Item 3 refers to the following paragraph.

(1) Tom jogs each morning. (2) Macon and Gary join him on Mondays and Thursdays. (3) The Robinson twins likes jogging too. (4) Jogging now replaces basketball as the neighborhood pastime.

3. Sentence 3: **The Robinson twins likes jogging too.**

   What correction should be made to this sentence?

   (1) change Robinson to Robinsons ① ② ③ ④ ⑤
   (2) change twins to twinns
   (3) change twins to twin
   (4) replace likes jogging with likes to jog
   (5) change likes to like

Items 4 and 5 refer to the following paragraph.

(1) Each year local artists participate in an art show. (2) The Community Center offers a perfect gallery. (3) One artist wins in each of five categories. (4) The winning artists displays their works in the Town Hall.

4. Sentence 1: **Each year local artists participate in an art show.**

What correction should be made to this sentence?

(1) replace Each year with Every year ① ② ③ ④ ⑤
(2) change participate to participates
(3) replace in an with as a part of an
(4) change show to showing
(5) no correction is necessary

5. Sentence 4: **The winning artists displays their works in the Town Hall.**

Which of the following is the best way to write the underlined portion of the sentence? If you think the original is the best way, choose option (1).

(1) artists displays their works ① ② ③ ④ ⑤
(2) artists display their works
(3) artist's display their works
(4) artists displays their work
(5) artists displays there works

The above paragraphs had errors in *number.* In the following exercise, look for errors in *time* and *number.*

PRACTICE VI

Directions: The following items are based on paragraphs that contain numbered sentences. Some of these sentences may contain errors in the time and number of the action words. Other sentences are correct as they appear in the paragraphs. Read the paragraphs and answer the items based on them. Choose the one best answer to each item.

Items 1 and 2 refer to the following paragraphs.

(1) In the spring the honeysuckle droops over the hillside. (2) Its sweet smell

hangs heavily in the air outside. (3) The fragrance floats into the room when the doors are open.

(4) A hummingbird dives daily in and out of the honeysuckle. (5) He bombs past the doors with his heavy load and balanced on a branch of the little olive tree.

1. Sentence 2: **Its sweet smell hangs heavily in the air outside.**

   What correction should be made to this sentence?

   (1) change Its to It's ① ② ③ ④ ⑤
   (2) change hangs to will be hanging
   (3) change hangs to hang
   (4) change hangs to hung
   (5) no correction is necessary

2. Sentence 5: **He bombs past the doors with his heavy load and balanced on a branch of the little olive tree.**

   Which of the following is the best way to write the underlined portion of the sentence? If you think the original is the best way, choose option (1).

   (1) load and balanced ① ② ③ ④ ⑤
   (2) load while balancing
   (3) load and will balance
   (4) load and balances
   (5) load and has balanced

Item 3 refers to the following paragraph.

(1) A teenage driver causes one out of every three automobile accidents. (2) Many people accuse teen drivers of not concentrating on the road. (3) Three out of six parents interviewed fears for their children's safety.

3. Sentence 3: **Three out of six parents interviewed fears for their children's safety.**

   What correction should be made to this sentence?

   (1) change parents to parent's ① ② ③ ④ ⑤

(2) replace interviewed with say that they
(3) replace fears with are always fearing
(4) change fears to fear
(5) change children's safety to childrens' safety

Items 4 and 5 refer to the following paragraph.

(1) The farmer and his hired men gathers the corn. (2) The farmer, along with his hired men, harvests the wheat. (3) Neither the corn nor the wheat is neglected. (4) The farmer's wife and daughter argue a great deal.

4. Sentence 1: **The farmer and his hired men gathers the corn.**

Which of the following is the best way to write the underlined portion of the sentence? If you think the original is the best way, choose option (1).

(1) men gathers ① ② ③ ④ ⑤
(2) men gathering
(3) man gathers
(4) men is gathering
(5) men gather

5. Sentence 2: **The farmer, along with his hired men, harvests the wheat.**

What correction should be made to this sentence?

(1) replace farmer, along with farmer, and along ① ② ③ ④ ⑤
(2) change men to man
(3) insert he's going to before harvests
(4) change harvests to harvest
(5) no correction is necessary

ANSWER KEY

Chapter 2

Performer and Action: Understanding Time and Number

Practice I *Page 21.*

1. Willie Farris *worked* overtime last week.
2. We must *work* a certain number of hours each day.
3. Four employees *will work* overtime next week.

Practice II *Page 21.*

Remember, *filed* set the time (past) for the other action words in the paragraph.

1. (3) The chairman *rapped* his gavel.
2. (4) Quiet finally *settled* over the room.
3. (2) The chairman *began* his report.

Practice III *Page 23.*

P
1. women

P
2. Mr. Smith and his son

P
3. Flour, sugar, and milk

S
4. Connie Martine

P
5. grandchildren

Practice IV *Page 24.*

1. wants — Use the singular form of the action word (wants) when the performer is singular (company).
2. own — Use the plural form of the action word (own) when the performer is plural (people).
3. does — Use the singular form of the action word (does) when the performer is singular (car).
4. stumps — Use the singular form of the action word (stumps) when the performer is singular (test).
5. listen — Use the plural form of the action word (listen) when the performer is plural (friends).

Practice V *Page 25.*

1. (1) *Makes* is the singular form of the action word, which agrees with the singular performer, *trip.*
2. (2) *Change* is the plural form of the action word, which agrees with the plural performer *prices.*
3. (5) *Like* is the plural form of the action word, which agrees with the plural performer, *twins.*
4. (5) No correction is necessary. *Participate* is the plural form of the action word, which agrees with the plural performer, *artists.*
5. (2) *Display* is the plural form of the action word, which agrees with the plural performer, *artists.*

Practice VI *Page 27.*

1. (5) No correction is necessary.
2. (4) The paragraph begins and continues in the present time. *Balances* agrees in time with the first two action words, *dives* and *bombs.*
3. (4) *Fear* is the plural form of the action word, which agrees with the plural performer, *three.*
4. (5) *Gather* is the plural form of the action word, which agrees with the plural performer, *farmer and his hired men.*
5. (5) No correction is necessary. *Harvests* is the singular form of the action word, which agrees with the singular performer, *farmer.*

3.

Adding Descriptive Words

Vic: We have to advertise, Charley. No wonder no one comes into our store.

Charley: I hate all those phony ads where they hit you in the head with one lie after another.

Vic: We don't have to lie. The truth will bring the suckers in.

Charley: This is a fruit store—that's it, a fruit store. What else can we say about it?

Vic: Use your head, Charles, my boy. Our fruit isn't just fruit, it's *delectable* fruit; we've got *golden* bananas, our cherries are *heavenly delicious*, the *sugar-sweet* pears would kill a diabetic.

Charley: I dunno, to me fruit is fruit.

L.I. Meyers
A Lovely Bunch of Coconuts

A Word With You . . .

Vic and Charley, the owners of Plaza Fruit, appear in a one-act play called *A Lovely Bunch of Coconuts*. As you can see, their personalities are different. Charley lacks romance—to him an apple is an apple. But Vic has the Madison Avenue approach to glamorizing his product.

Actually, what Vic did in this brief slice from the play is to add meaning by the use of descriptive words. You'll learn more about the technique in the next few pages.

Descriptive Words: Adding Meaning

You know that an English sentence must have a person or thing (performer) performing an action. You might say that these words are the core of every sentence. But we don't speak in such simple sentences: *He ran. She jumped.* Other words are added to the core to make a sentence more meaningful and interesting. These words may tell you more about the performer, or they may tell you more about the action. Look at the following example:

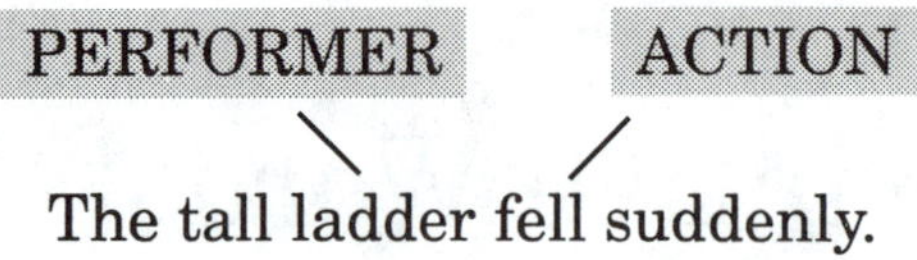

The performer is *ladder* and the action is *fell.* Note the words *the, tall,* and *suddenly.* These are descriptive words. *The* tells which *ladder; tall* tells you more about the performer, *ladder;* and *suddenly* tells you more about *fell,* the action.

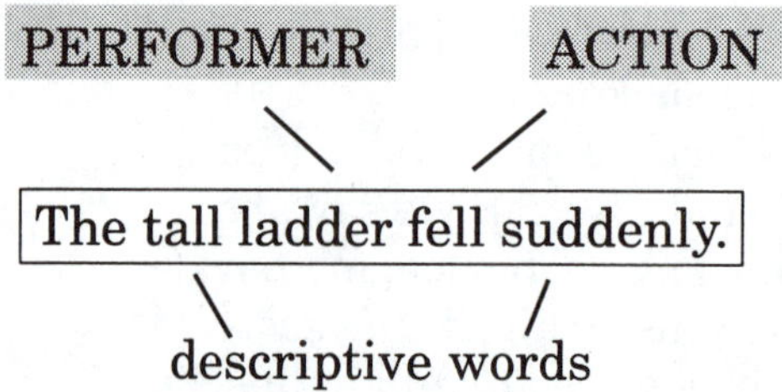

Now study the two sentences below. Label the performer, action, and descriptive words in each sentence.

The fire alarm rang loudly.

Fire describes the *alarm*. *Loudly* describes *rang.*

The decaying tooth throbbed painfully.

Decaying describes *tooth. Painfully* describes *throbbed.*

PRACTICE

I **Directions:** Complete the pattern in each of the following sentences by adding a descriptive word.

1. A ______________ man entered the store.
2. ______________ music annoys me.
3. The cat jumped ______________.
4. The ______________ book slipped to the floor.
5. Dolores Bremmer walked ______________ from the room.

PRACTICE II

Directions: Write five sentences of your own. Use descriptive words to tell more about the performer, the action, or both.

1. ______________________________
2. ______________________________
3. ______________________________
4. ______________________________
5. ______________________________

PRACTICE III

Directions: In each of the following sentences, one word is underlined. If the underlined word is the performer, blacken circle 1. If the underlined word is the action, blacken circle 2. If the underlined word describes the performer, blacken circle 3. If the underlined word describes the action, blacken circle 4.

1. The gooey candy stuck to the seat of the unsuspecting moviegoer's pants. ① ② ③ ④
2. Mr. McCarthy strode away angrily. ① ② ③ ④
3. The sweet old man winked. ① ② ③ ④
4. My friend cooks well. ① ② ③ ④
5. Ricardo gave me a good suggestion. ① ② ③ ④
6. We sat down beneath some trees. ① ② ③ ④
7. Four hungry children arrived for lunch. ① ② ③ ④
8. Northern merchants paid little for raw materials. ① ② ③ ④
9. Rita came directly home after work. ① ② ③ ④
10. A violent storm of controversy raged at our council meeting. ① ② ③ ④

PRACTICE IV

Directions: The descriptive words in the following sentences have been underlined. In each sentence, draw an arrow from the descriptive word to the word that it describes.

Example: The subway lurched *wildly.*

1. The telephone rang unexpectedly.
2. A heavy rain ruined our picnic.
3. The talented fingers knit the sweater.
4. The speeding truck swerved abruptly.
5. The soft snow fell gently.

PRACTICE V

Directions: Blacken the circle that corresponds to the number of the action word in each sentence.

1. *Barbra Streisand* (1) *sings* (2) *emotionally* (3) charged *songs.* (4) ① ② ③ ④
2. The *rumbling* (1) truck *sped* (2) *down* (3) the *highway.* (4) ① ② ③ ④
3. A *monotonous* (1) *tapping* (2) *annoyed* (3) the *students.* (4) ① ② ③ ④
4. My foreman, Roy, *bought* (1) beer for *all* (2) the men *on* (3) the *shift.* (4) ① ② ③ ④
5. The *President of the United States* (1) *walked* (2) *slowly* (3) *toward* (4) the microphone. ① ② ③ ④

PRACTICE VI

Directions: Draw an arrow from each descriptive word to the word that it describes.

1. Mr. Hudson displays a cheerful disposition.
2. The dull day passed slowly.

3. The fast car raced quickly.

4. The cool, clear water shimmered.

5. A hungry seagull greedily grabbed the fish.

6. That working mom leaves early in the morning.

7. Another new position opened unexpectedly.

8. You should write often.

9. The exhausted salesperson spoke harshly.

10. Adrianna held on tightly.

Descriptive Words: Special Problems

Many words that are used to describe performers must add *-ly* in order to describe actions. *For example:*

The *nice* woman spoke at the meeting.
The woman spoke *nicely* at the meeting.

In the above sentences, *nice* and *nicely* do two very different jobs. *Nice* describes the performer, *woman. Nicely* describes the action, *spoke.* You would never say, "The nicely woman spoke at the meeting." However, a common error is "The woman spoke nice." You can avoid that common error by recognizing that most words that describe actions end in *-ly.*

- *Well* describes actions, unless referring to the state of health.
  Good never describes an action.
  Examples:
  My neighbor paints *well*.
  My neighbor is a *good* painter.
  I don't feel *well* today.

- *Real* describes a person, place, or thing.

  Examples:

  The shoes were made of *real* leather.
  I prefer *real* butter to imitation.
  His loyalty makes him a *real* friend.

- *Really* describes another descriptive word.

  Examples:

  Many of the events in our history are *really* exciting.
  His story was not *really* believable.
  Jan's shoes were *really* too small.

- *Very* describes another descriptive word.

  Examples:

  The basketball game was *very* exciting.
  The members of this community work *very* well together.
  The guitarist played *very* quickly.

PRACTICE VII

Directions: Underline the correct descriptive word to complete each sentence.

1. My sister and I used to get along (bad, badly).
2. We were always (ready, readily) to fight.
3. She said that I played my radio too (loud, loudly).
4. I said that she did not behave (polite, politely) toward me.
5. Now we get along (good, well).
6. Since I'm never at fault, it must be that she is acting (immature, immaturely).
7. While I'm thinking of my sister, I will call her (quick, quickly) on the telephone.

PRACTICE VIII

Directions: Choose the word that best completes each sentence and draw an arrow to the word it describes.

1. Jose will call (immediate, immediately) after he arrives.

2. An abject Terry apologized (sincere, sincerely).
3. The chorus sings (good, well).
4. A good singer breathes (deep, deeply).
5. My nine year old runs (quick, quickly).
6. Did you ever have a neighbor who loved (loud, loudly) music?
7. The old dog walked (lazily, lazy) down the street.
8. The authors say, "Study each chapter (careful, carefully)."
9. A (quick, quickly) call will tell me everything I need to know.
10. That software works (good, well) for this project.

ANSWER KEY

Chapter 3

Adding Descriptive Words

Page 32.

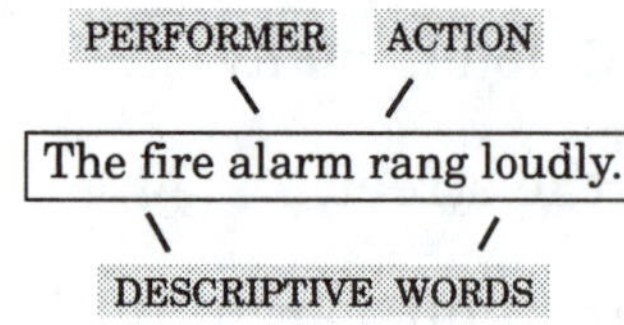

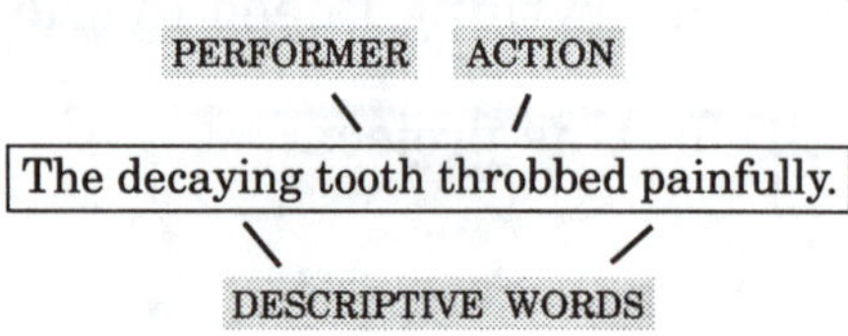

Practice 1 *Page 32.*

Answers may vary.

Sample answers:

1. A *tall* man entered the store.
2. *Loud* music annoys me.
3. The cat jumped *suddenly*.
4. The *heavy* book slipped to the floor.
5. Dolores Bremmer walked *quickly* from the room.

Practice II *Page 33.*

Answers may vary.

Sample answers:

The shy girl spoke softly.

The delicate jonquils announced spring

Practice III *Page 33.*

1. (3) *gooey* describes *candy,* the performer.
2. (4) *angrily* describes *strode,* the action.
3. (2) *winked* is the action.
4. (1) *friend* is the performer.
5. (2) *gave* is the action.
6. (2) *sat* is the action.
7. (1) *children* is the performer.
8. (3) *northern* describes *merchants,* the performers.
9. (4) *directly* describes *came,* the action.
10. (3) *violent* describes *storm,* the performer.

Practice IV *Page 33.*

1. rang — *unexpectedly* describes *rang.*
2. rain — *heavy* describes *rain.*
3. fingers — *talented* describes fingers.
4. swerved — *abruptly* describes *swerved.*
5. snow, fell — *soft* describes *snow, gently* describes *fell.*

Practice V *Page 34.*

1. (2) sings
2. (2) sped
3. (3) annoyed
4. (1) bought
5. (2) walked

Practice VI *Page 34.*

1. *Cheerful* describes disposition.
2. *Dull* describes day, *slowly* describes *passed.*
3. *Fast* describes car, *quickly* describes *raced.*
4. *Cool* describes water, *clear* describes *water.*
5. *Hungry* describes seagull, *greedily* describes *grabbed.*
6. *Early* describes *leaves.*
7. *Unexpectedly* describes *opened.*
8. *Often* describes *write.*
9. *Harshly* describes *spoke.*
10. *Tightly* describes *held on.*

Practice VII *Page 36.*

1. *Badly* describes *used to get along.*
2. *Ready* describes *to fight.*
3. *Loudly* describes *played.*
4. *Politely* describes *behave.*
5. *Well* describes *get along.*
6. *Immaturely* describes *is acting.*
7. *Quickly* describes *will call.*

Practice VIII *Page 36.*

1. *Immediately* describes *will call.*
2. *Sincerely* describes *apologized.*
3. *Well* describes *sings.*
4. *Deeply* describes *breathes.*
5. *Quickly* describes *runs.*
6. *Loud* describes *music.*
7. *Lazily* describes *walked.*
8. *Carefully* describes *study.*
9. *Quick* describes *call.*
10. *Well* describes *works.*

4.

Using Descriptive Words Correctly

Maury Wills has described a player as having good running speed. "I knew it was hit good," said Mike Schmidt of the Philadelphia Phillies, "but the ball doesn't carry good in the Astrodome." It carried bad. When James J. Braddock died, there were stories about the fight in which he lost his heavyweight championship to Joe Louis. In the first round Braddock knocked Louis down. Louis got up. Braddock: "I thought if I hit him good, he'll stay down." It did not work out that way. Braddock was a brave man, a light-heavyweight, really, who returned to fighting when he was unemployed and on relief and went on to win the heavyweight championship. He was a longshoreman and uneducated. Tom Seaver of the New York Mets is a college graduate: "Cedeno hit the ball pretty good." Budd Schulberg is a novelist. Said he, after the Ali-Foreman fight, "The fight turned out pretty good."

—Edwin Newman
A Civil Tongue

A Word with You . . .

Obviously, many people's use of *good* isn't their *best* grammar. The sports figures quoted by Edwin Newman are not alone in their misuse of that common adjective. Remember, no matter how good a player you are, you *play well*. This chapter will help you *use* descriptive words *well*.

Descriptive Words: Using Comparisons

Many descriptive words follow this pattern:

Mr. Smith built a tall fence.
Mr. Jones built a taller fence.
Mr. White built the tallest fence *of the three.*

Why is the fence in sentence 1 described as *tall,* the fence in sentence 2 described as *taller,* and the fence in sentence 3 described as *tallest? Tall* is a descriptive word that describes *fence. Taller* is a descriptive word that describes and compares *two fences. Tallest* is a descriptive word that compares *more than two fences.*

As you have seen in the above sentence, *-er* is added to a descriptive word to show a comparison between two people or things; *-est* is added to a descriptive word to show a comparison among more than two people or things. This is the general rule for comparison of descriptive words. *Study the examples below*:

DESCRIPTION	COMPARISON OF TWO	COMPARISON OF MORE THAN TWO
pretty	prettier	prettiest
small	smaller	smallest
fast	faster	fastest
near	nearer	nearest
soon	sooner	soonest
rude	ruder	rudest
shrewd	shrewder	shrewdest
spicy	spicier	spiciest
green	greener	greenest
stout	stouter	stoutest

Many descriptive words sound awkward when *-er* or *-est* is added. These words use more instead of *-er* and most instead of *-est* when making a comparison. *Study the examples below:*

DESCRIPTION	COMPARISON OF TWO	COMPARISON OF MORE THAN TWO
beautiful	more beautiful	most beautiful
tenacious	more tenacious	most tenacious
enormous	more enormous	most enormous
quickly	more quickly	most quickly
torrid	more torrid	most torrid

DESCRIPTION	COMPARISON OF TWO	COMPARISON OF MORE THAN TWO
valuable	more valuable	most valuable
legible	more legible	most legible
difficult	more difficult	most difficult
wonderful	more wonderful	most wonderful
sympathetic	more sympathetic	most sympathetic

Some descriptive words have entirely different forms to express different degrees of comparison. *Study the examples below:*

DESCRIPTIVE	COMPARISON OF TWO	COMPARISON OF MORE THAN TWO
good	better	best
bad	worse	worst

PRACTICE I

Directions: Complete the pattern in each of the following sentences by adding the *proper form* of one of the descriptive words below.

boring magnificent long high good

1. This is the ___________ meeting I've ever attended.
2. We chose the ____________ day of the summer for our office picnic.
3. Mr. Valdez is one of the ___________ people I know.
4. Ricky works _____________ than anyone else in the plant.
5. Our plants grew _____________ this year than last year.

PRACTICE II

Directions: Blacken the circle containing the number that corresponds to the number of the incorrect sentence in each group.

1. (1) This week's show was more funnier than last week's show. ① ② ③
   (2) A tiny, delicate bird flew quietly away.
   (3) That loud noise is very irritating.

2. (1) The nervous woman seemed very impatient. ① ② ③
(2) Only close relatives visited the very old man.
(3) John received the job because he was the efficientest competitor.

3. (1) Seven of the candidates competed vigorously for the local mayoralty. ① ② ③
(2) This dinner is the most delicious I've ever had.
(3) Willie is the better basketball player of the three.

4. (1) Harry Truman read continually. ① ② ③
(2) Of the two, Freddie runs quicker.
(3) The delightful aroma drifted across the room.

5. (1) Ed suggests a better solution. ① ② ③
(2) This coffee pot makes the badest coffee I've ever had.
(3) He handled the bus more skillfully than any other driver.

6. (1) The worst damage occurred in the rear. ① ② ③
(2) Of the two books, I like this one the most.
(3) This is the shortest of the three books.

7. (1) I like Indian sand paintings better than modern art. ① ② ③
(2) The corner market always has the best cheese.
(3) I chose the evergreen because it is the beautifulest of the three.

8. (1) Navajo artwork is more elaborate than Pueblo artwork. ① ② ③
(2) The morning trains are slower than the afternoon trains.
(3) This horse wins frequentlyer than any other.

9. (1) We liked this movie more better than any other. ① ② ③
(2) Our team is the best in our plant.
(3) Colonel Eden was a better officer than anyone else in the brigade.

10. (1) He lost his composure during the worse battle of the war. ① ② ③
(2) The science teacher carefully explained that this was the best technique.
(3) The record showed that their team was stronger than any other in the conference.

PRACTICE III **Directions:** Complete the paragraph below by adding descriptive words. Make certain you use the correct form of each descriptive word.

Marie sat on the _______ beach and stared _______ at the ______ waves. She _______ jumped up and ran _______ toward the ocean. She laughed when she realized that the dog she thought was drowning was a ________, stuffed animal.

PRACTICE IV **Directions:** In the paragraphs below, change each of the underlined words to its correct form and write it in the space provided. If the underlined word is correct, rewrite it in the space provided.

1. The skaters glided *smooth* across the ice. Their movements were as *graceful* as those of *professional* trained dancers. With rapt attention, the audience watched every *skillfully* turn.

The skaters glided _______ across the ice. Their movements were as ________ as those of ________ trained dancers. With rapt attention, the audience watched every ________ turn.

2. The department meeting this month was the *boringest* one yet. Each speaker was *most difficult* to understand than the one before. The meeting notes were *difficult* to read, and the refreshments were the *worse* I've ever had.

The department meeting this month was the _________ one yet. Each speaker was __________ to understand than the one before. The meeting notes were ________ to read, and the refreshments were the ________ I've ever had.

ANSWER KEY

Chapter 4

Using Descriptive Words Correctly

Practice I *Page 41.*

Answers may vary.

Sample answers:

1. longest
   most boring
   best
2. best
   most magnificent
3. most boring
   most magnificent
   best
4. better
   longer
5. higher
   better

Practice II *Page 41.*

1. (1) This week's show was *funnier* than last week's show. Do not use *more* with a descriptive word that ends in *-er*.
2. (3) John received the job because he was the *most efficient* competitor. Use *most* rather than *-est* with *efficient*.
3. (3) Willie is the *best* basketball player of the three. Use *best* when comparing three or more.
4. (2) Of the two, Freddie runs *more quickly*. Quickly describes run; therefore, *more quickly* compares how two people run.
5. (2) This coffee pot makes the *worst* coffee I've ever had. *Worst* is the form of *bad* used when comparing three or more.
6. (2) Of the two books, I like this one *more.* Use *more* to compare two items.
7. (3) I chose the evergreen because it is the *most beautiful* of the three. Use *most* rather than *-est* with *beautiful.*
8. (3) This horse wins *more frequently* than any other. Use *more* with *frequently* rather than *-er*.
9. (1) We liked this movie *better* than any other. Do not use *more* with *better.*
10. (1) He lost his composure during the *worst* battle of the war. *Worst* is the form of *bad* used when comparing three or more.

Practice III *Page 43.*

Answers will vary, of course.

Marie sat on the *empty* beach and stared *blankly* at the *huge* waves. She *suddenly* jumped up and ran *quickly* toward the ocean. She laughed when she realized that the dog she thought was drowning was a *large,* stuffed animal.

Practice IV *Page 43.*

1. The skaters glided *smoothly* across the ice. Their movements were as *graceful* as those of *professionally* trained dancers. With rapt attention, the audience watched every *skillful* turn.
2. The department meeting this month was the *most boring* one yet. Each speaker was *more difficult* to understand than the one before. The meeting notes were *difficult* to read, and the refreshments were the *worst* I've ever had.

5.

Adding Descriptive Phrases

"I spoke to Jerry at the office party about his need to get more education," said Mr. Grogan.

"You mean that there was an office party just to consider Jerry's lack of education," Mrs. Grogan sweetly replied. "Maybe Jerry should ask you to go back to school if you use sentences like that."

Mrs. Grogan ducked as the pillow came sailing at her head. Lions don't like to have their tails tugged.

Les Camhi
V.I.P. at I.B.M.

A Word With You . . .

Mrs. Grogan was having some fun at her husband's expense because he had been tarred with his own brush. Instead of coming across as the friendly vice-president who points out a weakness to his employee, he had the tables turned on him by the clever Mrs. Grogan, who spotted an error in her husband's sentence structure. Do you see the mistake? In Chapter 5 you will learn how to avoid it.

Descriptive Phrases: Adding Meaning

You have just been working with descriptive words that help to make the sentence more meaningful and interesting. Frequently, one descriptive word is not enough. We need a group of words (a phrase) to expand the meaning.

Example: The coffee cup fell *on the floor.*

How does *on the floor* expand the meaning of the sentence? It describes where the cup *fell.* You can say that this phrase is descriptive, just as a single word is descriptive. Look at the single words that describe *cup* and *fell* below; then, look back at the phrase, *on the floor*. It describes the action word, *fell*, in the example above.

Each word describes cup — Describes fell

Single word / / / /

Example: The delicate coffee cup fell unexpectedly.

You can see that a descriptive phrase does not contain the performer or the action word. Consequently, descriptive phrases can be found more easily if you find the core (performer and action) of the sentence first. Finding the action word first helps you to choose the performer. Look at the following sentence:

The movie *at our local theater* terrifies audiences.

1. What is the *action word* in the sentence?
   Terrifies

2. Who or what is *performing* the action?
   Movie

Note: You might have chosen *theater* as the performer if you had not chosen the action word (*terrifies*) first. Does the *theater* terrify audiences? No. The *movie* does.

3. What does *at our local theater* describe?
   Movie

4. How does *at our local theater* describe *movie?*
   The phrase tells which movie you are talking about—the one *at our local theater.*

PRACTICE

I **Directions:** Each of the sentences below contains at least one descriptive phrase. Draw an arrow from each descriptive phrase to the word it describes. The first one is done for you.

1. The company solved its financial problems through efficiency techniques.

2. The fire in the fireplace crackled into the night.

3. The dentist's ultrasonic cleaner sped along the surfaces of the patient's teeth.

4. Shrubbery grew around the house.

5. A contestant with a soprano voice won the talent competition.

6. During the training session, the recruits crawled under the fence.

7. A lonely figure waited on the bridge.

8. Everyone except him cheered.

9. The dealer divided the cards among the four players.

10. An argument raged between the two teams.

PRACTICE II

Directions: These words frequently begin descriptive phrases. Choose from among them to complete the following sentences. More than one answer may be correct.

of	at	between	after	under	on
in	from	through	beside	over	before
to	into	around	except	off	along
for	among	by	alongside	up	with

1. A brief summary of World War I is ______________ the first chapter.
2. A large crowd walked ____________________ the stairs in the historic building.
3. Surprised by the house owner's return, the intruder hurried ______________ the door.

4. The unseasoned traveler put his hand ____________ his pocket in search of the proper coin.
5. The book ____________ the top shelf belongs _________ Ada.
6. ________________ more peaceful methods had failed, the government seized control of the newspapers and radio stations.
7. Combined ____________ the bank's inter-office banking service is their policy of all-day, all-night depositing.
8. In dull winter weather, African violets will bloom __________ 100 watt grow lights.
9. Sitting ____________ me was a man who laughed and clapped loudly.
10. The unfortunate children were scattered __________ many homes.

PRACTICE III

Directions: Each of the sentences below contains a descriptive phrase. Complete the Practice in this order: (1) Choose the action word and label it A. (2) Choose the performer and label it P. (3) Find the descriptive phrase and draw an arrow from it to the word it describes. The first one is done for you.

Descriptive Phrase

P / A

1. Frequently, workers [in manufacturing jobs] need more training.
2. Business sometimes moves to new products and areas.
3. Successful training taps into an employee's knowledge and experience.
4. Lectures about ancient history bore me.
5. Some lectures put me into a deep sleep.

PRACTICE IV

Directions: In each sentence below, circle the descriptive phrase. Draw an arrow from it to the word it describes.

1. The trouble-ridden *Galileo* reached Jupiter after six years.

2. Scientists had launched the spacecraft from the shuttle *Atlantis*.
3. On its way, *Galileo* flew through a powerful dust storm.
4. *Galileo* will deliver significant information to astronomers.
5. The spacecraft will orbit around Jupiter for two years.

Descriptive Phrases: Correct Placement

A descriptive phrase should be placed next to the word that it describes. Misplacement of a descriptive phrase results in confused meaning. *For example:*

> The congressman made an unfavorable comment at a White House reception *about rising prices*.

The reception was not *about rising prices*; the congressman's comment was *about rising prices*. The sentence should read:

> The congressman made an unfavorable comment *about rising prices* at a White House reception.

PRACTICE V

Directions: The underlined descriptive phrase in each of the following sentences is correctly placed. Draw an arrow from each descriptive phrase to the word that it describes. The first one is done for you.

1. The American way <u>of life</u> changes constantly.
2. The economy has grown <u>over the years.</u>
3. This course <u>of action</u> is intolerable.
4. The prosecutor spoke <u>to Steve.</u>

5. John Canady writes about art.

6. Several angry commuters walked to the bus stop.

7. Representatives of the different factions spoke.

8. The actors dine after the show.

9. The panelist at the table's end spoke decisively.

10. Mr. Simmons spoke at length.

Notice that each descriptive phrase is next to the word that it describes. In the following exercise, each descriptive phrase is incorrectly placed.

PRACTICE VI

Directions: On the line provided, rewrite each sentence so that each descriptive phrase is next to the word it describes.

1. Amazingly, the man ran down the stairs in a leg cast.

____

2. That gentleman often walks to the corner in the trenchcoat.

____

3. Tom did not see across the street the accident.

____

4. Show Ella in the baggy pants the clown.

____

5. That boy runs around the track in the sweatsuit each day.

____

6. The dog belongs to that child with the brown spots.

____

All of the above sentences had simple placement errors. Each incorrectly placed phrase began with a clue word such as: of, in, to, at, from, with, across, etc.

PRACTICE VII

Directions: One sentence in each group has a placement error in it. Blacken the circle containing the number that corresponds to the number of the incorrect sentence.

1. (1) The man in the tweed suit ran toward the departing bus. ① ② ③
   (2) A woman in a raincoat hailed a passing taxi.
   (3) The man in the drawer found his handkerchief.

2. (1) The grateful veteran relaxed after years of battle in his living room. ① ② ③
   (2) The battery in my car died.
   (3) The woman on the park bench smiled warmly.

3. (1) Cher sang as she sauntered across the stage. ① ② ③
   (2) Michael Jordan will play in next Tuesday's game.
   (3) Mrs. Smith hung on the wall her favorite painting.

4. (1) The car drove 7,000 miles in the driveway. ① ② ③
   (2) The new sports car in the parking lot was stolen.
   (3) The man in the moon winked at the astronauts.

5. (1) The registration desk was located in the gymnasium. ① ② ③
   (2) Voter registration took place at three o'clock.
   (3) The voters on the table completed the forms.

Frequently, a descriptive phrase separates the performer and the action. You must remember that *the action agrees in number with the performer. For example:*

Correct: The *man* in the black high boots *walks slowly.*

Notice that the correct action word is *walks.* The number of that word is not affected by any word in the descriptive phrase. The action word, *walks,* agrees with *man.* It does not, for example, change to agree with *boots.*

Incorrect: The *man* in the black high boots *walk* slowly.

PRACTICE VIII

Directions: Write a four- or five-sentence paragraph for each group of phrases below. Place descriptive phrases close to the words they describe.

1. in a hurry — out the door — over the couch — into her car — before the soap opera

____
____
____
____
____

2. except Marie — among the applicants — after the deadline — for two positions — with excellent qualifications

____
____
____
____
____

ANSWER KEY

Chapter 5

Adding Descriptive Phrases

Practice 1 *Page 46.*

1. *through efficiency techniques* describes *solved.*
2. *in the fireplace* describes *fire.*
   into the night describes *crackled.*
3. *along the surfaces* describes *sped.*
4. *around the house* describes *grew.*
5. *with a soprano voice* describes *contestant.*
6. *under the fence* describes *crawled.*
7. *on the bridge* describes *waited.*
8. *except him* describes *everyone.*
9. *among the four players* describes *divided.*
10. *between the two teams* describes *raged.*

Practice II *Page 47.*

Answers will vary.
Sample answers:

1. in, after, before
2. up
3. through, to, from
4. into
5. on, to
6. After, Before
7. with
8. under
9. beside
10. among

Practice III *Page 48.*

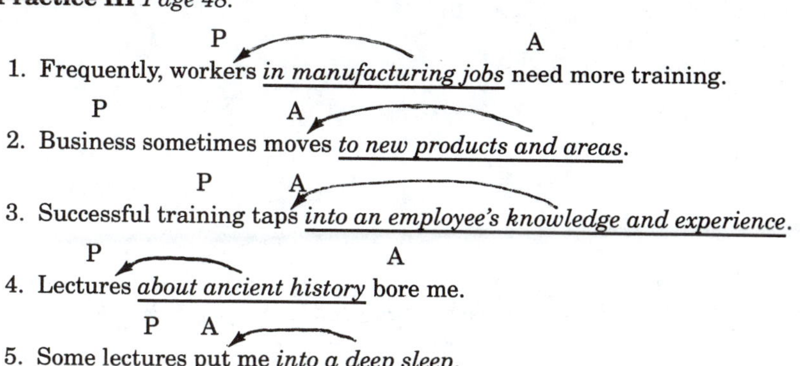

P
A
1. Frequently, workers *in manufacturing jobs* need more training.
P
A
2. Business sometimes moves *to new products and areas*.
P
A
3. Successful training taps *into an employee's knowledge and experience*.
P
A
4. Lectures *about ancient history* bore me.
P
A
5. Some lectures put me *into a deep sleep*.

Practice IV *Page 48.*

1. The trouble-ridden *Galileo* reached Jupiter *after six years*.
2. Scientists had launched the spacecraft *from the shuttle* Atlantis.
3. *On its way, Galileo* flew *through a powerful dust storm.*
4. *Galileo* will deliver significant information *to astronomers.*
5. The spacecraft will orbit *around Jupiter* *for two years*.

Practice V *Page 49.*

1. *of life* describes *way.*
2. *over the years* describes *has grown.*
3. *of action* describes *course.*
4. *to Steve* describes *spoke.*
5. *about art* describes *writes.*
6. *to the bus stop* describes *walked.*
7. *of the different factions* describes *representatives.*
8. *after the show* describes *dine.*
9. *at the table's end* describes *panelist.*
10. *at length* describes *spoke.*

Practice VI *Page 50.*

1. Amazingly, the man *in a leg cast* ran down the stairs.
2. That gentleman *in the trenchcoat* often walks to the corner.
3. Tom did not see the accident *across the street.*
4. Show Ella the clown *in the baggy pants.*
5. That boy *in the sweatsuit* runs around the track each day.
6. The dog *with the brown spots* belongs to that child.

Practice VII *Page 51.*

1. (3) The man found his handkerchief in the drawer.
2. (1) The grateful veteran relaxed in his living room after years of battle.
3. (3) Mrs. Smith hung her favorite painting on the wall.
4. (1) The car in the driveway drove 7,000 miles.
5. (3) The voters completed the forms on the table.

Practice VIII *Page 52.*

Answers will vary.

Sample answers:

1. Helen was *in a hurry*. She leapt *over the couch* and ran *out the door.* Another leap put her through the sunroof and *into the car.* Helen bought a candy bar and returned home just *before the soap opera* began.

2. Everyone *except Marie* had brought a resume to the interview. *Among the applicants*, there were only two college graduates. Seven people were applying *for two positions.* If not hired immediately, those *with excellent qualifications* would be kept in mind. Applications received *after the deadline* were not considered.

6.

Cumulative Review

This review covers:

- Performer and Action: Agreement in Number
- Action Words: Agreement in Time
- Correct Use of Descriptive Words

—After completing the Cumulative Review exercises and checking your answers with the ANSWER KEY, evaluate your ability using the SUMMARY OF RESULTS chart on page 63. Acceptable scores for each practice section are given.

—To learn your areas for skill improvement, find the question numbers you answered incorrectly on the SKILLS ANALYSIS table. The table will show which of your skills need improvement and the necessary chapters to review.

PRACTICE

Directions: The following items are based on paragraphs that contain numbered sentences. Some of the sentences may contain errors in usage. Other sentences are correct as they appear in the paragraphs. Read the paragraphs and then answer the items based on them. For each item, choose the one best answer that would result in the most effective sentence or sentences.

Items 1 to 7 refer to the following paragraphs.

(1) The flu and TB doesn't worry the American people in the 1990s. (2) Those diseases, the second-most-common cause of death in the 1930s, have lost their death grip on Americans. (3) Penicillin and immunization, as well as healthier living conditions, was the weapons used against the big three killers. (4) Can we consider our health problems solved? (5) No, we can't. (6) Now, the killer diseases of the early 20th century has been replaced by others.

(7) It is true that the genes we inherit from our parents decide, to some extent, what our health was like. (8) But most experts today agree that changing the

way we live will help us to reach a healthier old age. (9) To fight heart disease, cancer, and stroke, there's three basic "no's" to remember: no cigarettes, no (or less) salt and saturated fat, and no (or minimal) stress. (10) Along with a healthful diet of whole grains, beans, fruits, vegetables, fish, and chicken, adding regular exercise to fend off the avoidable health problems.

1. Sentence 1: **The flu and TB doesn't worry the American people in the 1990s.**

   What correction should be made to this sentence?

   (1) insert a comma after TB ① ② ③ ④ ⑤
   (2) change doesn't to don't
   (3) change the American people to the Americans
   (4) change in to during
   (5) no correction is necessary.

2. Sentence 2: **Those diseases, the second-most-common cause of death in the 1930s, have lost their death grip on Americans.**

   Which of the following is the best way to write the underlined portion of this sentence? If you think the original is the best way, choose option (1).

   (1) have lost ① ② ③ ④ ⑤
   (2) having lost
   (3) has lost
   (4) will lose
   (5) will be losing

3. Sentence 3: **Penicillin and immunization, as well as healthier living conditions, was the weapons used against the big three killers.**

   What correction should be made to this sentence?

(1) change immunization to immunizing ① ② ③ ④ ⑤
(2) remove the comma after immunization
(3) change well to good
(4) change was to were
(5) change weapons to weapon

4. Sentence 6: **Now, the killer diseases of the early 20th century has been replaced by others.**

What correction should be made to this sentence?

(1) remove the comma after Now ① ② ③ ④ ⑤
(2) change diseases to disease
(3) change has to have
(4) remove the period after others
(5) no correction is necessary

5. Sentence 7: **It is true that the genes we inherit from our parents decide, to some extent, what our health was like.**

Which of the following is the best way to write the underlined portion of this sentence? If you think the original is the best way, choose option (1).

(1) was ① ② ③ ④ ⑤
(2) has been
(3) wasn't
(4) will be
(5) won't be

6. Sentence 9: **To fight heart disease, cancer, and stroke, there's three basic "no's" to remember: no cigarettes, no (or less) salt and saturated fat, and no (or minimal) stress.**

What correction should be made to this sentence?

(1) change there's to there are ① ② ③ ④ ⑤

(2) change the colon after remember to a semicolon

(3) remove the parentheses around or less

(4) remove the comma after fat

(5) no correction is necessary

7. Sentence 10: **Along with the healthful diet of whole grains, beans, fruits, vegetables, fish, and chicken, adding regular exercise to fend off the avoidable health problems.**

What correction should be made to this sentence?

(1) change healthful to healthy ① ② ③ ④ ⑤

(2) change fish to fishes

(3) change adding to add

(4) replace off the with off of the

(5) insert a comma after avoidable

Items 8 to 15 refer to the following paragraphs.

(1) You must exercise regular; it is necessary for good health. (2) Experts have studied this real thoroughly. (3) They've concluded that exercising does more than just help you lose weight quick. (4) In fact, research offers many compelling reasons for including exercise in your life.

(5) Have you ever felt "blue"? (6) Is it harder to get a good night's sleep at these times? (7) Exercise performed often and moderate will help to lift your spirits. (8) According to studies done with mildly depressed people, aerobic activity calms the central nervous system and relieves anxiety. (9) In one study, it took only two to three weeks for the patients to feel good and sleep good.

(10) Doctors have tracked the physical effects of exercise, too. (11) One conclusion that no one can ignore is that exercise reduces the risk of heart disease. (12) The exercised heart, as a matter of fact, simply pumps more efficient. (13) In addition, exercise raises the level of "good" cholesterol, or H.D.L.'s (14) H.D.L.'s, experts think, remove the worse cholesterol from blood and arteries.

8. Sentence 1: **You must exercise regular; it is necessary for good health.**

What correction should be made to this sentence?

(1) change exercise to exercising ① ② ③ ④ ⑤
(2) change regular to regularly
(3) replace for with if you want
(4) replace health with muscles
(5) no correction is necessary

9. Sentence 2: **Experts have studied this real thoroughly.**

Which of the following is the best way to write the underlined portion of this sentence? If you think the original is the best way, choose option (1).

(1) real thoroughly ① ② ③ ④ ⑤
(2) real thorough
(3) really thoroughly
(4) really; thoroughly
(5) real, thorough

10. Sentence 3: **They've concluded that exercising does more than just help you lose weight quick.**

What correction should be made to this sentence?

(1) replace They've concluded with They think ① ② ③ ④ ⑤
(2) insert a comma after that
(3) change than to then
(4) change lose to loose
(5) change quick to quickly

11. Sentence 4: **In fact, research offers many compelling reasons for including exercise in your life.**

What correction should be made to this sentence?

(1) remove the comma after fact ① ② ③ ④ ⑤
(2) insert a colon after fact
(3) change compelling to compellingly
(4) change reasons to reason
(5) no correction is necessary

12. Sentence 7: **Exercise performed often and moderate will help to lift your spirits.**

Which of the following is the best way to write the underlined portion of this sentence? If you think the original is the best way to write the sentence, choose option (1).

(1) often and moderate ① ② ③ ④ ⑤
(2) often and moderately
(3) frequent and moderate
(4) frequently and moderate
(5) moderate and often

13. Sentence 9: **In one study, it took only two to three weeks for the patients to feel good and sleep good.**

Which of the following is the best way to write the underlined portion of this sentence? If you think the original is the best way, choose option (1).

(1) feel good and sleep good ① ② ③ ④ ⑤
(2) feel good and sleep goodly
(3) feel well and sleep better
(4) feel goodly and sleep well
(5) feel good and sleep best

14. Sentence 12: **The exercised heart, as a matter of fact, simply pumps more efficient.**

What correction should be made to this sentence?

(1) change exercised to exercising ① ② ③ ④ ⑤
(2) remove the comma after heart
(3) remove the commas around as a matter of fact
(4) change more to most
(5) change efficient to efficiently

15. Sentence 14: **H.D.L.'s, experts think, remove the worse cholesterol from blood and arteries.**

What correction should be made to this sentence?

(1) remove the comma after H.D.L.'s ① ② ③ ④ ⑤
(2) change experts to expert's
(3) change worse to bad
(4) remove the word worse
(5) no correction is necessary

Items 16 to 20 refer to the following paragraph.

(1) We spent a perfect day at the company picnic because the wind was real calm and the sun wasn't too hot. (2) Before anyone makes a decision about what activities to pursue, I had weighed all the alternatives and had chosen the best—baseball. (3) As usual, not everyone wanted to play baseball. (4) Finally, because Ellen and her friends enjoys exercise, we were able to get on with the game. (5) As it turned out, Ellen played so good that one of the men asked her to play first base on his neighborhood team.

16. Sentence 1: **We spent a perfect day at the company picnic because the wind was real calm and the sun wasn't too hot.**

What correction should be made to this sentence?

(1) insert a comma after picnic ① ② ③ ④ ⑤
(2) change real to really
(3) change wasn't to weren't
(4) change the spelling of too to to
(5) no correction is necessary

17. Sentence 2: **Before anyone makes a decision about what activities to pursue, I had weighed all the alternatives and had chosen the best—baseball.**
Which of the following is the best way to write the underlined portion of this sentence? If you think the original is the best way, choose option (1).

(1) anyone makes ① ② ③ ④ ⑤
(2) everyone makes
(3) anyone make
(4) anyone made
(5) anyone will make

18. Sentence 3: **As usual, not everyone wanted to play baseball.**
What correction should be made to this sentence?

(1) remove the comma after usual ① ② ③ ④ ⑤
(2) change everyone to anyone
(3) change wanted to wants
(4) insert a game of after play
(5) no correction is necessary

19. Sentence 4: **Finally, because Ellen and her friends enjoys exercise, we were able to get on with the game.**

What correction should be made to this sentence?

(1) remove the comma after Finally ① ② ③ ④ ⑤
(2) change enjoys to enjoy
(3) change the comma after exercise to a semicolon
(4) replace get on with continue
(5) change the period to an exclamation point

20. Sentence 5: **As it turned out, Ellen played so good that one of the men asked her to play first base on his neighborhood team.**

What correction should be made to this sentence?

(1) remove the comma after out ① ② ③ ④ ⑤
(2) change played to plays
(3) change good to well
(4) insert a comma after men
(5) change asked to asks

SUMMARY OF RESULTS

After reviewing the Answer Key on page 65, chart your scores below for each practice section.

Items	**Your Number Right**	**Your Number Wrong** (Including Omissions)	**Acceptable Score**
Items 1 to 7			5 correct
Items 8 to 15			5 correct
Items 16 to 20			4 correct

SKILLS ANALYSIS

To discover your areas for skill improvement, locate the question numbers you got wrong and circle them on this Skills Analysis chart. Then refer to the chapters listed in column 3.

Skill	Question Number	Chapter Reference
Items 1 to 7 Performer and Action: Agreement in Number	1, 2, 3, 4, 6	2
Action Words: Agreement in Time	5	2
Performer and Action: the Complete Thought	7	1
Items 8 to 15 Correct Use of Descriptive Words: Comparison	13b, 15	4
Correct Use of Descriptive Words	8, 9, 10, 11, 12, 13a, 14	3
Items 16 to 20 Performer and Action: Agreement in Number	19	2
Correct Use of Descriptive Words	16, 20	3
Performer and Action: Agreement in Time	17, 18	2

ANSWER KEY

Chapter 6

Cumulative Review

Items 1 to 7 *Page 56.*

1. (2) *Don't* agrees with the plural performer, *flu and TB.*
2. (1) No correction is necessary.
3. (4) *Were* agrees with the plural performer, *penicillin and immunization.*
4. (3) *Have* agrees with the plural performer, *diseases.*
5. (4) The paragraph discusses reaching a healthier old age. *Will be* suggests the future.
6. (1) *There are* agrees with the plural performer, *"no's."*
7. (3) *Add* is the action word that completes the thought: *Along with . . . diet . . . add . . . exercise.*

Items 8 to 15 *Page 59.*

8. (2) *Regularly* describes the action word, *exercise.*
9. (3) *Really* describes the descriptive word, *thoroughly.*
10. (5) *Quickly* describes the action word, *lose.*
11. (5) No correction is necessary.
12. (2) *Moderately* describes the action word, *performed.*
13. (3) a) *Well* is used to describe a state of health.
    b) *Better* is the comparative form of *good.*
14. (5) *Efficiently* describes the action word, *pumps.*
15. (3) *Bad* is used when there is no comparison; *worse* is used when there is a comparison of two things.

Items 16 to 20 *Page 61.*

16. (2) *Really* describes the descriptive word, *calm.*
17. (4) The action word, *made* agrees in past time with the rest of the paragraph. The time is set by the first action word in the paragraph, *spent.*
18. (5) No correction is necessary.
19. (2) *Enjoy* agrees with the plural performer, *Ellen and her friends.*
20. (3) *Well* describes the action word, *played.*

7.
Linking Words

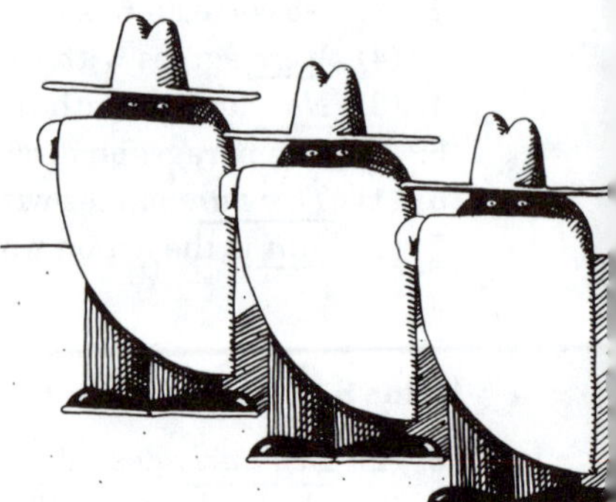

The murderer is . . ."
"Yes, yes," exclaimed Colonel Van Raalte, speaking for everyone in the living room. "Tell us who it is."

Detective Ling went on: "The murderer is . . . a real villain."

"We don't need any genius of a Chinese detective to tell us that," sneered the Colonel. "You might just twist that sentence around and tell us that 'the real villain is . . . a murderer.' It makes just as much sense—or stupidity!"

"Patience, my friend, patience," said Ling. "Before the evening is much older, I will point my finger in the direction of the killer."

Stillwell Kee
The Inscrutable Detective Ling

A Word With You . . .

The murderer is a villain.
A villain is the murderer.
Colonel Van Raalte was right in that he didn't learn anything from Detective Ling's statement.
You, however, are going to learn what a *linking word* is, why certain sentences can be reversed without changing their meanings—and you might even discover who killed Mrs. Van Raalte.

The Flink Is Pretty: The Subject Is *Being*, not *Doing*

You have been working with the simplest complete thought: a performer and an action. *For example:*

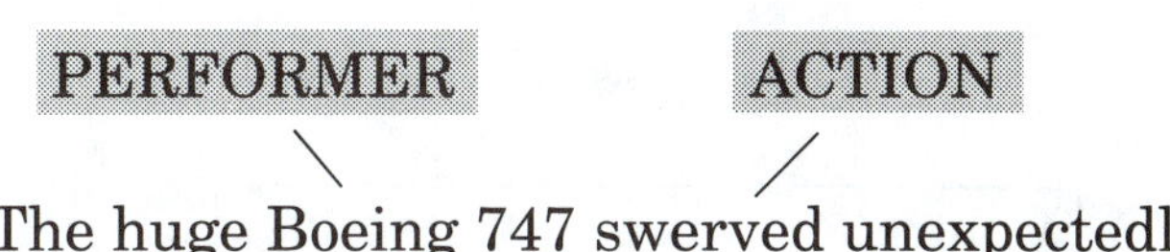

Another simple, complete thought in the English language is one in which a person or thing is *being* something rather than *doing* something. *For example:*

The Boeing 747 is huge.

As you see, the word *Boeing 747* in this sentence cannot be called the performer since it is not performing any action (swerving, flying, landing, departing). It is actually being described (huge). *Huge* describes *Boeing 747*. *Is* links the descriptive word *huge* to the subject, *Boeing 747*. The subject is the word which the sentence is about.

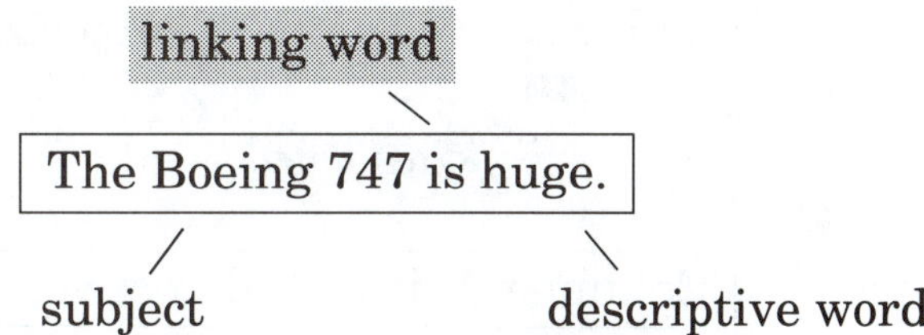

The word *is* is not an action word; it is a *linking word*. Study these examples of linking words:

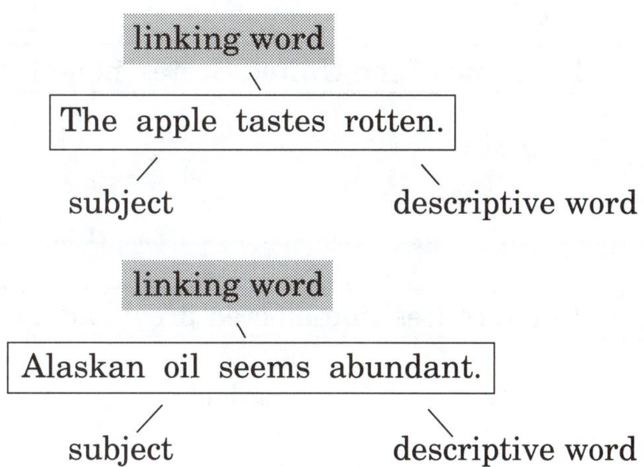

Sometimes *is* links the subject with another word that equals the subject. *For example:*

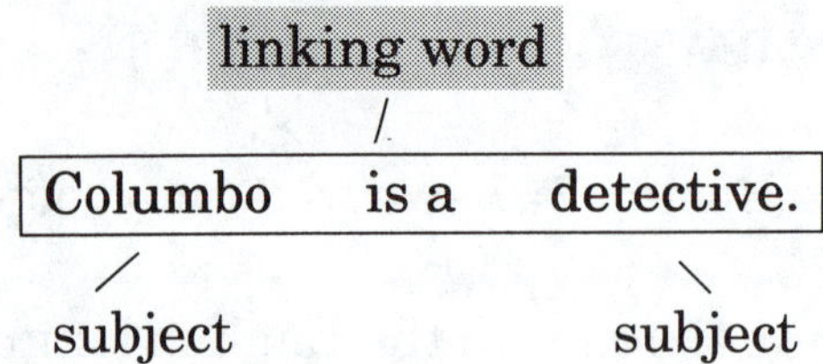

It is interesting to note that whenever the word linked with the subject *equals* the subject, the sentence can be reversed without changing its meaning. The reversed sentences may sound awkward; however, the meaning remains clear. *For example:*

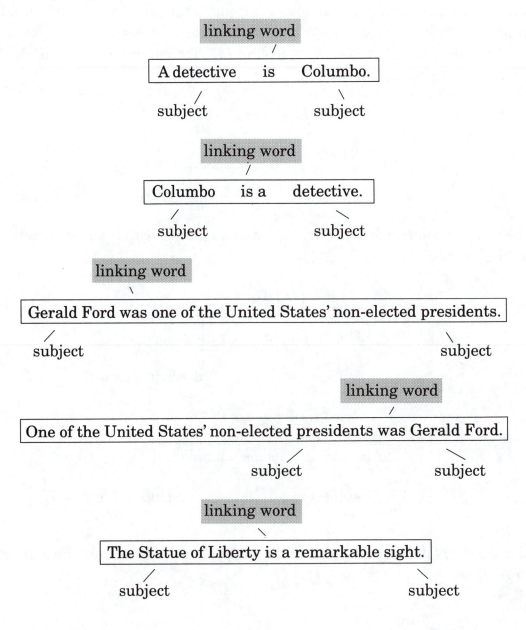

linking word

A detective is Columbo.

subject subject

linking word

Columbo is a detective.

subject subject

linking word

Gerald Ford was one of the United States' non-elected presidents.

subject subject

linking word

One of the United States' non-elected presidents was Gerald Ford.

subject subject

linking word

The Statue of Liberty is a remarkable sight.

subject subject

linking word

A remarkable sight is the Statue of Liberty.

subject subject

Linking Words

appear	remain	become	seem
feel	smell	grow	sound
look	taste	be	is
are	am	was	were

PRACTICE I

Directions: Complete each sentence using the correct form of a linking word from the above list. Several words may be appropriate. Choose one.

1. After the Lakers game, the players ________ tired.
2. The labor representative ____________ angry during the extensive negotiations.
3. The late Dwight Eisenhower ____________ once a general.
4. The watchman ________________ restless.
5. While shooting hoops, the teens never ________ exhausted.

PRACTICE II

Directions: Locate the subject in each sentence, and label it. Then underline the linking word that connects the subject and the descriptive word. Draw an arrow from the descriptive word to the subject.

subject

Example: An extensive renovation <u>seems</u> wasteful.

1. The entire class felt more ambitious after the coffee break.

2. The rosebushes in the park are breathtaking.

3. Seven noisy children suddenly grew still.

4. Theodore Roosevelt had been President of the United States for eight years.

5. The smoke in the kitchen became unbearable.

PRACTICE III

Directions: Each of the sentences below contains either an action word or a linking word. If the sentence contains an action word, blacken circle 1. If the sentence contains a linking word, blacken circle 2.

1. The snowmobile raced down the hill. ① ②
2. The tone of the meeting became threatening. ① ②
3. That candidate was our favorite. ① ②
4. We eat only organic foods. ① ②
5. Our day at the lake was pleasant. ① ②
6. Maximum individual choice is the democratic ideal. ① ②
7. Alvin Toffler, author of *Future Shock*, conjures up a bleak picture of the future. ① ②
8. People turn to a variety of experts. ① ②
9. The situation appeared uncomfortable. ① ②
10. Most people do not consider their own lives as typical life-styles. ① ②
11. It was I at the door. ① ②

Use the descriptive word correctly in the *Subject—Linking Word—Descriptive Word* pattern. Usually descriptive words that end in -ly are reserved for describing actions. Exceptions, such as *friendly*, exist. *For example:*

Our crossing guard has a *friendly* face.

CORRECT: The child *is* adorable. (linking word)
INCORRECT: The child is adorably.

CORRECT: She *speaks* too softly. (action)
INCORRECT: She speaks too soft.

PRACTICE IV

Directions: The following items are based on the paragraph that contains numbered sentences. Some of the sentences may contain errors in usage. Other sentences are correct as they appear in the paragraph. Read the paragraph and then answer the items based on it. For each item, choose the one best answer that would result in the most effective writing of the sentence.

(1) Math seems easily to accomplish when you use a calculator. (2) That's what teachers discovered when they gave students calculators to use in problem solving. (3) One fifth grader said, "I used to feel badly when I couldn't get my classroom work done in time. (4) Now I seem really quick." (5) It appears certain that classroom calculators are here to stay, especially to solve problems that require more than one operation.

1. Sentence 1: **Math seems easily to accomplish when you use a calculator.**

   Which of the following is the best way to write the underlined portion of this statement? If you think the original is the best way, choose option (1).

   (1) seems easily ① ② ③ ④ ⑤
   (2) will seem easily
   (3) seem easily
   (4) seems easy
   (5) seemed easily

2. Sentence 3: **One fifth grader said, "I used to feel badly when I couldn't get my classwork done in time."**

What correction should be made to this sentence?

(1) replace said with complained ① ② ③ ④ ⑤
(2) change badly to bad
(3) change classwork to two words
(4) insert a comma after done
(5) remove quotation marks before I

3. Sentence 5: **It appears certain that classroom calculators are here to stay, especially to solve problems that require more than one operation.**

What correction should be made to this sentence?

(1) change certain to certainly ① ② ③ ④ ⑤
(2) insert a comma after that
(3) insert they after calculator
(4) replace than with then
(5) no correction is necessary

Subject and Linking Word: Agreement in Number

You have already studied agreement of performer and action in number. The same concept applies to the subject and the linking word. For example, look at the following incorrect sentences:

1. *All* of our relatives *is* coming to dinner.
2. Those *cars appears* fast.
3. The *house are* on a hill.

Of course, these sentences sound awkward. Look at the same sentences written correctly. What changes have been made?

1. *All* of our relatives *are* coming to dinner.
2. Those *cars appear* fast.
3. The *house is* on a hill.

You see that a singular subject needs a singular linking word, and a plural subject needs a plural linking word.

Every linking word must agree with its subject in time and number. Notice that agreement in the past tense is easier to achieve than agreement in the present. *For example:*

Linking word: *appear*

Present Time, Singular and Plural

	I appear nervous.
	You appear confident.
(He)	David appears belligerent.
(She)	Pam appears calm.
(It)	The dog appears ill.
	Who appears contented?
(We)	Michael and I appear relaxed.
(You)	You and Marcel appear tired.
(They)	Ellen and Linda appear friendly.

Linking word: *appear*

Past Time, Singular and Plural

	I appeared nervous.
	You appeared nervous.
(He)	David appeared belligerent.
(She)	Pam appeared calm.
(It)	The dog appeared ill.
	Who appeared contented?
(We)	Michael and I appeared relaxed.
(You)	You and Marcel appeared tired.
(They)	Ellen and Linda appeared friendly.

Linking word: *be*

Be is a difficult word to understand. *Be* is used when preceded by *to, will, can, could, would,* or *should*. *Examples:*

The policeman wants *to be* helpful.
Next time, I *will be* more thoughtful.
Crowded supermarkets *can be* annoying.
This *could be* one chance in a lifetime.
The supervisor *would be* grateful if you could work late.
World peace *should be* everyone's goal.

Other forms of *be* are used in sentences which do not have the helping words *to, will, can, could, would,* or *should.* You already are familiar with these forms: *am, is, are, was, were*. The following lists show you the proper use of these words.

Linking word: *be*

Present Time, Singular and Plural

	I am a nurse.
	You are a policeman.
(He)	David is a crossing guard.
(She)	Pam is a teacher.
(It)	The dog is a Collie.
	Who is that lady?
(We)	Bill and I are co-chairmen.
(You)	You and your brother are partners.
	Who are those ladies?
(They)	Ellen and Linda are sisters.

Linking word: *be*

Past Time, Singular and Plural

	I was a nurse.
	You were a policeman.
(He)	David was a crossing guard.
(She)	Pam was a teacher.
(It)	The dog was a Collie.
	Who was that lady?
(We)	Bill and I were co-chairmen.

(You) You and your brother were partners.

Who were those ladies?

(They) Ellen and Linda were sisters.

PRACTICE V

Directions: Use *is, are, was,* or *were* in each of the following sentences.

1. Fritz ____________________ always late.
2. The Murphys ____________ home from their vacation.
3. The woman and her child ____________ in the park.
4. The books __________________ interesting.
5. He _______________ a member of the group when it was first formed.

PRACTICE VI

Directions: Use the *correct form* of one of the following linking words to complete each of the following sentences. Use at least one form of each word.

be *grow* *become* *appear* *feel*

1. The soldiers ________________ weary after the long march.
2. The crowd ___________________ angry.
3. The child quickly ___________________ tired of his new toy.
4. Mr. and Mrs. Smith __________________ elated after winning the lottery.
5. The football players __________________ traded.

PRACTICE VII

Directions: Items 1 to 5 are based on the following paragraphs that contain numbered sentences. Some of the sentences may contain errors in usage. Other sentences are correct as they appear in the paragraphs. Read the paragraphs and then answer the items based on them. For each item, choose the one best answer that would result in the most effective writing of the sentence.

(1) Ecology is emerging into an exact science. (2) At last, the function of waste products are being discovered. (3) Glass, plastic, and paper finally have been recognized as reusable and are being recycled. (4) Now, as their multiple functions are gradually being studied, their importance is more apparent than ever before.

(5) Finally, man's belief that his own actions, at least in part, control his destiny are being justified. (6) Each local ecology group, through its efforts, have been instrumental, in recent years, in identifying and solving solid waste problems. (7) The chairman of one local organization believes that the advent of recycling waste products are just beginning. (8) The same is true of nonpolluting detergents, which may perhaps be even more important.

1. Sentence 2: **At last, the function of waste products are being discovered.**

   What correction should be made to this sentence?

   (1) replace the comma after last with a semicolon ① ② ③ ④ ⑤
   (2) change function to functioning
   (3) insert way they before function
   (4) change waste to wasted
   (5) change are to is

2. Sentence 3: **Glass, plastic, and paper finally have been recognized as reusable and are being recycled.**

   What correction should be made to this sentence?

   (1) insert a comma after paper ① ② ③ ④ ⑤
   (2) change have been to must be
   (3) change have been to has been
   (4) change are being to is being
   (5) no correction is necessary

3. Sentence 5: **Finally, man's belief that his own actions, at least in part, control his destiny are being justified.**

   What correction should be made to this sentence?

   (1) change man's belief to man is believing ① ② ③ ④ ⑤
   (2) replace his with their
   (3) remove the words at least in part
   (4) change control to controls
   (5) change are to is

4. Sentence 6: **Each local ecology group, through its efforts, have been instrumental, in recent years, in identifying and solving solid waste problems.**

Which of the following is the best way to write the underlined portion of this sentence? If you think the original is the best way, choose option (1).

(1) Each local ecology group, through its efforts, have been ① ② ③ ④ ⑤
(2) Each local ecology group, through their efforts, have been
(3) Each local ecology group, through its efforts, has been
(4) Each local ecology group through its effort, have been
(5) Each local ecology group through their effort, have been

5. Sentence 7: **The chairman of one local organization believes that the advent of recycling waste products are just beginning.**

What correction should be made to this sentence?

(1) change believes to believe ① ② ③ ④ ⑤
(2) change advent to advents
(3) change are just beginning to are beginning
(4) change are to is
(5) no correction is necessary

The Missing Link(ing Word)

Often, a linking word is combined with another word. In combining, the initial letters of the linking word are dropped and replaced by an apostrophe.

Example: *There is* one answer to that question.
There's one answer to that question.

There is = there's

Common missing link(ing word) combinations:

he is = he's	*He's* the most forward-looking senator.
she is = she's	*She's* the strongest voice in Congress.
we are = we're	*We're* eager to hear your proposal.

you are = you're	*You're* one of the few people I trust.
They are = they're	*They're* determined to interfere.
here is = here's	*Here's* your hat.
it is = it's	*It's* an active committee.

NOTE: *Its* **without the apostrophe indicates possession.**

Example: The committee concluded its hearing.

Missing link combinations with *not*:

is not = isn't	Destruction *isn't* my idea of fun.
are not = aren't	The striking workers *aren't* going to settle for less pay.
were not = weren't	Lou and Toby *weren't* on the train.
was not = wasn't	I *wasn't* prepared for the crowd at the bus stop.

PRACTICE VIII

Directions: In each of the following sentences, there is an underlined phrase. Make a missing link combination from each underlined phrase and write it on the line provided.

Example: If it is convenient for Lucy, the bowling team will meet at 6 PM.
it's

1. They are the best approaches to the problem. __________
2. If you can understand management-labor relations, you are a better businessman than I. __________________
3. Agreement is not as important as understanding. _______
4. We did not realize that the job action had ended. __________________
5. Here is the name of an excellent mechanic. ____________
6. The legislators were not expecting such a strong consumer lobby. ______________
7. He is the least competent programmer in the company. __________________
8. There is only one best product in each line of merchandise. ______________

ANSWER KEY

Chapter 7

Linking Words

Practice I *Page 69.*

Answers may vary.
Sample answers:

1. appeared, felt, looked
2. seemed, became, grew
3. was
4. became, grew, is, was
5. were, seemed

Practice II *Page 69.*

1. The entire class *felt* more ambitious after the coffee break. (subject: class)
2. The rosebushes in the park *are* breathtaking. (subject: rosebushes)
3. Seven noisy children suddenly *grew* still. (subject: children)
4. Theodore Roosevelt *had been* President of the United States for eight years. (subject: Roosevelt)
5. The smoke in the kitchen *became* unbearable. (subject: smoke)

Practice III *Page 70.*

1. (1) raced
2. (2) became
3. (2) was
4. (1) eat
5. (2) was
6. (2) is
7. (1) conjures
8. (1) turn
9. (2) appeared
10. (1) consider
11. (2) was

Practice IV *Page 71.*

1. (4) Math seems easy to acomplish . . .
2. (2) I used to feel bad . . .
3. (5) No correction is necessary.

Practice V *Page 75.*

Answers may vary.
Sample answers:

1. is, was
2. are, were
3. are, were
4. are, were
5. was

Practice VI *Page 75.*

Answers may vary.
Sample answers:

1. were, grew, became, appeared, felt, are, become, grow, appear, feel
2. was, grew, became, appeared, appears, becomes, grows, is
3. grew, became, is, grows, becomes
4. were, appeared, felt, are, appear, feel
5. were, are

Practice VII *Page 75.*

subject — linking word

1. (5) At last, the function (of waste products) *is* being discovered.
Is agrees in number with the singular subject, *function.*

subject — linking word

2. (5) Glass, plastic, and paper finally *have been* recognized as reusable . . .
Have been agrees in number with the plural subjects, *glass, plastic,* and *paper.*

subject — linking word

3. (5) Finally, man's belief (that his own actions, at least in part, control his destiny) *is* being justified.
Is agrees in number with the singular subject, *belief.*

subject — linking word

4. (3) Each local ecology group (, through its efforts,) *has been* instrumental . . . .
Has been agrees in number with the singular subject, *group.*

subject

5. (4) The chairman of one local organization believes that the advent (of recycling waste products)

linking word

is just beginning.
Is agrees in number with the singular word, *advent.*

Practice VIII *Page 78.*

1. They're
2. you're
3. isn't
4. didn't
5. Here's
6. weren't
7. He's
8. There's

8.

Agreement: Special Problems

Each of the veterinary surgeons gathered around Ruffian knew *his* job. *Neither* the doctors nor Mr. Janney *was* willing to give up on the magnificent filly, but despite *everyone's* desire to do *his* best, it became necessary to put the horse to sleep.

—Murray Bromberg
The Great Match Race

A Word With You . . .

The scene from the book took place in the early hours of Monday morning, July 7, 1975, as the veterinarians tried to save the life of a great horse whose leg had been shattered.

Our chief interest, however, is in the italicized words:
each—his
neither . . . nor—was
everyone's—his
Some people might not see the reason for using these word combinations. Their relationships will be made clear in the following pages.

You know that an action word must agree with its performer in number, and with the sentence or paragraph in time. *For example:*

The jury *enters* the courtroom. A hush *falls* over the crowd. The judge *asks* for the verdict.

You know that a linking word must agree with its subject in number and with the sentence or paragraph in time. *For example:*

Court *is* in session. Please *remain* silent.
The defendant *seems* apprehensive. The prosecutor *appears* angry.

Rules Concerning Special Problems of Agreement

- *Each*
  Each is singular when it is the performer or subject of the sentence. *Example:*

Performer — Action

Each *shows* promise.

PRACTICE I

Directions: Underline either the singular or plural action word or linking word that correctly completes the sentence.

1. Each (gives, give) a lecture.
2. Each of the teachers (gives, give) a lecture.
3. They each (gives, give) a lecture.
4. Each (is, are) a good candidate.

- *Either-Or*
  When using *either-or*, you are choosing *one* or the *other*. The action or linking word is *singular* if the performer or subject closest to it is singular.

  Example: Either Tom *or* Bill drives to school.

Drives agrees with the singular performer, *Bill*.
The action or linking word is *plural* if the performer or subject closest to it is plural.

Example: Either Tom *or* his friends drive to school.

Drive agrees with the plural performer, *friends*.

PRACTICE II

Directions: Underline either the singular or plural linking word that correctly completes each sentence.

1. Either the coach or the captain (is, are) late.

2. Either the coach or the players (is, are) late.
3. Either the players or the coach (is, are) late.
4. Either these players or those players (is, are) late.

- *Any*

Any is singular. It is used when a choice involves *three* or more. *Either* is used for a choice between *two*.

Example: <u>Any</u> of the <u>*three*</u> movies suits me.

PRACTICE III **Directions:** Underline either the singular or plural action or linking word that correctly completes the sentence.

1. Any of the sandwiches (is, are) fine.
2. Any of the four records (sounds, sound) good.
3. (Any, either) of the three books (serves, serve) well.

- *Here* and *There*

In sentences that begin with *here* or *there,* the action or linking word must agree with the performer or subject. *Here* and *there* are never performers or subjects.

Example: Here (is, are) my coat.
(WHAT is here? COAT. COAT is the SUBJECT.) *Coat* is singular; therefore the singular linking word *is* correctly completes the sentence.

PRACTICE IV **Directions:** Locate the performer or subject in each sentence. Underline the action or linking word that correctly completes each sentence.

1. There (is, are) my boots.
2. There (is, are) two sides to the argument.
3. Here (goes, go) my last chance.
4. There (is, are) no way out.

- *Who* and *That*

You are familiar with the following sentence structures:

performer action

The woman attends every meeting.

action performer

Woman is singular; attends agrees with woman.

performer action

One (of those women) attends every meeting.

action performer

One is singular: *attends* agrees with *one*.

The following example is significantly different from the above.

One (of those women) *who* ATTEND every meeting seldom SPEAKS.

Ready?

performer action

"One seldom speaks" is the core of the sentence.

One is singular: *speaks* agrees with *one*.

"Of those women who attend every meeting" describes or tells more about, *one*.

Who might be singular or plural. How do we decide? We look at the word to which *who* refers. In this case, that word is *women*. *Women* is plural; therefore, *who* is plural. Within the descriptive group of words, "of those women who attend every meeting," *attend* must agree with *who*. *Who* is plural; *attend* agrees with *who*.

This rule also applies to *that*.

performer action

Examples: The *ruler belongs* to me.
One (of those rulers) belongs to me.
One (of those rulers) *that* ARE on the desk BELONGS to me.

PRACTICE V

Directions: Underline either the singular or the plural action or linking word that correctly completes each sentence.

1. One of the musicians (plays, play) above the others.
2. Several of those pencils (belongs, belong) in this container.
3. John Kennedy was one of those leaders who (has, have) charisma.
4. One of those underdeveloped nations that (counts, count) upon outside sources for food will inevitably be disappointed.
5. One of those vocations that (has, have) always appealed to me (is, are) radio announcing.

- *Surprisingly Singular Subjects*
  Some words seem to refer to more than one person. In fact, they do not. They are singular. These include:

Everybody	means every *single* body.
Somebody	means some *one* body.
Anybody	means any *one* body.
None	means no *one*.
Everyone	means every *one*.

- *Some Plural Subjects*
  Six words that take plural action or linking words are:
  all few several both many some

PRACTICE VI

Directions: Underline the action word that correctly completes each sentence.

1. Everybody (hear, hears) a different drummer.
2. Somebody (call, calls) our office at 5:05 each day.
3. Anybody who (want, wants) to can join our cooperative supermarket.
4. None of the scout leaders (shirk, shirks) his reponsibility.

To Do

I do	we do
you do	you do
he, she, it does	they do

REVIEW EXERCISES

PRACTICE VII

Directions: Underline the action or linking word that agrees with the performer or subject in each of the following sentences.

Example: The coat (*is*, are) too large.

1. The books (is, are) on the shelf.
2. Each (selects, select) his own menu.
3. Each of the students (is, are) registered for ten weeks.
4. Any of the six choices (is, are) suitable.
5. Everybody (does, do) his job.
6. This kind of movie (is, are) boring.
7. Those kinds of flowers (seems, seem) delicate.
8. None of the candidates (speaks, speak) well.
9. There (was, were) several good items on the menu.
10. Neither the meats nor the vegetables (is, are) fresh.
11. Either the children or the babysitter (drinks, drink) the milk.
12. He (doesn't, don't) speak well.
13. She is one of those women who never (says, say) what they mean.
14. One of those tractors (is, are) broken.

TO DO STATEMENTS

She works with Allen.

Works agrees with *she.*

She does work with Allen.

Does agrees with *she; work* is used in the "to work" form.
(*Does* would be used in this sentence for emphasis or clarification.)

They work with Allen.

Works agrees with *they.*

They do work with Allen.

Do agrees with *they; work* is used in the "to work" form.

TO DO QUESTIONS

Does she work with Allen?

Does agrees with *she; work* is used in the "to work" form.
In a typical question, the subject (*she*) follows *does.*

Do they work with Allen?

When using a negative, *not* follows *do* or *does:*

Doesn't she work with Allen?

Don't they work with Allen?

PRACTICE VIII

Directions: If the action or linking word in each sentence agrees with the subject, blacken circle 1. If the action or linking word does not agree with the subject, blacken circle 2.

1. There were two planes outside the hangar. ① ②
2. Macaroni or potatoes go with this dinner. ① ②
3. Any of these dips are great with crackers. ① ②
4. Ten minutes of my time is all that I can offer. ① ②
5. Don't she know your address? ① ②
6. My son or my daughter are coming for me. ① ②
7. There's two overseas routes to Europe. ① ②
8. One of the most recent discoveries are in regard to aging. ① ②
9. Doesn't any famous politician ever arrive on time? ① ②

10. Here's Joanna's friends. ① ②
11. One of those library books is lost. ① ②
12. Either the coach or the players argue with the manager every week. ① ②
13. Oprah Winfrey is one of those people who says what she means. ① ②

PRACTICE IX

Directions: Items 1 to 8 are based on the following paragraphs that contain numbered sentences. Some of the sentences may contain errors in usage. Other sentences are correct as they appear in the paragraphs. Read the paragraphs and then answer the items based on them. For each item, choose the one best answer that would result in the most effective writing of the sentence.

(1) There's always some people who get more work done on the job than others. (2) How do they manage it? (3) The answer to this question don't necessarily depend upon what they know, but, rather, upon how they work. (4) Each of us need a plan for getting our work done. (5) Here's two ideas that will help to speed the job along.

(6) First, as each work week ends, make a general plan for the following one. (7) Then, on Monday, break down the plan into smaller tasks. (8) Each of your tasks take its place on your "to do" list. (9) Work to check off all the items on your list by the end of the day. (10) Second, decide to work uninterrupted for a certain amount of time. (11) Everybody in an office like to talk, but you can control how much you socialize. (12) Just tell anyone who stop by to chat that you'll talk to that person later.

1. Sentence 1: **There's always some people who get more work done on the job than others.**

What correction should be made to this sentence?

(1) change There's to There are ① ② ③ ④ ⑤
(2) replace always some with always a few
(2) change who to whom
(4) insert a comma after who
(5) replace on with at

2. Sentence 3: **The answer to this question don't necessarily depend upon what they know, but, rather, upon how they work.**

What correction should be made to this sentence?

(1) change this question to these questions ① ② ③ ④ ⑤
(2) change necessarily to necessary
(3) change don't to doesn't
(4) remove the comma after know
(5) insert a semicolon after rather

3. Sentence 4: **Each of us need a plan for getting our work done.**

Which of the following is the best way to write the underlined portion of this sentence? If you think the original is the best way, choose option (1).

(1) Each of us need ① ② ③ ④ ⑤
(2) Each of you need
(3) Each and everyone of us need
(4) Each of us needs
(5) Each of them need

4. Sentence 5: **Here's two ideas that will help to speed the job along.**

What correction should be made to this sentence?

(1) change Here's to Here are ① ② ③ ④ ⑤
(2) insert a comma after ideas
(3) replace that with who
(4) remove help to
(5) no correction is necessary

5. Sentence 6: **First, as each work week ends, make a general plan for the following one.**

What correction should be made to this sentence?

(1) remove the comma after First ① ② ③ ④ ⑤
(2) insert a semicolon after ends
(3) change make to makes
(4) replace general with specific
(5) no correction is necessary

6. Sentence 8: **Each of your tasks take its place on your "to do" list.**

Which of the following is the best way to write the underlined portion of this sentence? If you think the original is the best way, choose option (1).

(1) tasks take ① ② ③ ④ ⑤
(2) tasks takes
(3) tasks taking
(4) tasks; take
(5) tasks is taking

7. Sentence 11: **Everybody in an office like to talk, but you can control how much you socialize.**

What correction should be made to this sentence?

(1) replace Everybody with Everyone ① ② ③ ④ ⑤
(2) remove an
(3) change like to talk to like talking
(4) change like to likes
(5) insert a comma after but you

8. Sentence 12: **Just tell anyone who stop by to chat that you'll talk to that person later.**

Which of the following is the best way to write the underlined portion of this sentence? If you think the original is the best way, choose option (1).

(1) anyone who stop ① ② ③ ④ ⑤
(2) anyone to stop
(3) anyone who stops
(4) anyone that stop
(5) each who stop

ANSWER KEY

Chapter 8

Agreement: Special Problems

Practice I *Page 82.*

1. Each *gives* — *Gives* agrees with the singular performer, *each*.
2. Each *gives* — *Gives* agrees with the singular performer, *each*.
3. They *give* — *Give* agrees with the plural performer, *they*.
4. Each *is* — *Is* agrees with the singular subject, *each*.

Practice II *Page 82.*

1. captain *is* — *Is* agrees with the singular subject, *captain*.
2. players *are* — *Are* agrees with the plural subject, *players*.
3. coach *is* — *Is* agrees with the singular subject, *coach*.
4. players *are* — *Are* agrees with the plural subject, *players*.

Practice III *Page 83.*

Linking Word

1. Any (of the sandwiches) *is* fine.
   Is agrees with the singular subject, *any*.

Linking Word

2. Any (of the four records) *sounds* good.
   Sounds agrees with the singular subject, *any*.

Action Word

3. Any (of the three books) *serves* well.
   Serves agrees with the singular performer, any.

Practice IV *Page 83.*

1. There *are* my boots.
   Are agrees with the plural subjects, *boots*.
2. There *are* two sides to the argument.
   Are agrees with the plural subject, *sides*.
3. Here *goes* my last chance.
   Goes agrees with the singular performer, *chance*.
4. There *is* no way out.
   Is agrees with the singular subject, *way*.

Practice V *Page 85.*

1. One of the musicians *plays* . . .
   Plays agrees with the singular subject, *One*.

2. Several of those pencils *belong* . . .
   Belong agrees with the plural subject, *several*.
3. John Kennedy was one of those leaders who *have* charisma.
   Have agrees with its subject *who*, which refers to the plural word, *leaders*.
4. One of those underdeveloped nations that *count* . . .
   Count agrees with its subject *that*, which refers to the plural word, *nations*.
5. One of those vocations that *have* always appealed to me *is* . . .
   Have agrees with its subject, *that*, which refers to the plural word, *vocations*; *is* agrees with the singular subject, *One*.

Practice VI *Page 86.*

1. Everybody *hears* a different drummer.
2. Somebody *calls* our office at 5:05 each day.
3. Anybody who *wants* to can join our cooperative supermarket.
4. None of the scout leaders *shirks* his responsibility.

The performer in each sentence is singular and requires a singular action word.

REVIEW

Practice VII *Page 86.*

The correct action or linking word in each sentence is underlined twice.
The subject in each sentence is underlined once.

1. The books are on the shelf.
2. Each selects his own menu.
3. Each (of the students) is registered for ten weeks.
4. Any (of the six choices) is suitable.
5. Everybody does his job.
6. This kind (of movie) is boring.
7. Those kinds (of flowers) seem delicate.
8. None (of the candidates) speaks well.
9. There were several good items on the menu.
10. Neither the meats nor the vegetables are fresh.
11. Either the children or the babysitter drinks the milk.
12. He doesn't speak well.
13. She is one of those women who never say what they mean.
14. One (of those tractors) is broken.

Practice VIII *Page 87.*

1. (1) planes were there
   Were agrees with the plural subject, *planes*.
2. (1) potatoes go
   Go agrees with the plural subject, potatoes.
3. (2) Any (of these dips) is
   Is agrees with the singular subject, *any*.
4. (1) ten minutes (as a unit of time) is
   Is agrees with the singular subject, *ten minutes*.
5. (2) Doesn't she know
   Doesn't agrees with the singular performer, *she*.

6. (2) my daughter is
Is agrees with the singular subject, *daughter*.
7. (2) two routes are there
Are agrees with the plural subject, *routes*.
8. (2) One (of the most recent discoveries) is
Is agrees with the singular subject, *one*.
9. (1) Doesn't any famous politician ever arrive
Doesn't agrees with the singular performer, *any*.
10. (2) Joanna's friends are here
Are agrees with the plural subject, *friends*.
11. (1) One (of those library books) is
Is agrees with the singular subject, *one*.
12. (1) players argue
Argue agrees with the plural performer, *players*.
13. (2) people who say what they mean
Say agrees with the plural performer, *who*.
They agrees with the plural performer, *who*.
Mean agrees with *they*.

Practice IX *Page 88.*

1. (1) There *are* always people . . .
The plural linking word, *are*, agrees with the plural subject, *people*.
2. (3) The answer to this question *doesn't* . . .
The singular helping word, *does (does not)*, agrees with the singular subject, *answer*.
3. (4) Each of us *needs* . . .
The singular action word, *needs*, agrees with the *singular* performer, *Each*.
4 (1) *Here are* two ideas . . .
The plural linking word, *are*, agrees with the plural subject, *ideas (Two ideas are here . . .)*
5. (5) No correction is necessary.
6. (2) Each of your *tasks* takes . . .
The singular action word, *takes*, agrees with the singular peformer, *Each*.
7. (4) Everybody in an office *likes* . . .
The singular action word, *likes*, agrees with the singular performer, *Everybody*.
8. (3) Just tell anyone who *stops* . . .
The singular action word, *stops*, agrees with the singular performer, who, which refers to *anyone*.

9.

Time: Special Problems

Eddie's father insisted that he pay attention. If Dad was going to give up a half hour of Archie Bunker in order to help Eddie with his homework, he wanted to make sure that Eddie was all ears.

"Now, there are the *present perfect,* the *past perfect,* and the *future perfect,*" explained Eddie's father. "Why can't you understand that?"

"Well, nobody's perfect, Dad," quipped Eddie.

"Okay, wise guy," his father said. "Just listen to this example of the *future perfect tense*: 'By next week, you *will have discovered* a decrease in your allowance.'"

Carol Lehrer
Tenting Out in the Suburbs

A Word With You . . .

It might not be cricket to cut a youngster's allowance because he had trouble with tenses (time), but Eddie's father seemed to know what he was doing in grammar, as well as in child-rearing.

The hapless Eddie was not concentrating—but you will, we are sure. Fortunately, you won't have to grapple with the "perfect" terms.

You know that sentences express time:

Present Action	-	I commute to work each day.
Past Action	-	I commuted to work each day.
Future Action	-	I will commute to work each day.

Occasionally, time is more complicated than the simple expression of past or future.

- Sometimes an action that began in the past continues into the present.

  Examples: I *have commuted* to work for six years.

  Marie *has commuted* to work for five years.

The addition of the helping word *have* or *has* expresses the idea of an action that began in the past, but is continuing into the present. In the above examples, the helping words, *have* and *has*, are in the present and the action word, *commuted*, is in the past.

Common Misuses of *Has* and *Have*

a. I *commuted* to work for six years and I am tired of commuting.

b. I *commuted* to work for six years and I have been tired of commuting.

The only correct use of the helping word have in these examples is:

I *have commuted* to work for six years and I am tired of commuting.

PRACTICE I

PART A **Directions:** Write the correct form of each action word on the left to combine it with the helping word on the right. The correct form may already appear.

watch have ____________________

draw has ____________________

learn has ____________________

see have ____________________

prepared has ____________________

go have ____________________

PART B **Directions:** Write a sentence for each combination you developed in Part A. The first one is already done for you.

Example: I have watched my last hockey game.

1. ______________________________
2. ______________________________
3. ______________________________
4. ______________________________
5. ______________________________

PRACTICE II

Directions: The following items are based on a paragraph that contains numbered sentences. Some of the sentences may contain errors in time. Other sentences are correct as they appear in the paragraph. Read the paragraph and then answer the items based on it. For each item, choose the one best answer that would result in the correct use of time in the sentence.

(1) Matthew was the last in line since he began school. (2) He has always resented that. (3) Occasionally, Matthew refused to go to the end of the line. (4) We have continually reminded him that the end of the line is common when your last name is Zarrow.

1. Sentence 1: **Matthew was the last in line since he began school.**

   Which of the following is the best way to write the underlined portion of this sentence? If you think the original is the best way, choose option (1).

   (1) was ① ② ③ ④ ⑤
   (2) has been
   (3) had been
   (4) is
   (5) will have been

2. Sentence 3: **Occasionally, Matthew refused to go to the end of the line.**

   Which of the following is the best way to write the underlined portion of this sentence? If you think the original is the best way, choose option (1).

(1) refused ①②③④⑤
(2) refuses
(3) had refused
(4) has refused
(5) would have refused

- Sometimes a past action has occurred before another past action.

  Example: I *had commuted* for two hours each way before I *moved* to the city.

The addition of the helping word *had* shows that the commuting occurred in the past *before* the moving occurred.

Common Misuses of *Had*

a. I *had commuted* two hours each way before I had moved to the city.
b. I *commuted* two hours each way before I *had moved* to the city.

The only correct use of the helping word *had* in this sentence is:

I *had commuted* two hours each way before I *moved* to the city.

PRACTICE III

PART A **Directions:** Write the correct form of each action word on the left to combine it with *had* on the right.

show had ____________________
copy had ____________________
apply had ____________________
fall had ____________________

PART B **Directions:** Write a sentence for each combination you developed in Part A. The first one is already done for you.

Example: Before she asked for a reduced price, Maria *had shown* the pull in the sweater to the salesperson.

1. ______________________________
2. ______________________________
3. ______________________________

PRACTICE IV

Directions: The following items are based on a paragraph that contains numbered sentences. Some of the sentences may contain errors in time. Other sentences are correct as they appear in the paragraph. Read the paragraph and then answer the items based on it. For each item, choose the one best answer that would result in the correct writing of the sentence.

(1) If I knew I could have a paying job, I never would have volunteered my services. (2) Now, I am volunteering for three months, and the agency advertises for an assistant for me. (3) An assistant would be great, but not one earning money while I don't. (4) I think I figured out a solution to this problem. (5) I will apply for the assistant's job.

1. Sentence 1: **If I knew I could have a paying job, I never would have volunteered my services.**

   Which of the following is the best way to write the underlined portion of this sentence? If you think the original is the best way, choose option (1).

   (1) I knew I could have ① ② ③ ④ ⑤
   (2) I'd a known I could have
   (3) I knew I could of
   (4) I had known I could have
   (5) I had know I could have

2. Sentence 2: **Now, I am volunteering for three months, and the agency advertises for an assistant for me.**

   Which of the following is the best way to write the underlined portion of this sentence? If you think the original is the best way, choose option (1).

(1) am volunteering ①②③④⑤
(2) volunteer
(3) have been volunteering
(4) am volunteered
(5) had been volunteering

3. Sentence 4: **I think I figured out a solution to this problem.**

Which of the following is the best way to write the underlined portion of this sentence? If you think the original is the best way, choose option (1).

(1) I think I figured out ①②③④⑤
(2) I think I have figured out
(3) I think I had figured out
(4) I thought I had figured out
(5) I thought I have figured out

- Sometimes a future action can occur before another future action.

  Example: I *will have commuted* four million miles by the time I retire.

The addition of the helping word *have* shows that the commuting will be completed before the retiring.

Common Misuses of *Will Have*

a. I *will have commuted* four million miles by the time I *will have retired.*

b. I *will commute* four million miles by the time I *will have retired.*

The only correct use of *will have* in this sentence is:

I *will have commuted* four million miles by the time I retire.

PRACTICE V

PART A

Directions: Write the correct form of each action word on the left to combine it with *will have* on the right.

leave — will have ____________________
complete — will have ____________________
see — will have ____________________
adjourn — will have ____________________
call — will have ____________________

PART B

Directions: Write sentences using the combinations you developed in Part A. The first one is already done for you.

Example: By the time I close up the office, the last train *will have left* the station.

1. ____
2. ____
3. ____
4. ____

PRACTICE VI

Directions: The following items are based on a paragraph that contains numbered sentences. Some of the sentences may contain errors in time. Other sentences are correct as they appear in the paragraph. Read the paragraph and then answer the items based on it. For each item, choose the one best answer that would result in the correct use of time in the sentence.

(1) John is always one step behind Sue. (2) They plan to meet in Seattle. (3) By the time John's plane lands in Chicago for his connecting flight, Sue will arrive in Seattle. (4) Before John gets to the hotel in Seattle, Sue will be checked in. (5) Sue will have had dinner before John unpacks.

1. Sentence 3: **By the time John's plane lands in Chicago for his connecting flight, Sue will arrive in Seattle.**

   Which of the following is the best way to write the underlined portion of this sentence? If you think the original is the best way, choose option (1).

(1) will arrive ① ② ③ ④ ⑤
(2) arrived
(3) has arrived
(4) will have arrived
(5) will have arriven

2. Sentence 4: **Before John gets to the hotel in Seattle, Sue <u>will have checked in.</u>**

Which of the following is the best way to write the underlined portion of this sentence? If you think the original is the best way, select option (1).

(1) will have checked in. ① ② ③ ④ ⑤
(2) will check in.
(3) had checked in.
(4) will get to check in.
(5) checks in.

- When two actions occur simultaneously, their time must be the same.

Example: As the curtain *rises*, the audience *applauds*.
As the curtain *rose*, the audience *applauded*.

Common Errors Regarding Simultaneous Actions

a. As the curtain *rose* to reveal the elaborate set, the enthusiastic audience *had applauded*.
b. As the curtain *had risen* to reveal the elaborate set, the enthusiastic audience *applauded*.

In sentences a and b, the audience applauded *as* the curtain rose. Since both actions occurred *at the same time*, neither action word should be accompanied by *had*.

PRACTICE VII **Directions:** Select the incorrect sentence in each group and rewrite it correctly on the line below.

1. (1) As the class filed out of the room, David noticed the trampled book on the floor.
   (2) When the power failed, all of our food was ruined.
   (3) As soon as you finish rereading *The Client*, please call me.
   (4) As it bit the worm, the fish had realized its error.

   ____

2. (1) As we began our trip in our brand-new convertible, gray clouds hovered threateningly above.
   (2) When the automobile industry's strike ended, our car was delivered.
   (3) When I lifted the papers, I had found Ellen's missing glasses.
   (4) As soon as you gave me your requirements, I shipped the order.

   ____

- Linking words express time, also. *Has*, *have*, and *had* are used with linking words in order to clarify time.

  Examples: Tom *has been* irritable all morning.
  Tom *had been* irritable before he received his promotion.
  Tom *will have* been president for two years, by the time he retires.

PRACTICE VIII **Directions:** Select the incorrect sentence in each group and rewrite it correctly on the line below.

1. (1) I have felt tired since my illness.
   (2) Jules always has been a good sport.
   (3) Before she began working full-time, Erica seemed more relaxed.
   (4) By the time this very long documentary ends, I will have grown bored.

   ____

2. (1) The amplifier had sounded distorted for several hours before it stopped working.
   (2) The court claimed that the children had been neglected.
   (3) For the past three days, your socks have been in the same place on the floor.
   (4) As I looked across the room at the woman who bore an uncanny resemblance to me, I had felt as though I were looking into a mirror.

____

REVIEW EXERCISES

PRACTICE IX

Directions: Select the incorrect sentence for each group and rewrite it correctly on the line below.

1. (1) I am teaching for twenty years.
   (2) Betty Friedan has been a pioneer in the women's movement.
   (3) The Thompsons have owned the drugstore since 1947.
   (4) Before he spoke, he had carefully prepared his speech.

____

2. (1) As the car pulled to the curb, a man jumped out.
   (2) Before the phone stopped ringing, Mary had answered it.
   (3) Before the music had stopped, a shot rang out.
   (4) When you arrive, we will begin the discussion.

____

3. (1) By next week, the price of lettuce will have doubled.
   (2) Before the doorbell rang, Ida seemed nervous.
   (3) Because he had known the temper of the crowd, he spoke calmly and clearly.
   (4) By the time the repairman arrives, I will have left.

____

4. (1) By this time tomorrow, I will have taken the test.
   (2) If you studied, you might have known the answer.
   (3) The historian carefully studied his subject.
   (4) Before boarding the plane, Tom had expressed a fear of flying.

____

5. (1) These sentences have been difficult.
   (2) Last week, they would have been impossible.
   (3) By next week, you will have mastered the problem.
   (4) Before he passed the test, the man studied for many hours.

____

PRACTICE
X **Directions:** Which is the best way to write the underlined portion of each sentence? If you think the original is the best way, choose option (1).

1. I signed the letter several days after I <u>wrote it.</u>
   (1) I wrote it. ① ② ③ ④ ⑤
   (2) I writed it.
   (3) it was written.
   (4) I had written it.
   (5) I have written it.

2. On this, his anniversary, Simpson <u>was</u> with the bank for forty years.
   (1) was ① ② ③ ④ ⑤
   (2) had been
   (3) is
   (4) has been
   (5) will be

3. I received a ticket because I parked in a no parking zone.
   (1) received a ticket because I parked ① ② ③ ④ ⑤
   (2) received a ticket because I had parked
   (3) had received a ticket because I parked
   (4) had received a ticket because I had parked
   (5) received a ticket because parking

4. If you arrive after 10, the kitchen will have closed.
   (1) will have closed. ① ② ③ ④ ⑤
   (2) closes.
   (3) will close.
   (4) should close.
   (5) has closed.

5. As soon as the bell rings, the horses will begin to run.
   (1) will begin ① ② ③ ④ ⑤
   (2) shall begin
   (3) have begun
   (4) began
   (5) begin

PRACTICE XI

Directions: The following items are based on a paragraph that contains numbered sentences. Three of the sentences contain errors in time. Read the paragraph and then answer the items based on it. For each item, choose the one best answer that would result in the correct writing of the sentence.

(1) We had traveled extensively before we bought our summer home. (2) We traveled in Europe and Asia before we went to South America. (3) For the past year, however, we were inclined to stay home. (4) Travel became so expensive over the past few years that we can no longer afford it.

1. Sentence 2: **We traveled in Europe and Asia before we went to South America.**

   What correction should be made to this sentence?

   (1) replace before with since ① ② ③ ④ ⑤
   (2) change traveled to had traveled
   (3) change traveled to have traveled
   (4) change went to were gone
   (5) replace went with had visited

2. Sentence 3: **For the past year, however, we were inclined to stay home.**

   What correction should be made to this sentence?

   (1) replace however with nevertheless ① ② ③ ④ ⑤
   (2) replace however with consequently
   (3) change were inclined to had been inclined
   (4) change were inclined to was inclined
   (5) change were inclined to have been inclined

3. Sentence 4: **Travel became so expensive over the past few years that we can no longer afford it.**

   What correction should be made to this sentence?

   (1) change became to has become ① ② ③ ④ ⑤
   (2) change became to had become
   (3) replace past with last
   (4) remove so
   (5) replace became with was

ANSWER KEY

Chapter 9

Time: Special Problems

Practice I *Page 95.*

Part A
have watched
has drawn
has learned
have seen
has prepared
have gone

Part B *Sample answers:*
1. John always *has drawn* cartoons.
2. Maria *has learned* that speeding tickets are expensive.
3. Since becoming crossing guards, Stuart and John *have seen* many happy children.
4. Susan *has prepared* a report on our committee's progress.
5. We *have gone* by that restaurant often.

Practice II *Page 96.*

1. (2) Matthew *has been* the last in line since he began school.
2. (4) Occasionally, Matthew *has refused* to go to the end of the line.

Practice III *Page 97.*

Part A
had shown
had copied
had applied
had fallen

Part B *Sample answers:*
1. By the time I decided on revisions, John *had copied* the entire report.
2. Before sunbathing, Carole *had applied* suntan lotion.
3. The vase *had fallen* before I realized that it was off center.

Practice IV *Page 98.*

1. (4) If *I had known I could have* a paying job, I never would have volunteered my services.
2. (3) Now, I *have been volunteering* for three months, and the agency advertises for an assistant for me.
3. (2) *I think I have figured out* a solution to this problem.

Practice V *Page 100.*

Part A
will have left

will have completed
will have seen
will have adjourned
will have called

Part B *Sample answers:*

1. By the time the meeting begins, I *will have completed* writing my introduction.
2. Before the interview process ends, I *will have seen* forty applicants.
3. By the time those figures are in final form, the meeting *will have adjourned.*
4. Before Sara arrives at the airport, I *will have called* to confirm her flight's landing schedule.

Practice VI *Page 100.*

1. (4) By the time John's plane lands in Chicago for his connecting flight, Sue *will have arrived* in Seattle.
2. (1) Before John gets to the hotel in Seattle, Sue *will have checked in.*

Practice VII *Page 102.*

1. (4) As it *bit* the worm, the fish *realized* its error.
   When two actions occur simultaneously, their forms must be the same. Omit *had* before *realized.*
2. (3) When I *lifted* the papers, I *found* Ellen's missing glasses.
   See explanation above. Omit *had* before *found.*

Practice VIII *Page 102.*

1. (3) Before she *began* working full-time, Erica *had seemed* more relaxed.
   Addition of the helping word *had* shows that *seemed* occured in the past before *began.*
2. (4) As I looked across the room at the woman who bore an uncanny resemblance to me, I *felt* as though I were looking into a mirror.
   Eliminate *had* before *felt. Looked* and *felt* are simultaneous actions.

REVIEW

Practice IX *Page 103.*

1. (1) I *have been teaching* for twenty years.
   The helping words *have been* show that the teaching began in the past and continues into the present.
2. (3) Before the music stopped, a shot *had rung* out.
   The helping word *had* shows that *rung* occurred in the past before the music stopped.
3. (2) Before the doorbell rang, Ida *had seemed* nervous.
   The helping word *had* shows that *seemed* occurred before the doorbell rang.
4. (2) If you *had studied*, you might have known the answer.
   The helping word *had* shows that *studied* began in the past before the knowing.
5. (4) Before he passed the test, the man *had studied* for many hours.
   The helping word *had* shows that *studied* began in the past before *passed.*

Practice X *Page 104.*

1. (4) I signed the letter several days after *I had written it.*
   The helping word *had* shows that the writing occurred in the past *before* the signing.

2. (4) On this, his anniversary, Simpson *has been* with the bank for forty years.
The helping word *has* shows that Simpson *has been* with the bank in the past and is continuing into the present.
3. (2) *I received a ticket because I had parked* in a no parking zone.
The helping word *had* shows that the parking occurred in the past *before* the receiving.
4. (1) If you arrive after 10, the kitchen *will have closed*.
The helping words *will have* show that the closing will be completed *before* the arrival.
5. (5) As soon as the bell rings, the horses *begin* to run.
Since both actions occur at the *same time*, the *same form* (present) is used for both action words.

Practice XI *Page 105.*

1. (2) We *had traveled* in Europe and Asia before we went to South America.
2. (5) For the past year, however, we *have been inclined* to stay home.
3. (1) Travel *has become* so expensive over the past few years that we can no longer afford it.

10.
Pronouns

Years ago when I was just out of graduate school and thought I could remake society by cleaning up slovenly grammar in the media, I sent some naive letters to the networks. Johnny Carson's quiz show should be called "*Whom* Do You Trust?" not "*Who* Do You Trust?" Arthur Godfrey should ask his Talent Scouts, "*Whom* did you bring to the show?" instead of "*Who* . . . ?" and the ABC situation comedy should be "My Sister and *I*" not "My Sister and *Me*."

The networks never made any changes, and now I sing "Ain't Misbehavin'" just like every other former purist.

—Bob Kassell
Surrounded by Assassins

A Word With You . . .

The words of critic Bob Kassell are amusing. There is a serious side to them, however, for students of language. Why, for example, are some people more comfortable while using the incorrect form of the language?

You might not find the answer to that question in Chapter 10—but you will learn why "I gave the books to Joe and *her*," "It is *I*," "Just between Edith and *me*," and "It is *we* players who must protest" all illustrate correct pronoun usage.

Pronouns are used as performers/subjects or as words which receive action. *For example:*

performer
/
Lloyd ran home.

performer pronoun
/
He ran home.

subject / Lloyd is pleasant. — subject pronoun / He is pleasant.

Lloyd is pleasant. (Lloyd = subject)

He is pleasant. (He = subject pronoun)

Elena gave a bright smile to Tom. (Elena = performer; Tom = receives action)

Elena gave a bright smile to him. (Elena = performer; him = pronoun which receives action)

Maria gave Tom an icy stare. (Maria = performer; Tom = receives action)

Maria gave him an icy stare. (Maria = performer; him = pronoun which receives action)

PERFORMER/SUBJECT PRONOUNS	PRONOUNS WHICH RECEIVE ACTION
I	me
you	you
he	him
she	her
it	it
we	us
they	them
who	whom

PRACTICE

I **Directions:** Using a pronoun from the above list, complete each sentence. More than one choice may be correct.

1. ______________________ won the election.
2. ______________________ campaigned all week.

3. The National Organization for Women gave the citation to ____________________.
4. The student hitchhiker got a lift from ______________.
5. __________________ was responsible for legislation providing consumer protection?
6. For ____________________ did the witness testify?

• **PRONOUN CLUE 1:**

Don't be confused by *who* and *whom*. As you can see in the preceding list, *who* is a subject/performer and *whom* is a pronoun that receives action.

If: *He* painted the house.
Then: *Who* painted the house?
If: The phone call is for *him*.
Then: For *whom* is the phone call?

PRACTICE II

Directions: Underline the pronoun that correctly completes each sentence.

Example: (*Who* - Whom) rang the doorbell?
Clue: *He* rang the doorbell.

1. (Who - Whom) did you call?
2. (Who - Whom) answered your letter?
3. (Who - Whom) will help with this project?
4. *Consumer Reports* cites manufacturers from (who - whom) we can expect quality products.
5. Mariah Carey is the singer (who - whom) Tony likes best.

• **PRONOUN CLUE 2:**

Don't be confused by more than one subject.

If: He won the election.
Then: Macon and *he* won the election.

Because it is incorrect to say:

Him won the election.

It is also incorrect to say:

Macon and *him* won the election

PRACTICE III **Directions:** Underline the pronoun that correctly completes each sentence.

1. Mr. Jones and (he, him) ran the fair.
2. (They, Them) and their father went fishing.
3. My friend and (I, me) are planning a camping trip.
4. (She, her) and (he, him) were delegates to the convention.
5. The Walters and (we, us) go to the shore each summer.
6. (Who, Whom), along with Susan, will work on this committee?

- **PRONOUN CLUE 3:**

Don't be confused by more than one word receiving the action.

If: I gave the present to *her*.

Then: I gave the present to Tom and *her*.

Because it is incorrect to say:

I gave the present to *she*.

It is also incorrect to say:

I gave the present to Tom and *she*.

If: Sam bought her lunch.

Then: Sam bought Robert and *her* lunch.

Because it is incorrect to say:

Sam bought *she* lunch.

It is also incorrect to say:

Sam bought Robert and *she* lunch.

PRACTICE IV **Directions:** Underline the pronoun that correctly completes each sentence.

1. When the plans for the new community center are completed, call Mr. Faldez and (I, me).
2. The supermarket manager gave discount coupons to Olga and (she, her).
3. When they question you about the accident, tell Paul and (they, them) the truth.
4. Will you be speaking to Hiroko and (he, him)?
5. The MacDonalds sent regards to Joanna and (we, us).

• **PRONOUN CLUE 4:**

Don't be confused by a condensed thought.

If: Elmer runs more quickly *than I do.*

Then: Elmer runs more quickly *than I.*

Because it is incorrect to say:

Elmer runs more quickly *than me* do.

It is equally incorrect to say:

Elmer runs more quickly *than me.*

PRACTICE V

Directions: Underline the pronoun that correctly completes each sentence.

1. Mary is a better cook than (I, me).
2. I sew better than (she, her).
3. You don't feel as sorry as (he, him).
4. The Ortegas are better swimmers than (we, us).
5. Their neighbors don't argue as often as (they, them).

• **PRONOUN CLUE 5:**

A sentence is reversible if it has a linking word that connects the subject to a word which means the same thing as the subject.

If: Carl is the mayor.

Then: The mayor is Carl.

If: He is the mayor.

Then: The mayor is *he.*

Because it is incorrect to say

Him is the mayor.

It is also incorrect to say:

The mayor is *him*.

PRACTICE VI

Directions: Underline the pronoun that correctly completes each sentence.

1. My secretary is (she, her).
2. The winner of the contest was (he, him).
3. (Who, Whom) seems most likely to get the promotion?
4. The culprits were (they, them).
5. The person who called you was (I, me).
6. If there is a couple who enjoys dancing, it is (we, us).

- **PRONOUN CLUE 6:**

Certain pronouns—*my, your, his, her, its, our, their*—may be used as descriptive words.

Example: I like the *red* hat.
I like *his* hat.

Descriptive pronouns are never a problem in the above context. However, errors tend to be made in sentences such as the following:

INCORRECT: I do not like *him* smoking.
CORRECT: I do not like *his* smoking.
INCORRECT: Of course I approve of *you* jogging.
CORRECT: Of course I approve of *your* jogging.

PRACTICE VII

Directions: Underline the pronoun that correctly completes each sentence.

1. Tom is very proud of (him, his) swimming.

2. I don't like (you, your) calling me at the office.
3. The professor was glad to hear about (me, my) writing a story.
4. We wondered (who's, whose) contribution to medicine was greatest
5. I don't like (them, their) refusing to take BHA and BHT out of foods.

- **PRONOUN CLUE 7:**

Words such as *to, from, between, except, among* are followed by pronouns that receive action (p. 111).

For example:

1. Between you and *me*, I don't enjoy cooking.
2. The package is for *her*.
3. Please divide the workload among *them*.
4. Everyone, except *us*, is attending the meeting.

PRACTICE VIII

Directions: Underline the pronoun that correctly completes each sentence.

1. From (who, whom) did you learn that myth about not eating before swimming?
2. Many secrets have passed between you and (he, him).
3. The personnel director gave notices to John and (they, them).
4. Everyone, except (she, her), plans to take the test.
5. The host and his friends divided the four bottles of beer among (they, them).

- **PRONOUN CLUE 8:**

A pronoun must agree in number with the word to which it refers.

For example:

1. One of the men in the back of the room could not project *his* voice.

   His refers to *one*. Both words are singular.

2. All of those women left *their* coats after the rally.
Their refers to *all*. Both words are plural.

PRACTICE IX

Directions: Select the word that correctly completes each sentence.

1. Everyone must decide for (himself, themselves).
2. Each of the painters worked (his, their) best.
3. They each performed to the best of (his, their) ability.
4. All of the members brought (his, their) wives.

REVIEW EXERCISES

PRACTICE X

Directions: Each of the following sentences has an error in pronoun usage. For each item, choose the one best answer that would result in the correct writing of the sentence.

1. He and his brother strenuously object to me smoking.

What correction should be made to this sentence?

(1) change He to Him ① ② ③ ④ ⑤
(2) insert he after brother
(3) insert they after brother
(4) change me to my
(5) insert cigarettes after smoking

2. The man who you called is out and his assistant insists that he will not return again today.

What correction should be made to this sentence?

(1) change who to whom ① ② ③ ④ ⑤
(2) change who to which
(3) replace who with that
(4) replace his assistant with the man's assistant
(5) remove that

3. If you are wondering who it was who called you earlier in the week, it was him.

   What correction should be made to this sentence?

   (1) change you are to you're ① ② ③ ④ ⑤
   (2) change wondering who to wondering whom
   (3) change who called to whom called
   (4) change earlier to early on
   (5) change him to he

4. Although he plays tennis better than I do, I play chess better than him.

   What correction should be made to this sentence?

   (1) replace I do with me ① ② ③ ④ ⑤
   (2) remove do
   (3) insert do before play
   (4) change than to then
   (5) change him to he

5. Don wanted us—John and I—to help him build his new garage.

   What correction should be made to this sentence?

   (1) insert he after Don ① ② ③ ④ ⑤
   (2) change us to we
   (3) change I to me
   (4) remove him
   (5) replace his with their

PRACTICE XI

Directions: The following items are based on paragraphs that contain numbered sentences. Some of the sentences may contain errors in pronoun usage. Other sentences are correct as they appear in the paragraphs. Read the paragraphs and then answer the items based on them. For each item, choose the one best answer that would result in the correct use of the pronouns in the sentence.

Items 1 and 2 refer to the following paragraph.

(1) Greg, Liz, and me went to the Mets game last night. (2) They sat their in the stands while I got hot dogs. (3) I missed Daryl Strawberry's home run. (4) We will go to another game this season, and they will get the hot dogs.

1. Sentence 1: **Greg, Liz, and me went to the Mets game last night.**

   Which of the following is the best way to write the underlined portion of this sentence? If you think the original is the best way, choose option (1).

   (1) Greg, Liz, and me ① ② ③ ④ ⑤
   (2) Me, Greg, and Liz
   (3) Me and Greg and Liz
   (4) Greg, Liz, and myself
   (5) Greg, Liz, and I

2. Sentence 2: **They sat their in the stands while I got hot dogs.**

   What correction should be made to this sentence?

   (1) change They to Them ① ② ③ ④ ⑤
   (2) replace They with Greg and Liz
   (3) change the spelling of their to there
   (4) change the spelling of their to they're
   (5) no correction is necessary

Items 3 and 4 refer to the following paragraph.

(1) I was very pleased with the Wilsons for thinking of me when they decided to expand there company. (2) I had worked with them on several projects last year. (3) Me and them always worked well together. (4) I feel that I can contribute to their team.

3. Sentence 1: **I was very pleased with the Wilsons for thinking of me when they decided to expand there company.**

   Which of the following is the best way to write the underlined portion of this sentence? If you think the original is the best way, choose option (1).

(1) of me when they decided to expand there company. ①②③④⑤
(2) of myself when the Wilsons they decided to expand there company.
(3) of me when the Wilsons they decided to expand the company.
(4) of me when they decided to expand their company.
(5) of me when they decided to expand they're company.

4. Sentence 3: **Me and them always worked well together.**

Which of the following is the best way to write the underlined portion of this sentence? If you think the original is the best way, choose option (1).

(1) Me and them ①②③④⑤
(2) Me and the Wilsons
(3) The Wilsons and me
(4) I and the Wilsons
(5) The Wilsons and I

Items 5 and 6 refer to the following paragraph.

(1) Sue and him always watch the soap opera. (2) They tape it during the day and watch it at night. (3) Whom does what to who in each day's story is very important. (4) If no one sets the VCR, Sue and he get very upset. (5) I don't understand them.

5. Sentence 1: **Sue and him always watch the soap opera.**

Which of the following is the best way to write the underlined portion of this sentence? If you think the original is the best way, choose option (1).

(1) Sue and him ①②③④⑤
(2) Sue and he
(3) Him and Sue
(4) Her and him
(5) She and him

6. Sentence 3: <u>**Whom does what to who**</u> **in each day's story is very important.**

Which of the following is the best way to write the underlined portion of this sentence? If you think the original is the best way, choose option (1).

(1) Whom does what to who ① ② ③ ④ ⑤
(2) Whom does what to whom
(3) Who does what to whom
(4) Who does what to who
(5) Whom does what to anyone

PRACTICE XII

Directions: Select the incorrect sentence for each group and rewrite it correctly on the line below. Some groups may not have an incorrect sentence.

1. (1) Them and us play gin rummy each Wednesday.
   (2) Please write to the folks and me while you're away.
   (3) The friendliest person on the street is he.
   (4) I did not give the information about the adverse effects of food additives to him.
   (5) No error

____

2. (1) Who told you that oil drilling equipment does not cause pollution?
   (2) Rita is a more knowledgeable gardener than me.
   (3) For whom did you buy that impractical gift?
   (4) The person responsible for creating the Equal Rights Amendment is she.
   (5) No error

____

3. (1) In the bright light, Theresa and I could see their faces clearly.
   (2) Either she or I am working late.

(3) A package just arrived, and it is marked for either him or her.
(4) The person who gave the lecture did not speak well.
(5) No error

____

4. (1) Since they went to Marriage Encounter, Simon fights more fairly than she.
(2) In 1954, Roberto and me saw Stan Musial hit five home runs in one game.
(3) Arthur and he claim to have seen several UFO's.
(4) At whose request do I announce the slate?
(5) No error

____

5. (1) Who's going to pay for education if all funding legislation is defeated?
(2) Please call Henry and I as soon as you know the election returns.
(3) Do you really approve of his playing football?
(4) Arlene will always be younger than I.
(5) No error

____

6. (1) Who called?
(2) After you've repaired the sink, give the tools to John and him.
(3) Mike and me will carry the steel beam.
(4) In case you didn't know, the new mayor is he.
(5) No error

____

7. (1) We hope the new police commissioner will be as friendly as him.
(2) The Jensens and they organize a block party each year to raise money for the Fresh Air Fund.

(3) Who do you think will run his campaign?

(4) Give responsible jobs to Kate and her because they have had the most experience.

(5) No error

____

8. (1) Daniel and I exchange information with them about the Bermuda Triangle.

(2) I have always worked harder than he.

(3) If you don't do the job, who will?

(4) He really shouldn't have objected to me leaving since my work had been finished.

(5) No error

____

9. (1) I was very pleased with them for thinking of me when they decided to expand their company.

(2) If it is his turn, then allow him to take it.

(3) Davis has always been more punctual than us.

(4) The Boss is one of those musicians who are full of surprises. .

(5) No error

____

10. (1) Give me your word that you and he will comply with our terms.

(2) Jean and I completed the forms and left them at the main desk.

(3) If I can find you and her, I will give you his instructions.

(4) According to a survey among writers, one of the finest authors of the century is Saul Bellow.

(5) No error

____

ANSWER KEY

Chapter 10

Pronouns

Practice I *Page 111.*

Answers will vary.

Sample answers

1. I, You, He, She, We, They
2. I, You, He, She, We, They
3. him, her, you, them, me, us
4. him, me, you, her, us, them
5. Who
6. whom

Practice II *Page 112.*

For explanations of these answers, see *Pronouns Clue 1.*

1. *Whom* did you call?
2. *Who* answered?
3. *Who* will help?
4. from *whom*
5. *whom* Tony likes

Practice III *Page 113.*

For explanations of these answers, see *Pronoun Clue 2.*

1. *he* ran
2. *They* went
3. My friend and *I* are
4. *She, he* were
5. *we* go
6. *Who* will work

Practice IV *Page 113.*

For explanations of these answers, see *Pronoun Clue 3.*

1. call *me*
2. gave to *her*
3. tell *them*
4. speaking to *him*
5. sent to *us*

Practice V *Page 114.*

For explanations of these answers, see *Pronoun Clue 4.*

1. than *I* (am)
2. than *she* (sews)
3. as *he* (feels)
4. than *we* (are)
5. as *they* (argue)

Practice VI *Page 115.*

For explanations of these answers, see *Pronoun Clue 5.*

1. *she* (is my secretary)
2. *he* (was the winner)
3. *Who* (seems)
4. *they* (were the culprits)
5. *I* (was the person)
6. *we* (are it)

Practice VII *Page 115.*

For explanations of these answers, see *Pronoun Clue 6.*

1. *his* swimming
2. *your* calling
3. *my* writing
4. *whose* contribution
5. *their* refusing

Practice VIII *Page 116.*

For explanations of these answers, see *Pronoun Clue 7.*

1. From *whom*
2. between you and *him*
3. to John and *them*
4. except *her*
5. among *them*

Practice IX *Page 117.*

For explanations of these answers,
see *Pronoun Clue 8.*

1. *Himself* refers to everyone (singular).
2. *His* refers to each (singular).
3. *Their* refers to they (plural).
4. *Their* refers to all (plural).

Practice X *Page 117.*

1. (4) He and his brother strenuously object to *my* smoking.
2. (1) The man *whom* you called is out and his assistant insists that he will not return again today.
3. (5) If you are wondering who it was who called you earlier in the week, it was *he.*
4. (5) Although he plays tennis better than I do, I play chess better than *he.*
5. (3) Don wanted us, John and *me,* to help him build his new garage.

Practice XI *Page 118.*

1. (5) *Greg, Liz, and I* went to the Mets game last night.
2. (3) They sat *there* in the stands while I got hot dogs.
3. (4) I was very pleased with the Wilsons for thinking *of me when they decided to expand their company.*
4. (5) *The Wilsons and I* always worked well together.
5. (2) *Sue and he* always watch the soap opera.
6. (3) *Who does what to whom* in each day's story is very important.

Practice XII *Page 121.*

1. (1) *They* and *we* play gin rummy each Wednesday.
2. (2) Rita is a more knowledgeable gardener than *I* (am).
3. (5) No error
4. (2) In 1954, Roberto and *I* saw Stan Musial hit five home runs in one game.
5. (2) Please call Henry and *me* as soon as you know the election returns.
6. (3) Mike and *I* will carry the steel beam.
7. (1) We hope the new police commissioner will be as friendly as *he* (is).
8. (4) He really shouldn't have objected to *my* leaving since my work had been finished.
9. (3) Davis has always been more punctual than *we* (have been).
10. (5) No error

11.

Cumulative Review

This review covers the following concepts that have been included in the preceding chapters:

- Agreement in Time and Number
- Correct Use of Descriptive Words and Phrases
- Recognizing Complete and Incomplete Thoughts
- Special Problems in Agreement
- Special Problems in Time
- Correct Use of Pronouns

After completing the Cumulative Review exercises and checking your answers with the ANSWER KEY, evaluate your ability using the SUMMARY OF RESULTS chart on page 134. Acceptable scores for each practice section are given.

To learn your areas for skill improvement, find the question numbers you answered incorrectly on the SKILLS ANALYSIS table. The table will show which of your skills need improvement and the necessary chapters to review.

PRACTICE

I **Directions:** Each of the following sentences contains an error in one of the concepts covered in Chapters 5 through 10. Read each sentence and answer the question that follows. For each item, choose the one best answer that would result in the correct writing of the sentence.

1. The angry man ran hurriedly into the crowded room and shouted loud at the guest.

What correction should be made to this sentence?

(1) change ran to had run ① ② ③ ④ ⑤
(2) replace hurriedly with fast
(3) change hurriedly to hurried

(4) change shouted to shouts
(5) change loud to loudly

2. What is the social implications of the small car?

What correction should be made to this sentence?

(1) replace What with Which ① ② ③ ④ ⑤
(2) change is to are
(3) insert serious before social
(4) replace small with tiny
(5) remove social

3. I must insist that I do not like you smoking in my home.

What correction should be made to this sentence?

(1) change insist to have insisted ① ② ③ ④ ⑤
(2) change do not to don't
(3) insert a comma after insist
(4) change you to your
(5) change home to house

4. Just between we two, I believe Jim did not write the contract properly.

What correction should be made to this sentence?

(1) change we to us ① ② ③ ④ ⑤
(2) change did not write to had not written
(3) change believe to believed
(4) change properly to proper
(5) change did not to didn't

5. Neither the Congressman nor the people whom he represents approves of this bill.

What correction should be made to this sentence?

(1) change nor to or ① ② ③ ④ ⑤
(2) change whom to who
(3) change represents to represent
(4) change bill to Bill
(5) change approves to approve

PRACTICE II

Directions: The following items are based on paragraphs that contain numbered sentences. Some of the sentences may contain errors in any of the concepts covered in Chapters 5 through 10. Read each sentence and answer the question that follows. For each item, choose the one best answer that would result in the correct writing of the sentence.

Items 1 and 2 refer to the following paragraph.

(1) A waiting room crowded with impatient patients were common at Dr. Rizzo's. (2) The doctor was known for the special care he gave all of his patients. (3) Even though each patient received quality time, they resented waiting.

1. Sentence 1: **A waiting room crowded with impatient patients were common at Dr. Rizzo's.**

Which of the following is the best way to write the underlined portion of this sentence? If you think the original is the best way, choose option (1).

(1) crowded with impatient patients were ① ② ③ ④ ⑤
(2) full with impatient patients were
(3) crowded with impatient patients was
(4) crowded with impatient patients had been
(5) crowded with impatient patients' was

2. Sentence 3: **Even though each patient received quality time, they resented waiting.**

Which of the following is the best way to write the underlined portion of this sentence? If you think the original is the best way, choose option 1.

(1) they resented waiting. ① ② ③ ④ ⑤
(2) they resent waiting.
(3) they will resent waiting.
(4) each resented waiting.
(5) each had resented waiting.

Items 3 to 5 refer to the following paragraph.

(1) Mrs. Stover is one of those teachers who relishes new ideas. (2) If anyone can be consistently supportive of students, it is her. (3) For as long as I have known her, she is a model teacher.

3. Sentence 1: **Mrs. Stover is one of those teachers who relishes new ideas.**

Which of the following is the best way to write the underlined portion of this sentence? If you think the original is the best way, choose option (1).

(1) is one of those teachers who relishes new ideas. ① ② ③ ④ ⑤
(2) is one of those teachers who relish new ideas.
(3) is a teacher who relish new ideas.
(4) a teacher, who relishes new ideas.
(5) who relish new ideas, is a teacher.

4. Sentence 2: **If anyone can be consistently supportive of students, it is her.**

Which of the following is the best way to write the underlined portion of this sentence? If you think the original is the best way, choose option (1)

(1) it is her. ① ② ③ ④ ⑤
(2) it isn't her.
(3) it is she.
(4) is it her?
(5) she's it.

5. Sentence 3: **For as long as I have known her, <u>she is a model teacher.</u>**

Which of the following is the best way to write the underlined portion of this sentence? If you think the original is the best way, choose option (1)

(1) she is a model teacher. ① ② ③ ④ ⑤
(2) she is no model teacher.
(3) she was a model teacher.
(4) she has been a model teacher.
(5) she is sure a model teacher.

PRACTICE III

Which is the best way to write the underlined portion of each sentence? If you think the original is the best way, choose option (1).

1. The shy girl <u>stood hesitantly</u> in the doorway before she entered the crowded bar.
(1) stood hesitantly ① ② ③ ④ ⑤
(2) standed hesitantly
(3) has stood hesitantly
(4) had stood hesitantly
(5) stands hesitantly

2. Either the grass or the shrubs need cutting weekly.
   (1) Either the grass or the shrubs need ① ② ③ ④ ⑤
   (2) Either the grass or the shrubs needs
   (3) Either the shrubs or the grass need
   (4) Either the grass or the shrubs needing
   (5) Either the shrubs or the grass needing

3. Here's my mother and father.
   (1) Here's ① ② ③ ④ ⑤
   (2) Here is
   (3) Here are
   (4) Here was
   (5) Here were

4. Last week I went to the boringest party.
   (1) went to the boringest party. ① ② ③ ④ ⑤
   (2) went to the most boringest party.
   (3) went to the more boring party.
   (4) had gone to the most boring party.
   (5) went to the most boring party.

5. David performed the difficult experiment more precisely than any student in the class.
   (1) more precisely than any student ① ② ③ ④ ⑤
   (2) most precisely than any student
   (3) more precise than any student
   (4) more precisely than any other student
   (5) more precisely than each student

PRACTICE IV

Directions: What correction should be made to each of the following sentences?

1. That painting hangs in my mother's hallway of which I am proud.
   (1) change That to The ① ② ③ ④ ⑤
   (2) delete my
   (3) insert , of which I am proud, after painting instead of after hallway
   (4) insert , of which I am proud, after hangs instead of after hallway
   (5) change mother's to mothers'

2. This excellent thesis surpasses all others and presented the facts most coherently.
   (1) delete excellent ① ② ③ ④ ⑤
   (2) delete others
   (3) change presented to presents
   (4) change coherently to coherent
   (5) insert had before presented

3. The tall, handsome man, wearing a plaid jacket and striped pants, stepping snappily off the curb.
   (1) change wearing to wears ① ② ③ ④ ⑤
   (2) change wearing to wore
   (3) delete snappily
   (4) change stepping to stepped
   (5) insert of after off

4. The stapler belongs to that woman on the table.
   (1) change belongs to belong ① ② ③ ④ ⑤
   (2) change belongs to belonged
   (3) replace belongs with is the property of
   (4) insert there after that
   (5) insert on the table after stapler instead of after woman

PRACTICE V

Directions: The following items are based on a paragraph that contains numbered sentences. Some of the sentences may contain errors in number. Other sentences are correct as they appear in the paragraph. Read the paragraph and then answer the items based on it. For each item, choose the one best answer that would result in the correct writing of the sentence.

(1) The air we breathe is sometimes hazardous to our health. (2) Our oceans are closed more frequently than ever before. (3) The closed landfills and the need for more modern disposal facilities has made "garbage crisis" a watchword of the times. (4) Since environmental care has become a public concern, paper and glass recycling are common in many communities.

1. Sentence 3: **The closed landfills and the need for more modern disposal facilities has made "garbage crisis" a watchword of the times.**

   Which of the following is the best way to write the underlined portion of this sentence? If you think the original is the best way, choose option (1).

   (1) has made "garbage crisis" ① ② ③ ④ ⑤
   (2) made "garbage crisis"
   (3) is making "garbage crisis"
   (4) have made "garbage crisis"
   (5) will have made "garbage crisis"

2. Sentence 4: **Since environmental care has become a public concern, paper and glass recycling are common in many communities.**

Which of the following is the best way to write the underlined portion of this sentence? If you think the original is the best way, choose option (1).

(1) paper and glass recycling are ① ② ③ ④ ⑤
(2) paper and glass recycling is
(3) paper and glass recycling will be
(4) paper and glass recycling is to be
(5) paper and glass recycling had been

SUMMARY OF RESULTS

After reviewing the Answer Key on page 136, chart your scores below for each practice section.

Practice Number	**Your Number Right**	**Your Number Wrong** (Including Omissions)	**Acceptable Score**
I			4 correct
II			4 correct
III			4 correct
IV			3 correct
V			2 correct

SKILLS ANALYSIS

To discover your areas for skill improvement, locate the question numbers you got wrong and circle them on this Skills Analysis chart. Then refer to the chapters listed in column 3.

Skill	Question Number	Chapter Reference
Practice I		*See Chapter*
Correct Use of Descriptive Words	1	3
Agreement of Subject and Action or Linking Word in Number	2	2
Correct Use of Pronouns	3, 4	10
Agreement: Special Problems	5	8
Practice II		
Agreement of Subject and Action of Linking Word in Number	1	2
Agreement: Special Problems	2, 3	8, 10
Correct Use of Pronouns	4	10
Time: Special Problems	5	9
Practice III		
Time: Special Problems	1	9
Agreement: Special Problems	2, 3	8
Correct Use of Descriptive Words	4,5	4
Practice IV		
Correct Use of Descriptive Phrases	1,4	5
Agreement of Action Words in Time	2	2
Complete and Incomplete Thoughts	3	1
Practice V		
Agreement of Subject and Action or Linking Words in Number	1,2	2

ANSWER KEY

Chapter 11

Cumulative Review

Practice I *Page 126.*

1. (5) The angry man ran hurriedly into the crowded room and shouted *loudly* at the guest.
2. (2) What *are* the social implications of the small car?
3. (4) I must insist that I do not like *your* smoking in my home.
4. (1) Just between *us* two, I believe Jim did not write the contract properly.
5. (5) Neither the Congressman nor the people whom he represents *approve* of this bill.

Practice II *Page 128.*

1. (3) A waiting room *crowded with impatient patients was* common at Dr. Rizzo's.
2. (4) Even though each patient received quality time, *each resented waiting.*
3. (2) Mrs. Stover *is one of those teachers who relish new ideas.*
4. (3) If anyone can be consistently supportive of students, *it is she.*
5. (4) For as long as I have known her, *she has been a model teacher.*

Practice III *Page 130.*

1. (4) *Stood* occurred *before* entered, so you must use the helping word *had* with *stood.*
2. (1) *Need* agrees with the closest performer, *shrubs*, which is plural.
3. (3) *Are* agrees with the plural subject, *mother and father.*
4. (5) Do not add *-er* or *-est* to a descriptive word ending in *ing;* use *more* or *most.*
5. (4) *Any other* is the correct form. (He did not perform more precisely than himself.)

Practice IV *Page 132.*

1. (3) That painting*, of which I am proud,* hangs in my mother's hallway.
2. (3) This excellent thesis surpasses all others and *presents* the facts most coherently.
3. (4) The tall, handsome man, wearing a plaid jacket and striped pants, *stepped* snappily off the curb.
4. (5) The stapler *on the table* belongs to that woman.

Practice V *Page 133.*

1. (4) The closed landfills and the need for more modern disposal facilities *have made "garbage crisis"* a watchword of the times.
2. (2) Since environmental care has become a public concern, *paper and glass recycling is* common in many communities.

12.

Balanced Sentences/ Coordinated Thoughts

One of the things that used to irritate me in my junior high English classes was the corrections some teachers made in the margins of my compositions. I didn't mind when they wrote "sp." and circled the misspelled word on the line, or "cap." to indicate that I had written "french" with a small "f."

What got me all riled up, however, were the mysterious jottings such as "awk." and "frag." And one term I had a former C.I.A. agent as a teacher, and he used secret codes, it seemed to me. His favorite was a couple of parallel lines in the margin—and his cryptic explanation to my query was "lack of parallelism." I never got to know what he meant, and, at the time, I couldn't see that anything was wrong with "I like swimming, hunting, and to fish."

Paul Allen
Trouble Deaf Heaven

A Word With You . . .

Paul Allen's teacher did a good job in spotting the error in "I like swimming, hunting, and to fish" but he failed to show his students why it was incorrect. The parallel slash marks in the margins were no substitute for a lesson explaining the need for balance in sentence structure.

You will find that the mystery is removed from that topic in the following pages and why in Paul Allen's later book we can find a sentence such as, *"Listening* to Beverly Sills, *looking* at a Rembrandt, and *sipping* Chivas Regal all give me goose pimples."

Balanced Sentences

Correctly and effectively written sentences are balanced. A *balanced sentence is one in which related actions, descriptions, or ideas are presented in the same form.* The following sentences are not balanced. Why not?

1. He liked swimming and *to dine.*
2. Tania is pleasant and *has intelligence.*
3. Working out is both stimulating and *makes me exhausted.*
4. Carlos is not only a good carpenter *but a fine electrician also.*

In sentence 1 the related actions are not expressed in the same form. One action word ends with *ing;* the other action takes on an entirely different form, using *to.* Now, you must choose which form you prefer. Either one would be correct, but the same form must be used for both action words.

He liked swimming and diving.

or

He liked to swim and to dive.

In sentence 2, what are the two terms that describe Tania? __________ and __________ . You've probably chosen *pleasant* and *has intelligence.* The sentence would be balanced if *has intelligence* were replaced by one word. *Pleasant* is a descriptive word, describing Tania. What descriptive word means *has intelligence?* In other words, how do you change the form of *has intelligence* to balance with *pleasant*?

Tania is pleasant and *intelligent.*

In sentence 3, what are the two terms that describe working out? __________ and __________ . You've probably chosen *stimulating* and *makes me exhausted.* The sentence would be balanced if *makes me exhausted* were replaced by one word. *Stimulating* is a descriptive word, describing working out. What descriptive word means *makes me exhausted*? In other words, how do you change the form of *makes me exhausted* to balance with *stimulating*?

Working out is both stimulating and *exhausting.*

In sentence 4, Carlos is two things. He is a *good carpenter* and a *fine electrician.*

What two phrases relate carpenter to electrician? ________________ and ______________ . You've probably chosen *not only* and *but.* The relationship is shown, however, by *not only* and *but also.* Just as *not only* comes immediately before *a good carpenter,* so must *but also* come immediately before *a fine electrician.*

Carlos is not only a good carpenter *but also a fine electrician.*

Look at a few more examples:

INCORRECT: I like to walk in the rain, to sing in the shower, and stamping in puddles.
CORRECT: I like to walk in the rain, to sing in the shower, and to stamp in puddles.
INCORRECT: The eagle has majesty, strength, and is graceful.
CORRECT: The eagle has majesty, strength, and grace.

PRACTICE
I

Directions: In the following practice, choose a word or phrase to balance and complete the sentence.

1. The longtime servant was faithful and
   (1) honestly. ① ② ③ ④
   (2) with honesty.
   (3) honest.
   (4) honesty.

2. Please write your evaluation carefully, truthfully, and
   (1) concise. ① ② ③ ④
   (2) concisely.
   (3) with concision.
   (4) be concise.

3. The advertisement said that at the "Y" Camps our children would learn to swim, play tennis, row boats, and
   (1) how to get along with others. ① ② ③ ④
   (2) getting along with others.
   (3) friendship.
   (4) get along with others.

4. Henry is not only a good doctor
   (1) but also an excellent friend. ① ② ③ ④
   (2) but he is also an excellent friend.
   (3) but he is an excellent friend also.
   (4) but is also an excellent friend.

5. If you want this job,
   (1) you must be prompt. ① ② ③ ④
   (2) one must be prompt.
   (3) they must be prompt.
   (4) you must have been prompt.

6. This book is a monument to its author and
   (1) it pays tribute to its subject. ① ② ③ ④
   (2) a tribute to its subject.
   (3) it tributes its subject.
   (4) pays tribute to its subject.

7. This weekend Cuong will fence in the backyard, mow the lawn, and
   (1) paints the house. ① ② ③ ④
   (2) he plans to paint the house.

(3) paint the house.
(4) will be painting the house.

8. The teenage boy's mother insisted that he hang up his clothes and
(1) make his bed. ① ② ③ ④
(2) he should make his bed.
(3) why doesn't he make his bed.
(4) to make his bed.

9. The volleyball game was invigorating and
(1) excitement. ① ② ③ ④
(2) had excitement.
(3) excited.
(4) exciting.

PRACTICE II

Directions: Each of the following sentences contains an error in balance. Read each sentence and answer the question that follows. Choose the one best answer to each item.

1. Soft drinks satisfy the appetite, offer absolutely nothing toward building health, taking up valuable space, and particularly crowd out milk needed for growth and normal bone and teeth structure.

What correction should be made to this sentence?

(1) change drinks to drink ① ② ③ ④ ⑤
(2) insert you after offer
(3) change taking to take
(4) change crowd to crowding
(5) insert you before needed

2. Personal health educators would be people who know the basic facts of nutrition, food buying, cooking, physical fitness, how to motivate people, and interviewing.

Which of the following is the best way to write the underlined portion of this sentence? If you think the original is the best way, choose option (1).

(1) how to motivate people ① ② ③ ④ ⑤
(2) motivating people
(3) when to motivate people
(4) working with motivating people
(5) and how to motivate people

3. Doctors are doing very little health education: they are not oriented or trained to be health educators, cannot make money dispensing health education, and there is no interest in being health educators.

What correction should be made to this sentence?

(1) change are not to aren't ① ② ③ ④ ⑤
(2) insert are not before trained
(3) remove the comma after educators
(4) change dispensing to having dispensed
(5) replace there is with have

PRACTICE III

Directions: Balance the following sentences. Rewrite them in the spaces provided.

1. The winner's attitude toward the loser was conciliatory yet not with condescension.

____

____

2. Mrs. Gonzalez is conservative not only in business but also politically.

____

____

3. The judge asked the defendant to swear to tell the truth and if he would cite the evidence.

____

____

4. I cannot abide congested subways or elevators with crowds in them.

____

____

5. This project is to be a benefit to the neighborhood and it will credit the sponsors.

____

____

6. Math, reading, and to write are my favorite subjects.

____

____

7. The professor lectured on anthropology, and he was outlining the child-rearing habits of the Polynesians.

____

____

8. I splashed cold water on my face and looking into the mirror.

____

____

9. The rain splashes onto the walk and soaked into the ground.

____

____

10. Outside the wind rustled the leaves in the trees, while inside the children sleep quietly.

____

____

PRACTICE IV

Directions: In each group below, find the sentence that lacks balance. Write the sentence correctly in the space provided.

1. (1) After killing his victim, the assassin jumped out of the window.
   (2) Harry S. Truman enjoyed reading not only fiction and sometimes he read some nonfiction.
   (3) The labor negotiations were deadlocked.

____

2. (1) Many people believe in stronger consumer protection and better informing of consumers.
   (2) While walking too quickly down the street, I lost my balance.
   (3) I enjoy roller blading and jogging.

____

3. (1) While reading a dull book, I was interrupted.
   (2) Neither the supervisor nor the assemblymen report directly to the president.
   (3) Doesn't automation deprive many of jobs and then it requires training?

____

4. (1) The reasons for shortening the workday are logical.
   (2) The attainment of freedom and achieving national security were their goals.
   (3) None of the representatives is lying.

____

5. (1) Although the system has defects, it still functions well.
(2) I not only endorse his candidacy, and you know I'll urge it.
(3) The mayor divided among his largest contributors the best municipal positions.

____

6. (1) A true Yoga must have discipline and concentrating is important, too.
(2) Dashing home from work, the busy woman prepared a menu in her mind.
(3) Clouds hang heavily in the sky, signaling rain.

____

7. (1) While talking on the telephone, I studied the painting on the kitchen wall.
(2) In the summer, the rosebushes climb along the side of the house.
(3) My feelings were hurt; so I cried a little, called a friend, and later I was going out with Bob.

____

8. (1) Spring is enjoyable, pretty, and fragrant.
(2) A duck swam across the lake and dived under the water.
(3) Many people in the wealthiest nation in the world are destitute, malnourished, and don't have jobs.

____

Coordinated Thoughts

Subordinating Words

Another test of an effective sentence is whether or not it combines ideas correctly. A group of words, including *since*, *although*, and *if*, are especially useful in combining ideas. These words are called *subordinating words* because they show that one idea in a sentence is less important than—or subordinate to—another idea in the sentence. Moreover, subordinating words add information and lend variety to a communication as a whole. A list of some of these words follows.

after
although
as
because
if
since
though
unless
when
where
whereas

To understand how subordinating words can be used to stress one idea over another, look at the following two sentences:

We've rented all the offices. We expect the building to show a profit this year.

The writer decided to combine the two sentences to emphasize the fact that now the building would show a profit. The subordinating word *since* makes *We've rented all the offices* less important than the rest of the sentence:

Since we've rented all the offices, we expect the building to show a profit this year.

PRACTICE V

Directions: In each item below, use the information to write a sentence in which one idea is more important than the other. Use a word from the preceding list to subordinate one idea to the other.

1. Give me all the data by January 15. The report won't be in on time.

___

2. We will arrive. We expect the meeting room to be ready.

___

3. We requested the parts three weeks ago. The parts have not arrived yet.

___

4. We worked hard. Our department has succeeded.

___

5. He programmed the computer. He had figured out which project would suit our needs.

___

Connecting Words

Another group of words plays an important role in combining ideas—the *connecting words*. Two lists of connecting words follow. The first contains words that combine ideas or sentences that the writer considers to be equal in importance. The words in the second group also link equal ideas, but these coordinating words are used in pairs.

1. Words That Link Coordinate Sentences or Ideas of Equal Importance:

and	also
but	besides
for	consequently
nor	further, furthermore
or	however
so	moreover
yet	then
	therefore
	thus

2. Words Used in Pairs to Relate One Sentence Element to Another:

    both—and

either—or
neither—nor
not only—but also
whether—or

The following examples show how you can use connecting words to combine sentences:

Separate: When you write an essay exam, jot down a few notes first. Use numbers to put the notes in proper sequence.

Combined: When you write an essay exam, jot down a few notes first; *then* use numbers to put the notes in proper sequence.

Separate: The police officers could not explain the cause of the accident. They could not locate a witness.

Combined: The police officers could not explain the cause of the accident, *nor* could they locate a witness.

Separate: Several employees have expressed an interest in a company childcare center. The personnel manager will investigate the possibility.

Combined: Several employees have expressed an interest in a company childcare center, *so* the personnel manager will investigate the possibility.

Separate: Style guides discuss the steps in researching your subject. They also discuss the steps in footnoting your sources.

Combined: Style guides discuss the steps *not only* in researching your subject *but also* in footnoting your sources.

(*Not only* and *but also* are both followed by descriptive phrases *in researching* and *in footnoting*. When you use pairs of connecting words, be sure that they are followed by words or word groups that are alike in form.)

Separate: The office manager filled the space with furniture that was not attractive. The furniture was not useful, either.

Combined: The office manager filled the space with furniture that was *neither* attractive *nor* useful.

One caution! Avoid relying too heavily on the word *and* when you combine related thoughts. *And* is sometimes useful, but it is often overworked. More important, it doesn't always show the precise relationship between two ideas. For example:

> A flowchart specifies the steps to be taken to complete a project, *and* many business managers use it in planning their department's schedules.

The sentence gives equal emphasis to the two ideas joined by *and*. In fact, the writer meant to say that the second part of the sentence was *a result* of the first part. A connecting word like *therefore* in front of the second idea would have made the point clearer:

> A flowchart specifies the steps to be taken to complete a project; *therefore*, many business managers use it in planning their department's schedules.

Notice that a semicolon comes before a connector like *therefore*, *however*, or *consequently* when it takes the place of *and* in a sentence. A comma usually comes after the connecting word.

PRACTICE VI

Directions: In each of the following items, combine the two sentences by using one of the connecting words from the list on page 147.

1. Orientation sets the stage for training. It smoothes the way for what is to come.

   ____

2. Transfers require planning. So do promotions.

   ____

3. We want you to have widgets for $1.49 each. We can offer the reduced price for two weeks only.

   ____

4. We hope that the new program will attract qualified applicants from among our employees. We are publicizing it in the company newsletter.

____

5. The prospectus didn't say how long the project would take. It didn't include an application form.

____

PRACTICE VII

Directions: The following items are based on paragraphs that contain numbered sentences. Some of the sentences may contain errors in sentence structure. Other sentences are correct as they appear in the paragraphs. Read the paragraphs and then answer the items based on them. For each item, choose the one best answer that would result in the most effective writing of the sentence or sentences.

Items 1 to 3 refer to the following paragraph.

(1) Our business plan should answer two important questions: how is our business doing right now? (2) And then another thing is where do we want the business to be in five years' time? (3) To write the plan, we'll have to take a careful look at such factors as our current products, our financial needs and resources, and how we are developing our management policies. (4) A critical look at the company's strengths and weaknesses will enable us to develop strategies to reach our long-term goal.

1. Sentences 1 and 2: **Our business plan should answer two important questions: how is our business doing right now? And then another thing is where do we want the business to be in five years' time?**

   The most effective combination of sentences 1 and 2 would include which of the following groups of words?

(1) now, and where do we ① ② ③ ④ ⑤
(2) now, and then another
(3) now, although another
(4) now; and then another thing
(5) now. Another thing is

2. Sentence 3: **To write the plan, we'll have to take a careful look at such factors as our current products, our financial needs and resources, and how we are developing our management policies.**

Which of the following is the best way to write the underlined portion of this sentence? If you think the original is the best way, choose option (1).

(1) how we are developing our management policies. ① ② ③ ④ ⑤
(2) when we'll develop our management policies.
(3) developing our management policies.
(4) our management policies.
(5) we'll develop a management policy.

3. Sentence 4: **A critical look at the company's strengths and weaknesses will enable us to develop strategies to reach our long-term goal.**

What correction should be made to this sentence?

(1) change look to looking ① ② ③ ④ ⑤
(2) change the spelling of company's to companies
(3) insert a comma after weaknesses
(4) replace our with their
(5) no correction is necessary

Items 4 to 8 refer to the following paragraph.

(1) All of the water we use leaves our homes as wasteflow. (2) It has to be treated to prevent pollution. (3) In addition, a large amount of the water has been heated. (4) Both procedures are costly not only in dollars, and then there is the energy use.

(5) You can cut down on your use of water and save both money and energy by starting a refit program for showerheads and faucets. (6) Add up the water used at all faucets in your house, and you'll discover a large part of household water use. (7) New faucets may have flow rates up to 2¾ gallons per minute. (8) The one you've had for years probably has a flow rate of 6 gallons per minute or more. (9) You don't need more than 1.0 gpm. (10) Can you see how much water and energy could be saved at your faucets?

4. Sentences 1 and 2: **All of the water we use leaves our homes as wasteflow. It has to be treated to prevent pollution.**

The most effective combination of sentences 1 and 2 would include which of the following groups of words?

(1) wasteflow, although that has ① ② ③ ④ ⑤
(2) wasteflow, so it has
(3) wasteflow, which has
(4) wasteflow, before it has
(5) wasteflow; and it has

5. Sentence 4: **Both procedures are costly, not only in dollars, and then there is the energy use.**

Which of the following is the best way to write the underlined portion of this sentence? If you think the original is the best way, choose option (1).

(1) and then there is the ① ② ③ ④ ⑤
(2) but also there is the
(3) and when there is the
(4) but also in
(5) but then there is the

6. Sentence 5: **You can cut down on your use of water and save both money and energy by starting a refit program for showerheads and faucets.**

If you rewrote sentence 5 beginning with

If you start a refit program for showerheads and faucets,

the next words should be

(1) use your money and energy ① ② ③ ④ ⑤
(2) you can cut down on water use
(3) we can cut down
(4) use water and money
(5) we can save money

7. Sentence 6: **Add up the water used at all faucets in your house, and you'll discover a large part of household water use.**

What correction should be made to this sentence?

(1) insert a comma between water and used ① ② ③ ④ ⑤
(2) replace the comma after house with a semicolon
(3) remove and
(4) change you'll to you will
(5) no correction is necessary

8. Sentences 7 and 8: **New faucets may have flow rates up to 2¾ gallons per minute. The one you've had for years probably has a flow rate of 6 gallons per minute or more.**

The most effective combination of sentences 7 and 8 would include which of the following groups of words?

(1) per minute, whereas ① ② ③ ④ ⑤
(2) per minute, and then the one
(3) per minute; while
(4) per minute and the one
(5) per minute, despite the one

ANSWER KEY

Chapter 12

Balanced Sentences/Coordinated Thoughts

Practice I *Page 139.*

1. (3) *Honest* agrees with faithful.
2. (2) *Concisely* agrees with carefully and truthfully.
3. (4) *Get (along with others)* agrees with swim, play, and row.
4. (1) Henry is two things: *a good doctor, an excellent friend. Not only* precedes *a good doctor*, and *but also* precedes *an excellent friend.*
5. (1) *You* agrees with you.
6. (2) *A tribute* agrees with a monument.
7. (3) *Paint* agrees with fence and mow.
8. (1) *Make* agrees with hang.
9. (4) *Exciting* agrees with *invigorating*.

Practice II *Page 141.*

1. (3) *Take* agrees with satisfy, offer, and crowd.
2. (2) *Motivating people* agrees with nutrition, buying, cooking, fitness, and interviewing.
3. (5) *Have no interest* agrees with are doing, are not oriented or trained, and cannot make.

Practice III *Page 142.*

(Note: Although there is more than one way of rewriting these sentences to make them balanced, the following answers indicate and explain one possible way.)

1. The winner's attitude toward the loser was conciliatory yet not condescending. *Yet not condescending* agrees with conciliatory.
2. Mrs. Gonzalez is conservative not only in business but also in politics. *In politics* agrees with in business.
3. The judge asked the defendant to swear to tell the truth and to cite the evidence. *To cite the evidence* agrees with to swear to tell the truth.
4. I cannot abide congested subways or crowded elevators. *Crowded elevators* agrees with congested subways.
5. This project is to be a benefit to the neighborhood and a credit to the sponsors. *A credit to the sponsors* agrees with a benefit to the neighborhood.
6. Math, reading, and writing are my favorite subjects. *Writing* agrees with math and reading.
7. The professor lectured on anthropology, and he outlined the child-rearing habits of the Polynesians. *Outlined* agrees with lectured.
8. I splashed cold water on my face and looked into the mirror. *Looked* agrees with splashed.
9. The rain splashes onto the walk and soaks into the ground. *Soaks* agrees with splashes.
10. Outside, the wind rustled the leaves in the trees, while inside the children slept quietly. *Slept* agrees with rustled.

Practice IV *Page 144.*

1. (2) Harry S. Truman enjoyed reading *not only* fiction *but also* nonfiction.
2. (1) Many people believe in stronger *consumer protection* and better *consumer products*.
3. (3) Doesn't automation *deprive* many of jobs and *require* training?

4. (2) *The attainment of* freedom and *the achievement of* national security were their goals.
5. (2) I *not only* endorse his candidacy, *but also* urge it.
6. (1) A true Yoga must have *discipline* and *concentration*.
7. (3) My feelings were hurt; so I *cried* a little, *called* a friend, and later *went* out with Bob.
8. (3) Many people in the wealthiest nation in the world are *destitute, malnourished,* and *jobless*.

Practice V *Page 146.*

Answers may vary.

1. Unless you give me all the data by January 15, the report won't be in on time.
2. When we arrive, we expect the meeting room to be ready.
3. Although we requested the parts three weeks ago, they have not arrived yet.
4. Because we worked hard, our department has succeeded.
5. He programmed the computer after he had figured out which project would suit our needs.

Practice VI *Page 149.*

Answers may vary.

1. Orientation not only sets the stage for training, but also smoothes the way for what is to come.
2. Both transfers and promotions require planning.
3. We want you to have the widgets for $1.49 each; however, we can offer this reduced price for two weeks only.
4. We hope that the new program will attract qualified applicants from among our employees; therefore (*or* consequently *or* accordingly), we are publicizing it in the company newsletter.
5. The prospectus didn't say how long the project would take, nor did it include an application form.

Practice VII *Page 150.*

1. (1) Our business plan should answer two important questions: how is our business doing right now, and where do we want the business to be in five years' time?
2. (4) To write the plan, we'll have to take a careful look at such factors as our current products, our financial needs and resources, and *our management policies*.
3. (5) No correction is necessary.
4. (3) All of the water we use leaves our homes as wasteflow, which has to be treated to prevent pollution.
5. (4) Both procedures are costly, not only in dollars, *but also* in energy use.
6. (2) If you start a refit program for showerheads and faucets, you can cut down on water use and save both money and energy.
7. (5) No correction is necessary.
8. (1) New faucets may have flow rates up to 2¾ gallons per minute, whereas the one you've had for years probably has a flow rate of 6 gallons per minute or more.

13.
Punctuation

To punctuate or not to punctuate that is the question is it better in the long run to omit the periods and question marks of English sentences or to include them against a large number of misunderstandings by using them we end all misinterpretation all the problems and confusion that the reader faces this is a result to be greatly valued

Adaptation of a monologue in
William Shakespeare's
Hamlet, Act III, Scene I

A Word With You . . .

Hamlet pondered the question, "To be or not to be." To punctuate or not to punctuate is not open to question. In order to write clearly and meaningfully, we must punctuate. Standard rules of punctuation help all of us gain the same meaning from written material. In this chapter, we review with you some of the more common rules of punctuation.

End Marks

Punctuation is simply a way of keeping ideas straight. The most commonly used forms of punctuation are marks that are used at the ends of sentences. These include the period (.), the question mark (?), and the exclamation mark (!). Read the following paragraph to see the confusion that results from not using end marks.

Paragraph I:

Preheat oven to 375° in a medium saucepan, melt 3 tablespoons butter stir in flour, salt, and pepper add milk and cook, stirring constantly, until thickened add mushrooms and parsley cook noodles as package directs.

Now place end marks where necessary in order to clarify the recipe.

Consider the following paragraph and place the proper end mark above each number.

Paragraph 2:

We have always considered heartbeat and breathing the basic

signs of life___Legally and medically, their absence indicates
1

death___But heartbeat and breathing are controlled by the
2

brain___Is a patient still alive when these functions occur only
3

through the use of a machine___A clinical decision to turn off
4

the machines is either a recognition that life is over or a form

of murder___Many agree with the former, but an equal
5

number will cry, "Murder___"
6

Turn to the answer key on page 168 to see if you've punctuated correctly.

Commas

The comma is the most difficult form of punctuation because of its varied uses. After studying the comma style sheet, take Practice I to determine where your comma strengths and areas for improvement lie.

COMMA STYLE SHEET

1. Commas are used to separate items in a series to ensure clarity.

   Example: Check the tires, the oil, and the battery.

2. Commas separate more than one descriptive word describing the same word.

   Example: Racing car drivers like long, streamlined cars.

3. Commas separate words or groups of words that interrupt the flow of the sentence.

   Examples: Jimmy Doolittle, Air Force squadron leader during WWII, was admired by those who flew with him.

   Chow mein, if you must know, is my favorite food.

4. The words *therefore, however, nevertheless, inasmuch as,* are set off by commas when they interrupt a complete thought.

   Examples: Unfortunately for Herbert Hoover, however, he became president a year before the crash of 1929.

   Can we, therefore, call environmentalists over-cautious?

5. A comma separates an introductory word or group of words from the complete thought.

   Examples: Before the New Deal, laissez-faire economics was practiced.

   Before Roosevelt introduced the New Deal, laissez-faire economics was practiced.

6. Commas separate two complete thoughts that are joined by a connecting word such as *and, or, but,* or *for.*

   Example: The office building will be torn down, and a parking lot will replace it.

7. A comma always separates the day from the year, and a comma separates the year from the rest of the sentence.

   Example: His son graduated on June 14, 1972, from New York University.

8. Separate a direct quotation from the rest of the sentence by using commas.

   Examples: "I cannot attend," he said.

The master of ceremonies shouted, “Attention, ladies and gentlemen!”

“I can understand how you feel,” he said, “but please try to see it my way.”

9. A comma separates the name of a city from the name of a state or country.

Examples: Madeline Manning Jackson is from Cleveland, Ohio.

Paul Martin will be stationed in Paris, France.

10. A comma follows the salutation in a friendly letter.
A comma follows the closing in a friendly letter, as well as in a business letter.

Examples: Dear Tom,
Sincerely,
Harvey

Friendly Letter

65 Eames Place
Boston, MA 02107
January 3, 1989

Dear Ann,

It was a pleasure seeing you again, and I want you to know how grateful I am for your advice and suggestions regarding my job search.

Since we met, I have had interviews at two of the three companies you mentioned. Our conversation prompted me to put several other companies on my list as well. Those interviews are set for the coming weeks.

Ann, I will let you know how my search progresses. As you requested, I am sending six more copies of my resume for your use. Thanks again for your help.

Sincerely,
Phil

Business Letter

65 Eames Place
Boston, MA 02107
January 11, 1989

Mr. Edward T. Adams, Vice-President
Major Distributing Company
203 Barton Road
Boston, MA 02120

Dear Mr. Adams:

Thank you again for the time you made available for me on Wednesday, December 28. I especially appreciated the comprehensive background you gave me of Descon Corporation and want you to know that it heightened my interest in the company. I am sure that my recent experience at XYZ Company will prove valuable in carrying out your plans for a new customer relations department.

You mentioned that your search for a manager would conclude in two weeks, so that I will anticipate hearing from you about January 20.

Very truly yours,
Phillip M. Smith
Phillip M. Smith

Common Comma Errors

Frequently, commas are included where they should not be. Following are two common examples.

1. A comma is *not* used to separate two actions if the sentence has one performer.

   INCORRECT: *I returned* to the library, and *left* the unread book.

   CORRECT: *I returned* to the library and *left* the unread book.

2. A comma is *not* used when a sentence begins with a complete thought followed by an incomplete thought.

INCORRECT: The party became lively,_when John arrived.
CORRECT: The party became lively_when John arrived.

PRACTICE I

Directions: Insert the missing commas in the following sentences.

1. The "Day in the City" tour included visits to the Metropolitan Museum the Museum of Natural History the Planetarium and Central Park Zoo.
2. The local theater group presented *Death of a Salesman* on June 14 1988.
3. The company transferred my brother from Cleveland Ohio to New York City.
4. After escaping from his pursuers the innocent victim ran breathlessly into the room and collapsed into a chair.
5. Dear Joe

   We arrived in Phoenix Arizona on July 10 and we were fortunate to find pleasant accommodations. We will come home on January 15 1989. Feed the cat.

   Love,

   Mother
6. Pélé the soccer star brought renewed interest to an old sport.
7. After reading the newspaper Terence Morgan decided to write to his congressman.
8. Will stood up when Mrs. Sullivan the mayor's wife entered the room.
9. "Please bring your camera to the game" said Jim.
10. "I would like to" Mitchell replied "but I can't afford the film."

PRACTICE II

Directions: The following items are based on paragraphs that contain numbered sentences. Some of the sentences may contain errors in the use of commas. Other sentences are correct as they appear in the paragraphs. Read the paragraphs and then answer the items based on them. Choose the one best answer to each item.

(1) For example, another story that appeared in the *Herald* on April 20, 1987 states, "Many home economists report that mothers overfeed their children and allow improper foods." (2) The story says serious future effects can result from such habits. (3) Many children are fed more than necessary and they have many unnecessary sweets on their menus. (4) These children may develop future incurable diseases.

(5) These same parents will donate generous sums, of money for research for cures for these diseases. (6) On the other hand, they don't realize that their overindulgence, spoiling, and doting are not in their children's best interests.

1. Sentence 1: **For example, another story that appeared in the *Herald* on April 20, 1987 states, "Many home economists report that mothers overfeed their children and allow improper foods."**

   What correction should be made to this sentence?

   (1) remove the comma after example — ① ② ③ ④ ⑤
   (2) replace the comma after states with a semicolon
   (3) insert a comma after 1987
   (4) remove the comma after states
   (5) no correction is necessary

2. Sentence 3: **Many children are fed more than necessary and they have many unnecessary sweets on their menus.**

   Which of the following is the best way to write the underlined portion of this sentence? If you think the original is the best way, choose option (1).

   (1) necessary and they — ① ② ③ ④ ⑤
   (2) necessary or they
   (3) necessary! And they
   (4) necessary, and they
   (5) necessary and in addition they

3. Sentence 5: **These same parents will donate generous sums, of money for research for cures for these diseases.**

What correction should be made to this sentence?

(1) insert a comma after parents
(2) insert a comma after generous
(3) remove the comma after sums
(4) insert a comma after money
(5) replace the comma after sums with a semicolon

① ② ③ ④ ⑤

4. Sentence 6: **On the other hand, they don't realize that their over-indulgence, spoiling, and doting are not in their children's best interests.**

What correction should be made to this sentence?

(1) remove the comma after hand
(2) remove the comma after spoiling
(3) insert a comma after realize
(4) insert a comma after doting
(5) no correction is necessary

① ② ③ ④ ⑤

Semicolons

The semicolon is a strong mark of punctuation. It signals the end of a thought. Unlike a period, it is used in the middle of a sentence because it connects two complete thoughts that are closely related.

Examples: The world acclaimed the Great Houdini's feats of escape. He earned the world's praise.

The world acclaimed the Great Houdini's feats of escape; he earned the world's praise.

The semicolon can also be used to separate two complete and related thoughts that would otherwise be separated by *and, but, or, nor, for, so.*

Examples: The world acclaimed the Great Houdini's feats of escape, and he earned the world's praise.

The world acclaimed the Great Houdini's feats of escape; he earned the world's praise.

PRACTICE III

Directions: Each of the following sentences is missing either a comma or a semicolon. If the sentence is missing a comma, blacken circle 1. If there is a missing semicolon, blacken circle 2.

1. In 1871, Kate O'Leary's cow kicked over a lamp_ the City of Chicago burned to the ground. ① ②
2. We accepted the invitation_but we cancelled because of illness. ① ②
3. Our backs were weak_but our spirit was strong. ① ②
4. The Louisiana Purchase enlarged America by about 140 percent in area_fifteen states were later carved from it. ① ②
5. Lemmings travel toward the sea_and they eat everything that is available on the way. ① ②
6. Dr. Toselli, our physician, was delayed at the hospital_my husband left. ① ②
7. An ancient temple in Mexico was cut out of a mountain_and water was the natural stonecutting tool used by its builders. ① ②
8. Please walk in_don't run. ① ②
9. Julius Caesar knew that it would be dangerous to transport an army across rough waters_but it was the only way he could learn more about Britain. ① ②
10. I am working late tonight_don't expect me for dinner. ① ②

Occasionally, one or both of two complete and related thoughts will contain commas.

Example: John, my older brother, is not a very good pool player; but even though he never wins, he enjoys the game.

Notice that in this type of sentence, in order to avoid confusion, a semicolon is used to separate the two complete thoughts even though a connecting word is present. *Study these examples:*

Although Jane is five years old, she has never been swimming; and personally, I think that is a shame.

When you are ready, please call me; and I, although occupied, will meet you at once.

The following large connecting words are always preceded by a semicolon and followed by a comma when connecting two complete thoughts:

therefore
nevertheless
however
inasmuch as

For example:

I don't like the terms of the contract; therefore, I will not sign it.

PRACTICE IV

Directions: The following items are based on a paragraph that contains numbered sentences. Some of the sentences may contain errors in the use of semicolons. Other sentences are correct as they appear in the paragraph. Read the paragraph and then answer the items based on it. Choose the one best answer to each item.

(1) Why do job training experts always suggest that you need to do homework before you go to an interview? (2) You may have thought that it's the interviewer's job to give you facts and background about the company, and it is but that doesn't mean that you shouldn't be prepared. (3) To begin with, there are practical reasons for getting information beforehand about the company.

(4) Suppose you need a certain, minimum salary in order to cover your expenses. (5) Through personal contacts and information from newspapers, you learn that the top salary can't meet your needs therefore, you decide not to waste your time interviewing. (6) On the other hand, if you do go to the interview, you should arrive with information and questions about the company in mind. (7) You will, undoubtedly, impress the interviewer with how well informed you are and therefore he or she will note your interest in the company, raising your interview rating considerably.

1. Sentence 2: **You may have thought that it's the interviewer's job to give you facts and background about the company, and it is but that doesn't mean that you shouldn't be prepared.**

   Which of the following is the best way to write the underlined portion of this sentence? If you think the original is the best way, choose option (1).

   ① ② ③ ❹ ⑤

   (1) company, and it is but
   (2) company, and, it is but
   (3) company and it is, but
   (4) company, and it is; but
   (5) company, and it is, but

2. Sentence 3: **To begin with, there are practical reasons for getting information beforehand about the company.**

   What correction should be made to this sentence?

   ① ② ③ ④ ❺

   (1) remove the comma after with
   (2) replace the comma after with with a semicolon
   (3) insert a comma after reasons
   (4) insert commas before and after beforehand
   (5) no correction is necessary

3. Sentence 5: **Through personal contacts and information from newspapers, you learn that the top salary can't meet your needs therefore, you decide not to waste your time interviewing.**

   What correction should be made to this sentence?

(1) insert a semicolon after needs ① ② ③ ④ ⑤
(2) remove the comma after newspapers
(3) replace the comma after newspapers with a semicolon
(4) insert a comma after needs
(5) insert a comma after time

4. Sentence 6: **On the other hand, if you do go to the interview, you should arrive with information and questions about the company in mind.**

What correction should be made to this sentence?

(1) remove the comma after hand ① ② ③ ④ ⑤
(2) replace the comma after hand with a semicolon
(3) replace the comma after interview with a semicolon
(4) insert a comma after information
(5) no correction is necessary

5. Sentence 7: **You will, undoubtedly, impress the interviewer with how well informed you are therefore he or she will note your interest in the company, raising your interview rating considerably.**

Which of the following is the best way to write the underlined portion of the sentence? If you think the original is the best way, choose option (1).

(1) are therefore, ① ② ③ ④ ⑤
(2) are; therefore,
(3) are, therefore
(4) are; therefore
(5) are; therefore;

ANSWER KEY

Chapter 13

Punctuation

Introductory Paragraph 1 *Page 156.*

Preheat oven to 375°. In a medium saucepan, melt 3 tablespoons butter. Stir in flour, salt, and pepper. Add milk and cook, stirring constantly, until thickened. Add mushrooms and parsley. Cook noodles as package directs.

Introductory Paragraph 2 *Page 157.*

We have always considered heartbeat and breathing the basic signs of life. Legally and medically, their absence indicates death. But heartbeat and breathing are controlled by the brain. Is a patient still alive when these functions occur only through the use of a machine? A clinical decision to turn off the machines is either a recognition that life is over or a form of murder. Many will agree with the former, but an equal number will cry, "Murder!"

Practice I *Page 161.*

1. The "Day in the City" tour included visits to the Metropolitan Museum, the Museum of Natural History, the Planetarium, and the Central Park Zoo.
2. The local theater group presented *Death of a Salesman* on June 14, 1988.
3. The company transferred my brother from Cleveland, Ohio, to New York City.
4. After escaping from his pursuers, the innocent victim ran breathlessly into the room and collapsed into a chair.
5. Dear Joe,

   We arrived in Phoenix, Arizona, on July 10, and we were fortunate to find pleasant accommodations. We will come home on January 15, 1989. Feed the cat.

   Love,
Mother
6. Pélé, the soccer star, brought renewed interest to an old sport.
7. After reading the newspaper, Terence Morgan decided to write to his congressman.
8. Will stood up when Mrs. Sullivan, the mayor's wife, entered the room.
9. "Please bring your camera to the game," said Juan.
10. "I would like to," Mitchell replied, "but I can't afford the film."

Practice II *Page 161.*

1. (3) For example, another story that appeared in the *Herald* on April 20, *1987,* states, "Many home economists report that mothers overfeed their children and allow improper foods."
2. (4) Many children are fed more than *necessary, and they* have many unnecessary sweets on their menus.
3. (3) These same parents donate generous *sums* of money for research for cures for these diseases.
4. (5) No correction is necessary.

Practice III *Page 164.*

1. (2) Use a semicolon to connect two complete, related thoughts when there is no connecting word such as *and, but, or.*
2. (1) Use a comma when connecting two complete thoughts joined by *and, but, or.*
3. (1) See answer 2.
4. (2) See answer 1.
5. (1) See answer 2.
6. (2) See answer 1.
7. (1) See answer 2.
8. (2) See answer 1.
9. (1) See answer 2.
10. (2) See answer 1.

Practice IV *Page 165.*

1. (4) The first thought already contains a comma. To avoid confusion, you need a semicolon before the connecting word, *but.*
2. (5) No correction is necessary.
3. (1) *Therefore* is one of those large connecting words always preceded by a semicolon and followed by a comma.
4. (5) No correction is necessary.
5. (2) See answer 3.

14.
Cumulative Review

This review covers the following concepts that have been included in the preceding chapters.

- Balanced Sentences
- Coordinated Thoughts
- Correct Sentence Structure
- Punctuation That Affects Sentence Structure

After completing the Cumulative Review exercises and checking your answers with the ANSWER KEY, evaluate your ability using the SUMMARY OF RESULTS chart on page 180. Acceptable scores for each practice section are given.

To learn your areas for skill improvement, find the question numbers you answered incorrectly on the SKILLS ANALYSIS table. The table will show which of your skills need improvement and the necessary chapters to review.

PRACTICE I

Directions: Which is the best way to write the underlined portion of each sentence? If you think the original is the best way, choose option (1).

1. In the autumn of 1984 we prepared for the colonization of Venus. We encountered <u>difficulties although</u> our technology was advanced.
(1) difficulties although ① ② ③ ④ ⑤
(2) difficulties, although
(3) difficulties! Although
(4) difficulties. Although
(5) difficulties; although

2. My Aunt Belle, the woman in the <u>green dress speakes five languages.</u>

(1) green dress speaks five languages. ① ② ③ ④ ⑤
(2) green dress, speaks five languages.
(3) green dress; speaks five languages.
(4) green dress. speaks five languages.
(5) green dress? She speaks five languages.

3. <u>After the baseball game we</u> bought lettuce, tomatoes, onions, luncheon meats, and Italian bread and made hero sandwiches.

(1) After the baseball game we ① ② ③ ④ ⑤
(2) After the baseball game. We
(3) After the baseball game, we
(4) After the baseball game ended we
(5) After the baseball game; we

4. She was an attractive woman, an excellent <u>speaker and a charming hostess; but,</u> she dressed outlandishly.

(1) speaker and a charming hostess; but, ① ② ③ ④ ⑤
(2) speaker and a charming hostess, but,
(3) speaker, and a charming hostess; but
(4) speaker, and a charming hostess, but,
(5) speaker, and a charming hostess but,

5. Because he did not enjoy last week's <u>lecture, Tom</u> decided to skip this week's.

(1) lecture, Tom ① ② ③ ④ ⑤
(2) lecture! Tom
(3) lecture Tom
(4) lecture; Tom
(5) lecture. Tom

6. The carnival was exciting, the games were fun but the children became very tired.
(1) fun but ① ② ③ ④ ⑤
(2) fun; but
(3) fun, but
(4) fun. But
(5) fun, the

7. We decided to play tennis, have lunch, and then we played bridge.
(1) , and then we played bridge. ① ② ③ ④ ⑤
(2) , and played bridge.
(3) ; and then we played bridge.
(4) , and play bridge.
(5) ; we played bridge.

8. Their living room lights were shining we decided to stop to say hello.
(1) shining we ① ② ③ ④ ⑤
(2) shining, we
(3) shining. And we
(4) shining; and we
(5) shining; we

9. We should first measure the room, then order the carpeting, and, finally, we will paint the walls.
(1) we will paint the walls. ① ② ③ ④ ⑤
(2) we would paint the walls.
(3) paint the walls.
(4) we will be painting the walls.
(5) to paint the walls.

10. Among all the causes of sedition and basic changes of the state; none is more important than excessive wealth of the few and extreme poverty of the many.
(1) the state; none ① ② ③ ④ ⑤
(2) the state none
(3) the state? None
(4) the state, none
(5) the state, so none

11. From a thousand feet, flapping his wings as hard as he could, he pushed over into a blazing steep dive toward the waves, and learned why seagulls don't make blazing steep power-dives.*
(1) waves, and ① ② ③ ④ ⑤
(2) waves and
(3) waves; and
(4) waves. And
(5) waves and,

PRACTICE II

Directions: The following items are based on paragraphs that contain numbered sentences. Some of the sentences may contain errors in balance or punctuation. Other sentences are correct as they appear in the paragraphs. Read the paragraphs and then answer the items based on them. For each item, choose the one best answer that would result in the most effective writing of the sentence or sentences.

Items 1 to 5 refer to the following paragraphs.

(1) Penny-wise consumers think twice before they buy foods packed in convenience-size containers. (2) True to their name, the smaller containers of premade foods do make packing lunches easier. (3) And they save time in the kitchen because they're likely to be premeasured for faster serving. (4) But do they save money? (5) Look at these comparative prices, decide for yourself.

(6) Individual packets of hot cereal cost about 20¢ for less than a cup. (7) Measure your own from a box of hot cereal, and the cost is about 5¢ per serving. (8) Juice, in the popular soft boxes adds up to 60¢ per cup. (9) The frozen concentrate will cost you about 18¢ a cup. (10) Although there are so many convenience foods tempting you; you should try to use these costly items only when it's absolutely necessary.

1. Sentence 2: **True to their name, the smaller containers of premade foods do make packing lunches easier.**

   What correction should be made to this sentence?

   (1) remove the comma after name ① ② ③ ④ ⑤
   (2) change containers to container
   (3) insert they after foods
   (4) change do to does
   (5) no correction is necessary

2. Sentence 3: **And they save time in the kitchen because they're likely to be premeasured for faster serving.**

   If you rewrote sentence 3 beginning with

   Premeasured for faster serving,

   the next words should be

   (1) because they're likely ① ② ③ ④ ⑤
   (2) you probably will save time
   (3) they save time
   (4) they will sometimes probably
   (5) you will save time

3. Sentence 5: **Look at these comparative prices, decide for yourself.**

Which of the following is the best way to write the underlined portion of this sentence? If you think the original is the best way, choose option (1).

(1) prices, decide ① ② ③ ④ ⑤
(2) prices; decide
(3) prices, then decide
(4) prices; Then decide
(5) prices; then deciding

4. Sentence 8: **Juice, in the popular soft boxes adds up to 60¢ per cup.**

What correction should be made to this sentence?

(1) remove the comma after Juice ① ② ③ ④ ⑤
(2) insert it's after Juice
(3) change adds to add
(4) insert a comma after boxes
(5) change per to for a

5. Sentence 10: **Although there are so many convenience foods tempting you; you should try to use these costly items only when it's absolutely necessary.**

What correction should be made to this sentence?

(1) change the spelling of there to their ① ② ③ ④ ⑤
(2) change are to is
(3) insert a comma after convenience
(4) change the semicolon after tempting you to a comma
(5) change it's to its

Items 6 to 10 refer to the following paragraph.

(1) The bicycle is a fairly pleasant machine for limited use by a few people, but claims that it can substitute for the automobile as a device for moving people around are grossly overstated. (2) Most elderly people will not be happy aboard it, and mothers who must take along small children during a shopping trip to the supermarket won't be either. (3) It is an exhausting and brutal machine in cities built on hills, and being the most unattractive way to travel wherever and whenever the temperature is over 90° and under 30°. (4) If parked, even chained, out of eyesight for more than 10 minutes; it is a cinch to be stolen. (5) And then, of course there is the awkward question of courage.*

6. Sentence 1: **The bicycle is a fairly pleasant machine for limited use by a few people, but claims that it can substitute for the automobile as a device for moving people around are grossly overstated.**

What correction should be made to this sentence?

(1) change the spelling of bicycle to bycicle ① ② ③ ④ ⑤
(2) change , but to ; but
(3) remove the comma after people
(4) insert commas after automobile and around
(5) no correction is necessary

7. Sentence 2: **Most elderly people will not be happy aboard it, and mothers who must take along small children during a shopping trip to the supermarket won't be either.**

Which of the following is the best way to write the underlined portion of this sentence? If you think the original is the best way, choose option (1).

(1) it, and mothers who must take along small children during a shopping trip to the supermarket won't be either. ① ② ③ ④ ⑤

*The paragraph for items 6 to 10 is adapted from Russell Baker's "Backwards Wheels the Mind," *The New York Times*, July 1, 1973.

(2) it, and mothers who must take along small children during a shopping trip to the supermarket won't be.
(3) it, nor will mothers who must take along small children during a shopping trip to the supermarket.
(4) it, or will mothers who must take along small children during a shopping trip to the supermarket.
(5) it; or mothers who must take along small children during a shopping trip to the supermarket.

8. Sentence 3: **It is an exhausting and brutal machine in cities built on hills, and being the most unattractive way to travel wherever and whenever the temperature is over 90° and under 30°.**

What correction should be made to this sentence?

(1) replace and brutal with or brutal ① ② ③ ④ ⑤
(2) insert a comma after machine
(3) replace the comma after hills with a semicolon
(4) replace and being with and it is
(5) no correction is necessary

9. Sentence 4: **If parked, even chained, out of eyesight for more than 10 minutes; it is a cinch to be stolen.**

Which of the following is the best way to write the underlined portion of this sentence? If you think the original is the best way, choose option (1).

(1) minutes; it ① ② ③ ④ ⑤
(2) minutes. It
(3) minutes, it
(4) minutes, and it
(5) minutes, but it

10. Sentence 5: **And then, of course there is the awkward question of courage.**

What correction should be made to this sentence?

(1) replace And with Although ① ② ③ ④ ⑤
(2) insert a comma after And
(3) remove the comma after then
(4) insert a comma after course
(5) change the spelling of there to their

Items 11 to 16 refer to the following paragraphs.

(1) Men are bent intently over chessboards. (2) They are men of all ages. (3) Most are closer to life's twilight than its dawn. (4) They are in battle with one another, the chessboard is their battlefield.

(5) The sun is hot. (6) Sometimes a drizzle begins. (7) Never mind. (8) This is not some silly pastime to idle time away, this is chess. (9) This outdoor chess congregation is the only one of its kind in the borough.

(10) Yet, it boasts not a single chess master. (11) Is this sad? (12) No, it's irrelevant. (13) For, if a man is seeking out excellence in chess he would do well to stay away from St. James Park. (14) What he would find here is grimness, determination, anguish, wisdom after the fact, bitterness under the breath, and there are a number of accidental brilliances.

11. Sentences 2 and 3: **They are men of all ages. Most are closer to life's twilight than its dawn.**

The most effective combination of sentences 2 and 3 would include which of the following groups of words?

(1) ages; but most ① ② ③ ④ ⑤
(2) ages. But most
(3) ages, but most
(4) ages. but most
(5) ages, most

12. Sentence 4: **They are in battle with one another, the chessboard is their battlefield.**

Which of the following is the best way to write the underlined portion of this sentence? If you think the original is the best way, choose option (1).

(1) another, the ① ② ③ ④ ⑤
(2) another. the
(3) another—The
(4) another; The
(5) another; the

13. Sentence 8: **This is not some silly pastime to idle time away, this is chess.**

What correction should be made to this sentence?

(1) change the spelling of idle to idol ① ② ③ ④ ⑤
(2) change is not to isn't
(3) insert a comma after pastime
(4) replace the comma after away with a semicolon
(5) no correction is necessary

14. Sentence 12: **No it's irrelevant.**

What correction should be made to this sentence?

(1) change the spelling of no to know ① ② ③ ④ ⑤
(2) change it's to its
(3) insert a comma after No
(4) insert a semicolon after No
(5) change the spelling of irrelevant to irrevelant

15. Sentence 13: **For, if a man is seeking out excellence in chess he would do well to stay away from St. James Park.**

What correction should be made to this sentence?

(1) remove the comma after For ① ② ③ ④ ⑤
(2) change is to was
(3) insert a comma after chess
(4) replace he with they
(5) change St. James to St. Jame's

16. Sentence 14: **What he would find here is grimness, determination, anguish, wisdom after the fact, and there are a number of accidental brilliances.**

Which of the following is the best way to write the underlined portion of this sentence? If you think the original is the best way, choose option (1).

(1) , and there are a number ① ② ③ ④ ⑤
(2) , and a number
(3) , and then there are a number
(4) . And there are a number
(5) ; and there are a number

SUMMARY OF RESULTS

After reviewing the Answer Key on page 182, chart your scores below for each practice section.

Practice Number	**Your Number Right**	**Your Number Wrong** (Including Omissions)	**Acceptable Score**
I			8 correct
II			12 correct

SKILLS ANALYSIS

To discover your areas for skill improvement, locate the question numbers you got wrong and circle them on this Skills Analysis chart. Then, refer to the chapters listed in column 3.

Skill	Question Number	Chapter Reference
Practice I		*See Chapter*
Balanced Sentences	7, 9	12
Punctuation That Affects Sentence Structure	1, 2, 3, 4, 5, 6, 8, 10, 11	13
Practice II		
Punctuation That Affects Sentence Structure	1, 3, 4, 5, 6, 9, 10, 12, 13, 14, 15	13
Balanced Sentences	8, 16	12
Coordinated Thoughts	7, 11	12
Correct Sentence Structure	2	13

ANSWER KEY

Chapter 14

Cumulative Review

Practice I *Page 170.*

1. (1) No correction is necessary.
2. (2) My Aunt Belle, the woman in the *green dress, speaks five languages.*
3. (3) *After the baseball game, we* bought lettuce, tomatoes, onions, luncheon meats, and Italian bread and made hero sandwiches.
4. (3) She was an attractive woman, an excellent *speaker, and a charming hostess; but* she dressed outlandishly.
5. (1) Because he did not enjoy last week's *lecture, Tom* decided to skip this week's.
6. (3) The carnival was exciting, the games were *fun, but* the children became very tired.
7. (4) We decided to play tennis, have lunch, *and play bridge.*
8. (5) Their living room lights were *shining; we* decided to stop to say hello.
9. (3) We should first measure the room, then order the carpeting, and, finally, *paint the walls.*
10. (4) Among all the causes of sedition and basic changes of *the state, none* is more important than excessive wealth of the few and extreme poverty of the many.
11. (2) From a thousand feet, flapping his wings as hard as he could, he pushed over into a blazing steep dive toward the *waves and* learned why seagulls don't make blazing steep power-dives.

Practice II *Page 173.*

1. (5) No correction is necessary.
2. (3) Premeasured for faster serving, they save time in the kitchen.
3. (2) Look at these comparative *prices; decide* for yourself.
4. (4) Juice, in the popular soft *boxes,* adds up to 60¢ per cup.
5. (4) Although there are so many convenience foods tempting *you, you* should try to use these costly items only when *it's* absolutely necessary.
6. (5) No correction is necessary.
7. (3) Most elderly people will not be happy aboard *it, nor will mothers who must take along small children during a shopping trip to the supermarket.*
8. (4) It is an exhausting and brutal machine in cities built on hills, *and it is* the most unattractive way to travel wherever and whenever the temperature is over 90° and under 30°.
9. (3) If parked, even chained, out of eyesight for more than 10 *minutes, it* is a cinch to be stolen.
10. (4) And then, of *course,* there is the awkward question of courage.
11. (3) There are men of all *ages, but most* are closer to life's twilight than its dawn.
12. (5) They are in battle with one *another; the* (OR *another, and the* OR *another. The*) chessboard is their battlefield.
13. (4) This is not some silly pastime to idle time *away; this* (OR *away. This*) is chess.
14. (3) *No, it's* irrelevant.
15. (3) For, if a man is seeking out excellence in *chess, he* would do well to stay away from St. James Park.
16. (2) What he would find here is grimness, determination, anguish, wisdom after the fact, *and a number* of accidental brilliances.

15.

Effective Expression

I never say, "The trip it was a lovely cruise,"
Nor make a boorish error of that type.
  "The reason is because" I hesitate to use
  And regard "he hardly never" as sheer tripe.
When it comes to proper style, I've paid my dues.

Lorraine Lockwood
from "Paying One's Dues" in
A Housewife and Her Poems

A Word With You . . .

The common errors pointed out by the poet are all treated in Chapter 15. She "paid her dues" by learning how to avoid such repetitive expressions and how to write in a clear, concise, uncluttered fashion.

Care to pay your dues?

Style and Clarity

Many sentences that seem correctly written are, in fact, incorrect because of:

the misuse of words or phrases.

the addition of unnecessary words or phrases.

the lack of logic in using a descriptive word or phrase.

See if you can locate the errors in style and clarity in the following paragraphs. Mark your corrections directly in the paragraph.

Paragraph A:

My reason for sending the children to Happy Days Camp was that I thought they might learn to swim. Much of the time, the weather was cloudy, but they didn't go swimming. At the end of the season, the campers gave a party for their parents, but they didn't seem to enjoy it. Since our expectations were not fulfilled, we signed the children up for the next year.

Did you find these errors?

1. INCORRECT: My reason for sending the children to Happy Days Camp was that I thought they might learn to swim.

PROBLEM: The incorrect sentence uses too many words to make the point. "My reason . . . was that" can be condensed simply to "I sent the children to Happy Days Camp because . . ."

CORRECT: I sent the children to Happy Days Camp *because* I thought they might learn to swim.

2. INCORRECT: Much of the time, the weather was cloudy, but they didn't go swimming.

PROBLEM: The sentence states that they didn't go swimming *in spite of* the cloudy weather. In fact, they didn't go swimming *because of* the cloudy weather.

CORRECT:

a. Much of the time, the weather was cloudy, so they didn't go swimming.
b. Much of the time, the weather was cloudy; therefore, they didn't go swimming.
c. Much of the time, they didn't go swimming because the weather was cloudy.

3. INCORRECT: At the end of the season, the campers gave a party for their parents, but they didn't enjoy it.

PROBLEM: It is unclear whether *they* refers to the campers or their parents. The sentence must be changed in order to convey the true meaning.

CORRECT:

a. At the end of the season, the campers gave a party for their parents, but the campers didn't enjoy it.
b. At the end of the season, the campers gave a party for their parents, but their parents didn't enjoy it.
c. Although they didn't enjoy it, at the end of the season, the campers gave a party for their parents.
d. At the end of the season, the campers gave a party for their parents who didn't enjoy it.

4. INCORRECT: Since our expectations were not fulfilled, we signed the children up for next year.

PROBLEM: The sentence states that we enrolled the children for next year *since* our expectations were not fulfilled. In fact, we enrolled the children for next year *although* our expectations were not fulfilled.

CORRECT: Although our expectations were not fulfilled, we enrolled the children for next year.

The corrected paragraph would look like this:

I sent the children to Happy Days Camp *because* I thought they might learn to swim. Much of the time, the weather was cloudy, *so* they didn't go swimming. At the end of the season, the campers gave a party for their parents, but *the campers* didn't enjoy it. *Although* our expectations were not fulfilled, we enrolled the children for next year.

Paragraph B:

The bus tour of Philadelphia on the bus was interesting. I don't never remember a livelier group. The highlight of the trip was when we saw the Liberty Bell. The reason I enjoyed that sight was because I love history. The bus driver, he gave an informative speech.

Did you find these errors?

1. INCORRECT: The bus tour on the bus of Philadelphia was interesting.

PROBLEM: The phrase *on the bus* is a repetition. Bus *tour* means that the tour was on the bus.

CORRECT: The bus tour of Philadelphia was interesting.

2. INCORRECT: I don't never remember a livelier group.

PROBLEM: The incorrect sentence uses a double negative, *don't never*. These two negative words, in effect, cancel each other. Other negative words that should not be used in combination are: hardly, scarcely, neither, only, never, no one, nobody, no, none, nothing, not.

CORRECT: I don't ever remember a livelier group.

3. INCORRECT: The highlight of the trip was when we saw the Liberty Bell.
PROBLEM: The use of *was when* is poor style. A more concise form of expression should be chosen.
CORRECT: The highlight of the trip was seeing the Liberty Bell.

4. INCORRECT: The reason I enjoyed that sight was because I love history.
PROBLEM: *The reason . . . was because* creates an awkward sentence. Simplify the sentence by stating A because B without the unnecessary words.
CORRECT: I enjoyed that sight because I love history.

5. INCORRECT: The bus driver, he gave an informative speech.
PROBLEM: Wordiness results from the repetition in the phrase *the bus driver, he*. Use one or the other, but not both terms. In this sentence you need to use *bus driver*, since there has been no prior reference to him.
CORRECT: The bus driver planned an informative speech.

The corrected paragraph would look like this:

The bus tour of Philadelphia was interesting. I don't *ever* remember a livelier group. The highlight of the trip was *seeing* the Liberty Bell. I enjoyed that sight *because* I love history. The *bus driver* gave an informative speech.

PRACTICE

I **Directions:** For each sentence below, blacken circle 1 if the sentence has an error in clarity or style. Blacken circle 2 if there is no error.

1. He hardly never writes home. ① ②
2. Charlie accepted the job because the pay was good. ① ②
3. Manuel doesn't like fishing. ① ②
4. Leonardo Da Vinci, he painted the *Last Supper*. ① ②
5. I hadn't scarcely opened the book when I fell asleep. ① ②
6. Since I enjoy music, I never attended concerts. ① ②

7. Britons and Americans have never spoken the same language. ① ②

8. Dolores visited her former employer, Mei Lin, and she gave her a lovely gift. ① ②

9. Although I like to play chess, I can't play now. ① ②

10. There isn't no easy way of solving the problem. ① ②

11. Since Martin Luther King had been an advocate of nonviolence, his violent death was particularly shocking. ① ②

12. If the play is not a success, the reason is because the actors never learned their lines well. ① ②

13. The babysitter gave the child lunch, and she continued to play. ① ②

14. The ancient, old castle still stood on the hill. ① ②

15. Since the weather had been unusually dry, forests are in danger of burning. ① ②

PRACTICE II

Direction: Which is the best way to write the underlined portion of each sentence? If you think the original is the best way, choose option (1).

1. The graduates and their teachers gathered in the auditorium, <u>where they received diplomas.</u>

(1) where they received diplomas. ① ② ③ ④ ⑤
(2) in which they received diplomas.
(3) where the graduates received their diplomas.
(4) to receive diplomas.
(5) where diplomas were received.

2. The mailman <u>he comes promptly</u> at 12 noon.

(1) he comes promptly ① ② ③ ④ ⑤
(2) who comes promptly
(3) comes promptly
(4) coming promptly
(5) he come promptly

3. The reason I bought the outfit was because it was on sale.
   (1) The reason I bought the outfit was because it was on sale. ① ② ③ ④ ⑤
   (2) The reason I bought the outfit was it was on sale.
   (3) I bought the outfit for the reason it was on sale.
   (4) I bought the outfit because it was on sale.
   (5) The reason it was on sale was because I bought the outfit.

4. The polite time to comment was when he finished his entire speech.
   (1) was when he finished his entire speech. ① ② ③ ④ ⑤
   (2) was when he had finished his entire speech.
   (3) was when he was finishing his speech.
   (4) was while he was finishing his speech.
   (5) came after he had finished his speech.

5. Don't you never have to work on weekends?
   (1) Don't you never ① ② ③ ④ ⑤
   (2) Don't you ever
   (3) Didn't you never
   (4) Haven't you never
   (5) Do you not never

6. All of the graduates who graduated in the class of '87 met at the school for a party.
   (1) who graduated in the class of '87 ① ② ③ ④ ⑤
   (2) whom graduated in the class of '87
   (3) graduated in the class of '87
   (4) who graduate in the class of '87
   (5) of the class of '87

7. Since I had cooked dinner, we did not go out to eat.

(1) Since I had cooked dinner, we did not go out to eat. ① ② ③ ④ ⑤

(2) Since I had cooked dinner, we went out to eat.

(3) We went out to eat since I had cooked dinner.

(4) We went out to eat because I cooked dinner.

(5) Since I cooked dinner, we did not go out to eat.

PRACTICE III

Directions: The following items are based on a paragraph that contains numbered sentences. Some of the sentences may contain errors in style and clarity. Other sentences are correct as they appear in the paragraph. Read the paragraph and then answer the items based on it. For each item, choose the one best answer that would result in the most effective writing of the sentence or sentences.

(1) Our family, we went to the craft show. (2) The craft show included displays of pottery, needlepoint, jewelry, leaded glass, and other crafts. (3) My favorite part of the afternoon was when I tried the potter's wheel. (4) I didn't never do anything that creative before. (5) I had difficulty with the spinning wheel. (6) I had never tried one before. (7) The artists permitted the children to try the media, and they enjoyed sharing this creative experience.

1. Sentence 1: **Our family, we went to the craft show.**

What correction should be made to this sentence?

(1) remove the comma after family ① ② ③ ④ ⑤

(2) replace went with are going

(3) remove the comma and we

(4) insert whole before family

(5) insert when before we

2. Sentence 2: **The craft show included displays of pottery, needlepoint, jewelry, leaded glass, and other crafts.**

Which of the following is the best way to write the underlined portion of this sentence? If you think the original is the best way, choose option (1).

(1) craft show ① ② ③ ④ ⑤
(2) show of crafts
(3) crafts shows
(4) show
(5) craft's show

3. Sentence 3: **My favorite part of the afternoon was when I tried the potter's wheel.**

What correction should be made to this sentence?

(1) change part to parts ① ② ③ ④ ⑤
(2) insert a comma after part
(3) replace afternoon with day
(4) replace when I tried with trying
(5) change potter's to potters

4. Sentence 4: **I didn't never do anything that creative before.**

What correction should be made to this sentence?

(1) change didn't to did not ① ② ③ ④ ⑤
(2) replace didn't never do with never did
(3) replace anything with nothing
(4) insert was before creative
(5) no correction is necessary

5. Sentences 5 and 6: **I had difficulty with the spinning wheel. I had never tried one before.**

The most effective combination of sentences 5 and 6 would include which of the following groups of words?

(1) wheel, and ① ② ③ ④ ⑤
(2) wheel because
(3) wheel, despite the fact that
(4) wheel, when
(5) wheel, it's because

6. Sentence 7: **The artists permitted the children to try the media, and they enjoyed sharing this creative experience.**

Which of the following is the best way to write the underlined portion of this sentence? If you think the original is the best way, choose option (1).

(1) they enjoyed ① ② ③ ④ ⑤
(2) then they enjoyed
(3) despite this, they enjoyed
(4) they also enjoyed
(5) the artists enjoyed

Problems with Logic

When you use a descriptive word or phrase in a sentence, be sure your sentence also includes the word described. Look at what happens to logic when the word described is left out of the sentence.

1. INCORRECT: Tired from the long climb, a rest seemed in order.

PROBLEM: As it is written, the sentence means that *a rest* was *tired*. The people being described as *tired* are missing from the sentence.

CORRECT: Tired from the long climb, *we* thought a rest seemed in order.

ANOTHER SOLUTION: Move the person or thing described to the beginning of the sentence.

CORRECT: Because *we* were *tired* from the long climb, a rest seemed in order.

2. INCORRECT: After signing the bill, the pen was given to the Boy Scout leader.

PROBLEM: As it is written, the sentence means that the pen—with no help from a person—signed the bill. The person who used the pen to sign the bill is missing from the sentence.

CORRECT: After signing the bill, the president gave the pen to the Boy Scout leader.

ANOTHER SOLUTION: After the president signed the bill, he gave the pen to the Boy Scout leader.

PRACTICE IV

Directions: The following items are based on a paragraph that contains numbered sentences. Some of the sentences may contain errors in logic. Other sentences are correct as they appear in the paragraph. Read the paragraph and then answer the items based on it. Choose the one best answer to each item.

(1) A computer collects the information, or data, as input. (2) Using a typewriter-like keyboard, information passes from the keyboard to the computer's storage area. (3) Stored, the computer will need to work with the information later. (4) After the computer processes the data in some way, the information is passed to an output machine called a visual display unit.

1. Sentence 1: **A computer collects the information, or data, as input.**

   What correction should be made to this sentence?

   (1) insert it after computer ① ② ③ ④ ⑤
   (2) change collects to collect
   (3) remove the comma after information
   (4) remove the comma after data
   (5) no correction is necessary

2. Sentence 2: **Using a typewriter-like keyboard, information passes from the keyboard to the computer's storage area.**

   If you rewrote sentence 2 beginning with

   Using a typewriter-like keyboard, the operator

   the next words should be

   (1) passes from the keyboard ① ② ③ ④ ⑤
   (2) passes information from the keyboard
   (3) computes the information from the keyboard
   (4) keyboards to the computer's storage area
   (5) passes to the computer's storage area

3. Sentence 3: **Stored, the computer will need to work with the information later.**

   If you rewrote sentence 3 beginning with

   The computer will need to

   the next words should be

   (1) store the work with ① ② ③ ④ ⑤
   (2) store the information
   (3) compute the work
   (4) work with the stored
   (5) work the information

Reminder: In Chapter 5 you learned to place descriptive phrases close to the words they describe. Follow that rule in order to ensure that your sentences are clear and logical.

1. INCORRECT: Problems are solved by computer scientists that are very complicated.

   PROBLEM: Written this way, the sentence states that scientists are very complicated.
   The descriptive words, that are very complicated are placed incorrectly.

   CORRECT: Problems that are very complicated are solved by computer scientists.

   ANOTHER SOLUTION: Computer scientists solve problems that are very complicated.

2. INCORRECT: The scientist types questions and the computer answers on the keyboard.

   PROBLEM: According to this sentence, answers appear on the keyboard. The descriptive words on the keyboard are placed incorrectly.

   CORRECT: The scientist types questions on the keyboard and the computer answers.

ANSWER KEY

Chapter 15

Effective Expression

Practice I *Page 186.*

1. (1) He *hardly ever* writes home. Do not use *hardly* with a negative word such as *never*.
2. (2)
3. (2)
4. (1) *Leonardo da Vinci painted* the *Last Supper*. *He* is repetitious.
5. (1) I *had scarcely* opened the book when I fell asleep. Do not use *scarcely* with a negative word such as *hadn't* (had *not*).
6. (1) Since I enjoy music, I *frequently attend* concerts. The second part of the sentence contradicted the first.
7. (2)
8. (1) Dolores *visited* her former employer, Mei Lin, *and gave* her a lovely gift. Eliminate *she* to get rid of the confusion.
9. (2)
10. (1) There *is no* easy way of solving the problem. Don't use *not* and *no* together.
11. (2)
12. (1) If the play is not a success, *it is because* the actors never learned their lines. *The reason is because* makes the sentence unwieldy.
13. (1) The babysitter gave the child lunch, and *the child* continued to play. The use of *she* makes the sentence unclear.
14. (1) The *ancient castle* still stood on the hill. *Old* is repetitious.
15. (2)

Practice II *Page 187.*

1. (3) The graduates and their teachers gathered in the auditorium, *where the graduates received their diplomas.*
2. (3) The mailman *comes promptly* at 12 noon.
3. (4) *I bought the outfit because it was on sale.*
4. (5) The polite time to comment *came after he had finished his speech.*
5. (2) *Don't you ever* have to work on weekends?
6. (5) All of the graduates *of the class of '87* met at the school for a party.
7. (1) *Since I had cooked dinner, we did not go out to eat.*

Practice III *Page 189.*

1. (3) *We* is repetitious. The sentence should read: Our *family went* to the craft show.
2. (4) *Craft* is repetitious. The sentence should read: The *show* included displays of pottery, needlepoint, jewelry, leaded glass, and other crafts.
3. (4) *Was when* is an awkward construction. The sentence should read: My favorite part of the afternoon was *trying* the potter's wheel.
4. (2) Don't use *didn't* and *never* together. The sentence should read: I *never did* anything that creative before.
5. (2) *Because* coordinates the two thoughts. The sentence should read: I had difficulty with the spinning *wheel because* I had never tried one before.

6. (5) The word to which *they* refers is unclear. The sentence should read: The artists permitted the children to try the media, and *the artists enjoyed* sharing this creative experience.

Practice IV *Page 192.*

1. (5) No correction is necessary.
2. (2) Using a typewriter-like keyboard, the operator passes information from the keyboard to the computer's storage area.
3. (4) The computer will need to work with the stored information later.

16.
More Punctuation

A Word With You . . .

Charlie Brown knows that strong writers don't just "sprinkle in the little curvy marks" or any other mark of punctuation. Punctuation, used correctly, guides your reader through your writing. This chapter introduces marks of punctuation that many people avoid. Learn to use them correctly, and your writing will stand out.

Quotation Marks

Quotation marks are used to set off the *exact* words said by somebody or taken from a source.

Direct quotation: The young mother remarked, "Thank Heavens for our community's parks and recreation program!"

Indirect quotation: The young mother remarked that she was grateful for her community's parks and recreation program.

In the first sentence, the woman's exact words are quoted. In the second sentence, the word *that* signals the fact that the sentence is a report of what was said, not a direct quotation.

QUOTATION MARK STYLE SHEET

1. Use quotation marks to set off the exact words of a speaker. Note the comma between the speaker and the words spoken in each example. Note the period *inside* the quotation marks at the end of the first sentence.

   Examples: The teacher instructed, "Complete the vocabulary list at home."

   "Review the vocabulary list for our last class," the teacher instructed.

2. Use quotation marks to set off both parts of a broken quotation. Do not capitalize the first word of the second part of the quotation unless it is the beginning of a new sentence.

   Examples: "Well," exclaimed Anita, "what did you expect?"

   "Stop complaining, Billy," said his brother. "It won't help."

3. Place a semicolon after the closing quotation marks.

   Example: You said, "Wait until your see me"; so I waited.

4. Never use two forms of punctuation at the end of a quotation. When the entire sentence is a question but the quoted portion is not, place a question mark *after* the closing quotation marks.

   Example: Did Jane say, "Meet at our house"?

5. Never use two forms of punctuation at the end of a quotation. When the entire sentence is an exclamation but the quoted portion is not, place the exclamation point *after* the closing quotation marks.

   When the quoted portion is an exclamation, place the exclamation mark *inside* the quotes.

   Examples: I could scream each time you call and say, "I'll be late for dinner tonight, dear"!

   The guard shouted, "Stop him! Stop him!"

6. Use single quotation marks for a quotation within a quotation.

   Example: The history student asked, "Is it true that Patrick Henry said, 'Give me liberty or give me death' when America's freedom was in question?"

7. Use quotation marks to enclose titles of poems, articles, chapters, or any part of a book or magazine. If the quoted title is followed by a comma, the comma should be placed inside the quotation marks.

   Example: The third chapter of *Our World,* entitled, "Views of the Middle East," is the most interesting.

Common Errors with Quotation Marks

Quotations require marks of punctuation in addition to quotation marks. The most common errors in quotations involve the omission or misuse of commas, periods, and capital letters. Following are common examples.

1. Place a comma between what is quoted and the person quoted.

INCORRECT: "When you finish packing the last box, start loading all of them onto the truck" the shipping manager instructed.

CORRECT: "When you finish packing the last box, start loading all of them onto the truck," the shipping manager instructed.

2. In a broken quotation, do not capitalize the first word of the second part of the quotation unless it is the beginning of a new sentence.

INCORRECT: "When you finish packing the last box," the shipping manager instructed. "Start loading all of them onto the truck."

CORRECT: "When you finish packing the last box," the shipping manager instructed, "start loading all of them onto the truck."

CORRECT: "You have finished packing the last box," the foreman said. "Start loading all of them onto the truck."

3. Place the period inside the quotation marks at the end of a sentence.

INCORRECT: Dr. D'Amato said, "Before you leave the office, please give your Medicare number to the nurse".

CORRECT: Dr. D'Amato said, "Before you leave the office, please give your Medicare number to the nurse."

4. Place a question mark *after* the closing quotation marks when the entire sentence is a question, but the quoted portion is not.

INCORRECT: Did Dr. D'Amato say, "Please leave your Medicare number with the nurse?"

CORRECT: Did Dr. D'Amato say, "Please leave your Medicare number with the nurse"?

5. Place a question mark *inside* the closing quotation marks when the quoted portion is a question, but the entire sentence is not.

INCORRECT: Dr. D'Amato asked, "Is this your correct Medicare number"?

CORRECT: Dr. D'Amato asked, "Is this your correct Medicare number?"

PRACTICE I

Directions: Punctuate the following sentences.

1. The manager said three men must work overtime
2. The manager said that three men must work overtime
3. Three men said the manager must work overtime
4. The manager asked who will work overtime
5. Why didn't the manager say everyone must work
6. Imagine if the manager had said everyone must work overtime
7. Imagine if the manager had said that everyone must work overtime
8. The manager shouted everyone must work overtime

PRACTICE II

Directions: Some of the following sentences contain errors in punctuation. Make corrections where necessary. Four sentences contain no errors.

1. Mrs. Romano exclaimed, Frankie, the parakeet has disappeared!"

2. Frankie answered, "Mom, I don't know why; it was there when I tried to clean it with the vacuum cleaner.
3. "You will never catch me!" shouted Batman. The pursuers vowed to catch him.
4. The student said that he now understands the theory behind these problems. He said, "Suddenly, everything falls into place."
5. The author said, "You can learn to write only through writing." He said that one can never learn to write by reading how-to books.
6. Alice told Marion she was to stay at home and be a babysitter. Marion exclaimed, "what a shame!"
7. Clean your room, take the laundry to the basement, and wash the car," instructed Mother.
8. After you turn over the earth, add some plant food and water. Then you'll be ready to plant the flower," concluded the gardener.
9. Was it Elsa who said, "Our sales meeting begins at 9:30 A.M. sharp?"
10. "When will you ever," asked the foreman, "Arrive at work on time?"
11. "I know when I will arrive on time," answered Marie. "it will be when my alarm clock is finished being repaired."
12. The show is called "Day After Day;" it starts at 2:30 P.M.
13. He replied encouragingly, "Remember that Ted said, "Let Irene wait. I'll interview her as soon as I return.' "
14. After having read the third chapter, entitled "Springtime Planting", I felt that I was ready to tackle the gardening job.
15. After the vicious dog had attacked the trespasser, the dog's owner said "Didn't you see the sign that reads 'Beware of the Dog' before you entered my property?".

Other Marks of Punctuation

You have already studied the major punctuation marks. There are several marks of punctuation that we encounter less frequently. These are the colon, the hyphen, the apostrophe, the dash, parentheses, and brackets.

OTHER MARKS OF PUNCTUATION STYLE SHEET

1. **Colon** Use a colon to introduce a list. Don't use a colon when the list is preceded by an action or linking word.

   Example: Bring the following equipment: a tent, a cot or sleeping bag, basic cooking utensils, and matches. Necessary equipment for such a trip includes a tent, a cot or sleeping bag, basic cooking utensils, and matches.

2. Use a colon after the salutation in a business letter.

   Examples: Dear Mr. Williams:

   Dear Sir:

3. Use a colon between numbers to show time.

   Example: 4:15 P.M.

4. **Hyphen** Use a hyphen to divide a word at the end of a line. Divide between syllables with a hyphen.

   Example: The new, downtown building is enormous, yet un-ornamented.

5. Use a hyphen to divide compound numbers from twenty-one to ninety-nine.

   Example: twenty-two, eighty-seven

6. Hyphenated descriptive words that are brought together to form a new word.

   Example: well-to-do, fly-by-night, half-yearly, self-supporting

7. Hyphenate certain prefixes and the words to which they are added. For example, ex-husband.

   Example: My favorite art form is pre-Columbian sculpture.

8. **Apostrophe** Use an apostrophe to show the omission of a letter from a word.

   Example: We aren't (are not) responsible for breakage.

9. Use an apostrophe to show possession. Note that apostrophes are placed differently according to whether the word is singular or plural and according to the way the word forms its plural. Exceptions: *It* is the possessive form of *it. It's* means *it is. His* and *hers* are the possessive forms of *he* and *she.*

   Example: the lamb's wool, the dog's kennels, the men's department, the ladies' club

10. Use an apostrophe to show the plural of letters when necessary to avoid confusion. Use the apostrophe with all lower case letters and with those upper case/lower case combinations that create words.

    Examples: A's, B's, I's, r's, v's, U's, T's

11. **Dash** Use dashes to emphasize an interruption within a sentence.

    Example: Be home on time—no later than midnight—or I will be very worried.

12. **Parentheses** Use parentheses for words not strictly related to the main thought of the sentence. Do not use a capital letter or final punctuation (except the question mark) within the parentheses.

    Examples: I managed (somehow or other) to drag three heavy suitcases to the terminal.

    I called you last night (or was it Friday?) to give you the message.

13. **Brackets** Use brackets within parentheses and within a quotation.

    Examples: They tried some French wines (Bordeaux [Medoc], Burgundy, and Chablis).

    We were asked to read a poem and Tom said, "The one I've chosen [by Wilde] is called 'The Ballad of Reading Gaol.'"

PRACTICE III

Directions: In the following sentences, find the errors in punctuation. Only two sentences are correctly punctuated. Choose the one best answer to each item.

1. The president's desk was covered with all sorts of business papers; invoices, receipts, minutes of his last meeting, and projected plans for the new building.

What correction should be made to this sentence?

(1) change president's to presidents
(2) insert a comma after desk
(3) change sorts to sort's
(4) replace the semicolon with a colon
(5) remove the comma after meeting

① ② ③ ④ ⑤

2. We expect to arrive at Kennedy Airport at 815 P.M. on Thursday, June 6, 1996.

What correction should be made to this sentence?

(1) insert a comma after P.M.
(2) change 815 P.M. to 8:15 P.M.
(3) remove the comma after Thursday
(4) insert a comma after Airport
(5) remove the comma after June 6

① ② ③ ④ ⑤

3. Although we had met only once, in Denver, he recognized me immediately and began to regale me with the following: he had just arrived in town; he had bought a house; and he had been promoted within his company.

Which of the following is the best way to write the underlined portion of this sentence? If you think the original is the best way, choose option (1).

(1) once, in Denver, he recognized ① ② ③ ④ ⑤
(2) once; in Denver he recognized
(3) once, in Denver, he recognized
(4) once in Denver he recognized
(5) once in Denver, he recognized

4. Do you really believe that you were a different person at twenty nine from the one you are at thirty?

What correction should be made to this sentence?

(1) insert a comma after believe ① ② ③ ④ ⑤
(2) change the spelling of believe to beleive
(3) insert a hyphen in twenty nine
(4) change the question mark to a period
(5) no correction is necessary

5. If you are planning to send a present to Laurie, go to the half-yearly sale in the childrens' department.

What correction should be made to this sentence?

(1) insert a comma after If ① ② ③ ④ ⑤
(2) replace the comma after Laurie with a semicolon
(3) replace the comma after Laurie with a dash
(4) remove the hyphen from half-yearly
(5) change childrens' to children's

6. Dont forget to write two r's in "deferred."

   What correction should be made to this sentence?

   (1) insert an apostrophe in Dont ① ② ③ ④ ⑤
   (2) replace two with too
   (3) remove the apostrophe from r's
   (4) remove the quotation mark before "deferred."
   (5) change "deferred." to "deferred".

7. When I arrived in Wilmington (after a four-hour drive), I found that my cousin's weren't at home.

   Which of the following is the best way to write the underlined portion of this sentence? If you think the original is the best way, choose option (1).

   (1) my cousin's weren't ① ② ③ ④ ⑤
   (2) my cousin's were not
   (3) my cousins' weren't
   (4) my cousins weren't
   (5) my cousin's werent

8. The ex Senator hoped that approval of his protege's bill would pass the two-thirds mark.

   What correction should be made to this sentence?

   (1) insert a hyphen between ex and Senator ① ② ③ ④ ⑤
   (2) insert a comma after hoped
   (3) remove the apostrophe from protege's
   (4) remove the hyphen from two-thirds
   (5) no correction is necessary

9. Although September, June, and April have thirty days, December and January have thirty-one days.

What correction should be made to this sentence?

(1) insert a comma after Although ① ② ③ ④ ⑤
(2) remove the comma after September
(3) insert a comma after April
(4) insert a hyphen between one and days
(5) no correction is necessary

10. At 11:45 A.M., the commuter's train pulled into the jam-packed station.

What correction should be made to this sentence?

(1) insert a comma after 11:45 ① ② ③ ④ ⑤
(2) insert parentheses around A.M.
(3) change commuter's to commuters'
(4) remove the apostrophe in commuter's
(5) remove the hyphen from jam-packed

PRACTICE IV

Directions: The following items are based on a paragraph that contains numbered sentences. Some of the sentences contain errors in punctuation. Only one sentence is correct as it appears in the paragraph. Read the paragraph and then answer the items based on it. Choose the one best answer to each item.

(1) Henrys new car seems to be a poor sample of this year's cars. (2) When he picked it up, Henry didn't realize that the car's wheels hadn't been aligned. (3) In fact, it's front end was completely out of line. (4) By the time Henry returned the car for service, many experts skills needed to be brought to bear upon the problem. (5) Henry listed the major problems worn tires, a shudder in the steering wheel, and a dangerous swerving to the right when he applied the brakes.

(6) If, in the future, Henry decides not to buy a new car every three or four years, do you think he'll be considered unAmerican?

1. Sentence 1: **Henrys new car seems to be a poor sample of this year's cars.**

   What correction should be made to this sentence?

   (1) change Henrys to Henry's ① ② ③ ④ ⑤
   (2) change Henrys to Henrys'
   (3) insert a comma after car
   (4) remove the apostrophe in year's
   (5) change year's to years'

2. Sentence 2: **When he picked it up, Henry didn't realize that the car's wheels hadn't been aligned.**

   What correction should be made to this sentence?

   (1) remove the comma after up ① ② ③ ④ ⑤
   (2) change didn't to did not
   (3) change car's to cars'
   (4) change wheels to wheel's
   (5) no correction is necessary

3. Sentence 3: **In fact, it's front end was completely out of line.**

   What correction should be made to this sentence?

   (1) replace the comma after fact with a colon ① ② ③ ④ ⑤
   (2) change it's to its
   (3) insert a comma after end
   (4) change out of line to out-of-line
   (5) no correction is necessary

4. Sentence 4: **By the time Henry returned the car for service, many experts skills needed to be brought to bear upon the problem.**

What correction should be made to this sentence?

(1) insert a comma after car ① ② ③ ④ ⑤
(2) remove the comma after service
(3) change experts to experts'
(4) change skills to skills'
(5) insert a comma after bear

5. Sentence 5: **Henry listed the major problems worn tires, a shudder in the steering wheel, and a dangerous swerving to the right when he applied the brakes.**

Which of the following is the best way to write the underlined portion of this sentence? If you think the original is the best way, choose option (1).

(1) problems worn tires, ① ② ③ ④ ⑤
(2) problems. Worn tires,
(3) problems; worn tires,
(4) problems: worn tires,
(5) problems: worn tires;

6. Sentence 6: **If, in the future, Henry decides not to buy a new car every three or four years, do you think he'll be considered unAmerican?**

What correction should be made to this sentence?

(1) remove the comma after If ① ② ③ ④ ⑤
(2) remove the comma after future
(3) replace the comma after years with a semicolon
(4) change unAmerican to un-American
(5) replace the question mark after unAmerican with an exclamation point

ANSWER KEY

Chapter 16

More Punctuation

Quotation Marks

Practice I *Page 199.*

1. The manager said, “Three men must work overtime.”
2. The manager said that three men must work overtime.
3. “Three men,” said the manager, “must work overtime.”
4. The manager asked, “Who will work overtime?”
5. Why didn’t the manager say, “Everyone must work”?
6. Imagine if the manager had said, “Everyone must work overtime”!
7. Imagine if the manager had said that everyone must work overtime!
8. The manager shouted, “Everyone must work overtime!”

Practice II *Page 199.*

For explanations of answers, refer to the punctuation rules on pages *196–199.*

1. Mrs. Romano exclaimed, “Frankie, the parakeet has disappeared!”
   See Rule 1.
2. Frankie answered, “Mom, I don’t know why; it was there when I tried to clean it with the vacuum cleaner.”
   See Rule 1.
3. No error
4. No error
5. No error
6. Alice told Marion she was to stay at home and be a babysitter. Marion exclaimed, “What a shame!”
   See Rule 1.
7. No error
8. “After you turn over the earth, add some plant food and water. Then you’ll be ready to plant the flower,” concluded the gardener.
   See Rule 1.
9. Was it Elsa who said, “Our sales meeting begins at 9:30 A.M. sharp”?
   See Rule 4.
10. “When will you ever,” asked the foreman, “arrive at work on time?”
    See Rule 2.
11. “I know when I will arrive on time,” answered Marie. “It will be when my alarm clock is finished being repaired.”
    See Rule 2.
12. The show is called “Day After Day”; it starts at 2:30 P.M.
    See Rule 3.
13. He replied encouragingly, “Remember that Ted said, ‘Let Irene wait. I’ll interview her as soon as I return.’ ”
    See Rule 6.
14. After having read the third chapter, entitled “Springtime Planting,” I felt that I was ready to tackle the gardening job.
    See Rule 7.
15. After the vicious dog had attacked the trespasser, the dog’s owner said, “Didn’t you see the sign that reads ‘Beware of Dog’ before you entered my property?”
    See Rule 4.

Other Marks of Punctuation

Practice III *Page 203.*

For explanations of answers, refer to the punctuation rules on *pages 201–202.*

1. (4) The president's desk was covered with all sorts of business papers*:* invoices, receipts, minutes of his last meeting, and projected plans for the new building. See Rule 1.
2. (2) We expect to arrive at Kennedy Airport at *8:15* P.M. on Thursday, June 6, 1996. See Rule 3.
3. (1) No correction is necessary. See Rule 4.
4. (3) Do you really believe that you were a different person at *twenty-nine* from the one you are at thirty? See Rule 5.
5. (5) If you are planning to send a present to Laurie, go to the half-yearly sale in the *children's* department. See Rule 9.
6. (1) *Don't* forget to write two r's in "deferred." See Rule 10.
7. (4) When I arrived in Wilmington (after a four-hour drive), I found that *my cousins weren't* at home. See Rule 8.
8. (1) The *ex-Senator* hoped that approval of his protege's bill would pass the two-thirds mark. See Rule 7.
9. (5) No correction is necessary.
10. (3) At 11:45 A.M., the *commuters'* train pulled into the jam-packed station. See Rule 9.

Practice IV *Page 206.*

For explanations of answers, refer to the punctuation rules on *pages 201–202.*

1. (1) *Henry's* new car seems to be a poor sample of this year's cars. See Rule 9.
2. (5) No correction is necessary.
3. (2) In fact, *its* front end was completely out of line. See Rule 9.
4. (3) By the time Henry returned the car for service, many *experts'* skills needed to be brought to bear upon the problem. See Rule 9.
5. (4) Henry listed the major *problems: worn tires,* a shudder in the steering wheel, and a dangerous swerving to the right when he applied the brakes. See Rule 1.
6. (4) If, in the future, Henry decides not to buy a new car every three or four years, do you think he'll be considered *un-American*? See Rule 7.

17.
Capitalization

When I was a young writer, submitting poems and thought pieces to arty little magazines, I refused to capitalize anything—not my own name, not kentucky, not broadway, not belgium, not even e. e. cummings or don marquis' cockroach, archy.

It was a period I was going through when I explained to my courtiers that only God was deserving of capitalization. You can't imagine how that nonsensical pose won approbation with my admirers, but, come to think of it, it never made much of an impression on the editors of *Partisan Review*. When they sent me my usual rejection slip, they always used CAPITAL LETTERS.

Tim Wolfe
The Child That's Got His Own

A Word With You . . .

Some writers, for purposes best known to themselves, use lowercase letters at all times, refusing to capitalize anything. Instead of "Dear Sir" in the salutation of a letter, they prefer "dear sir," that is, when they take the trouble to write a formal letter.

When one is a professional writer with a philosophical point of view about capitalization, one can afford to use lowercase letters. The rest of us had better learn where and when to capitalize. Chapter 17 will help.

CAPITALIZATION STYLE SHEET

Capitalization, like punctuation, is applied according to rules. Study the style sheet and then take the survey test that follows.

1. Capitalize the first letter of the first word in a sentence, unless it is a sentence within parentheses.

   Example: Language changes continually (note all the once-slang words in your current dictionary) but slowly.

2. Capitalize the first word of a direct quotation.

   Example: He cautioned, "If you buy a ticket beforehand, you will secure a seat for the performance."

3. Capitalize the word *I*.

   Example: In case you are late, *I* will cover for you.

4. Capitalize the deity, place names, street names, persons' names, organization names, languages, and specific course names.

   Example: God and His universe, Blue Ridge Mountains, Delaware River, Forty-second Street, John Masters, Knights of Columbus, Spanish, History II (not sociology, math, etc.)

5. Capitalize names of important historical events, documents, and ages.

   Example: World War I, Magna Carta, Declaration of Independence, Victorian Era

6. Capitalize days of the week, months, and special holidays.

   Example: Monday, January, Memorial Day

7. Capitalize east, west, north, and south only when they are used as sections of the country, not as directions.

   Examples: Rod Lewis lived in the East for three years, then moved to the Midwest.

   Turn east at the next corner.

8. In a title (of a play, book, poem, magazine, etc.) capitalize the first word and each important word.

   Example: *Death of a Salesman, The Odyssey, The Wasteland, The Last of the Mohicans*

9. Capitalize the initials of a person's name.

   Example: T. J. Phillips

10. Capitalize a title when it is used as a form of address.
    Do not capitalize a title when it is not used as a form of address.

Examples: Captain T. J. Phillips

T. J. Phillips, captain of *Star Lady,* . . .

The captain of *Star Lady,* T. J. Phillips . . .

11. Capitalize the first word in each line of poetry.

Example: "A thing of beauty is a joy forever:
Its loveliness increases . . ."

Survey Test

Directions: Capitalize letters as necessary in the following sentences.

1. after considering all the facts, i have chosen an appropriate action.
2. don't you think that fred might enjoy owning a french-english dictionary?
3. he said, "leave new jersey at noon, and you will reach new york city by 1 P.M. at the latest."
4. john is planning to take german, geography, history, and economics this year at city college.
5. we're expecting guests for dinner on friday night. i hope you can join us.
6. mary stark bought a chevrolet last tuesday, although she hadn't planned on buying a car this year.
7. in history II we will study the industrial revolution, world war I, world war II, and the atomic age.
8. this course will be offered to adults on mondays, wednesdays, and fridays in the spring only.
9. his original home, in california, was his favorite; and he plans on returning to the west in november.
10. captain and mrs. ryan made reservations at island beach motel on the cape's north shore for labor day.

Before beginning *Practice I,* check your answers on the Survey Test and review the rules relating to your areas for improvement.

PRACTICE

I **Directions:** Some of the following sentences contain errors in capitalization. Make corrections where necessary. Two sentences contain no errors.

1. Our history course this semester highlights civilizations of the East.
2. My family plans to move to cypress street in Millville, Ohio.
3. "If you plan to see the entire art exhibit," Joan said, "Be sure to arrive at 10 A.M."
4. The Thompkins' plans for labor day include a visit to the beach.
5. Proceed two blocks north to the traffic light, and turn right onto Rumson Lane.
6. I asked father to lend me the Chevrolet so that we can drive to the Rosemont Club, which is on the east side of town.
7. Speaking to the town's Community Action Council, Dr. j. l. Raio suggested revamping mental health services.
8. This September, both of my children, Bob and Ronny, will be attending Cedar High school.
9. Waiting for the Twenty-second Street bus, we had time to admire the arrow shirts displayed in Stone's Haberdashery.
10. "Why don't you read the Winston Item," said Mother, "and check for sales on air conditioners?"
11. Uncle John and my father are going to Crystal Lake on saturday to try out their new fishing gear.
12. I've already crossed the Atlantic ocean by air; but this summer, in July, I hope to make the crossing on an Italian freighter.
13. More and more elementary schools are also teaching in spanish in order to meet the needs of the community.
14. You recall Reverend Hempstead saying that he will study religious philosophies of the east.
15. The Ridgedale Garden club developed a hybrid rose and named it Everlasting Beauty.
16. Including caucasians, Blacks, and Asians, the population of Winfield has grown to one and a half million.

PRACTICE II

Directions: For each of the following sentences, choose the completion that is correctly capitalized.

1. Each year our community celebrates the
   (1) fourth of July with entertainment and fireworks. ① ② ③ ④ ⑤
   (2) fourth of july with entertainment and fireworks.
   (3) Fourth of July with entertainment and fireworks.
   (4) fourth of July with entertainment and Fireworks.
   (5) Fourth of July with entertainment and fire-works.

2. John works for the
   (1) Ford Motor Company in Cleveland. ① ② ③ ④ ⑤
   (2) Ford Motor company in Cleveland.
   (3) Ford motor company in Cleveland.
   (4) ford Motor Company in Cleveland.
   (5) Ford Motor Company in Cleveland.

3. I asked Gerry,
   (1) "do you think Mike will get to the bank in time?" ① ② ③ ④ ⑤
   (2) "do you think Mike will get to the Bank in time?"
   (3) "do you think mike will get to the bank in time?"
   (4) "Do you think Mike will get to the bank in time?"
   (5) "Do you think Mike will get to the Bank in time?"

4. Even Greene, who lives in
(1) Syracuse, new york, joined the Professional Photographers Association. ① ② ③ ④ ⑤
(2) Syracuse, New York, joined the Professional photographers Association.
(3) syracuse, new york, joined the professional photographers association.
(4) Syracuse, New York, joined the Professional Photographers association.
(5) Syracuse, New York, joined the Professional Photographers Association.

5. We plan to visit the
(1) Grand Canyon in the west, as well as southern California. ① ② ③ ④ ⑤
(2) Grand Canyon in the West, as well as southern California.
(3) Grand Canyon in the West, as well as Southern California.
(4) Grand Canyon in the West, as well as southern california.
(5) Grand Canyon in the West, as well as southern California.

6. Our curriculum stresses reading skills in
(1) science, social studies, and American literature. ① ② ③ ④ ⑤
(2) Science, Social Studies, and American Literature.
(3) science, Social Studies, and American Literature.

(4) science, social studies, and American Literature.

(5) Science, social studies, and American Literature.

7. Two years ago,

(1) judge Arthur D. Billings of Texas was appointed to the bench. ① ② ③ ④ ⑤

(2) Judge Arthur d. Billings of Texas was appointed to the bench.

(3) Judge Arthur D. Billings of texas was appointed to the bench.

(4) judge Arthur D. Billings of Texas was appointed to the Bench.

(5) Judge Arthur D. Billings of Texas was appointed to the bench.

8. Although it is no longer the tallest building in the world, the

(1) empire state building in New York City is still an impressive sight. ① ② ③ ④ ⑤

(2) Empire state building in New York City is still an impressive sight.

(3) Empire State building in New York City is still an impressive sight.

(4) Empire State Building in New York City is still an impressive sight.

(5) Empire State Building in New York city is still an impressive sight.

9. I have a subscription to the
   (1) *Reader's Digest*, and I wish they would serialize the book *Odessa File*. ① ② ③ ④ ⑤
   (2) *reader's Digest*, and I wish they would serialize the book *Odessa File*.
   (3) *Reader's Digest*, and i wish they would serialize the book *Odessa File*.
   (4) *Reader's Digest,* and I wish they would serialize the book *Odessa file*.
   (5) *reader's digest,* and I wish they would serialize the book *Odessa File*.

10. Did you hear Jack ask,
   (1) "can you imagine our history if we hadn't signed the Declaration of Independence?" ① ② ③ ④ ⑤
   (2) "Can you imagine our History if we hadn't signed the Declaration of Independence?"
   (3) "Can you imagine our history if we hadn't signed the Declaration of Independence?"
   (4) "Can you imagine our history if we hadn't signed the declaration of independence?"
   (5) "can you imagine our History if we hadn't signed the Declaration Of Independence?"

ANSWER KEY

Chapter 17

Capitalization

Survey Test *Page 213.*

1. *After* considering all the facts, *I* have chosen an appropriate action. See Rules 1 and 3.
2. *Don't* you think that *Fred* might enjoy owning a *French-English* dictionary? See Rules 1 and 4.
3. *He* said, "Leave *New Jersey* at noon, and you will reach *New York City* by 1 P.M. at the latest." See Rules 1, 2, 4.
4. *John* is planning to take *German*, geography, history, and economics this year at *City College*. See Rules 1 and 4.
5. *We're* expecting guests for dinner on *Friday* night. *I* hope you can join us. See Rules 1, 4, and 6.
6. *Mary Stark* bought a Chevrolet last *Tuesday*, although she hadn't planned on buying a car this year. See Rules 1, 4, and 6.
7. *In History* II we will study the *Industrial Revolution*, *World War* I, *World War* II, and the *Atomic Age*. See Rules 1, 4, and 5.
8. *This* course will be offered to adults on *Mondays*, *Wednesdays*, and *Fridays* in the spring only. See Rules 1 and 6.
9. *His* original home, in *California*, was his favorite; and he plans on returning to the *West* in *November*. See Rules 1, 4, 6, and 7.
10. *Captain* and *Mrs. Ryan* made reservations at *Island Beach Motel* on the *Cape's* north shore for *Labor Day*. See Rules 1, 4, and 6.

Practice I *Page 214.*

1. Our *history* course this semester highlights civilizations of the East.
   Capitalize only *specific* course names, e.g., History IA.
2. My family plans to move to *Cypress Street* in Millville, Ohio.
   Capitalize entire street names.
3. "If you plan to see the entire art exhibit," Joan said, "*be* sure to arrive at 10 A.M."
   Do not capitalize the first word of the second part of a broken quotation unless each part of the quotation is a complete thought.
4. The Thompkins' plans for *Labor Day* include a visit to the beach.
   Capitalize the name of a holiday.
5. No error
6. I asked *Father* to lend me the Chevrolet so that we can drive to the Rosemont Club, which is on the east side of town.
   Capitalize Father or Mother when they are used as names.
7. Speaking to the town's Community Action Council, Dr. *J. L.* Raio suggested revamping mental health services.
   Capitalize initials in a name.
8. This September, both of my children, Bob and Ronny, will be attending Cedar High *School*.
   Capitalize the entire name of a school.
9. Waiting for the Twenty-second Street Bus, we had time to admire the *Arrow* shirts displayed in Stone's Haberdashery.
   Capitalize brand names.
10. No error
11. Uncle John and my father are going to Crystal Lake on *Saturday* to try out their new fishing gear.
    Capitalize the names of the days of the week.

12. I've already crossed the Atlantic *Ocean* by air; but this summer, in July, I hope to make the crossing on an Italian freighter.
    Capitalize the entire name of an ocean.
13. More and more elementary schools are also teaching in *Spanish* in order to meet the needs of the community.
    Capitalize the name of a language.
14. You recall Reverend Hempstead saying that he will study religious philosophies of the *East*.
    Capitalize North, South, East, and West when they designate an area.
15. The Ridgedale Garden *Club* developed a hybrid rose and named it Everlasting Beauty.
    Capitalize the entire name of a club.
16. Including *Caucasians*, Blacks, and Asians, the population of Winfield has grown to one and a half million.
    Capitalize the name of a race.

Practice II *Page 215.*

1. (3) Each year our community celebrates the Fourth of July with entertainment and fireworks.
2. (1) John works for the Ford Motor Company in Cleveland.
3. (4) I asked Gerry, "Do you think Mike will get to the bank in time?"
4. (5) Evan Greene, who lives in Syracuse, New York, joined the Professional Photographers Association.
5. (2) We plan to visit the Grand Canyon in the West, as well as southern California.
6. (1) Our curriculum stresses reading skills in science, social studies, and American literature.
7. (5) Two years ago, Judge Arthur D. Billings of Texas was appointed to the bench.
8. (4) Although it is no longer the tallest building in the world, the Empire State Building in New York City is still an impressive sight.
9. (1) I have a subscription to the *Reader's Digest*, and I wish they would serialize the book *Odessa File*.
10. (3) Did you hear Jack ask, "Can you imagine our history if we hadn't signed the Declaration of Independence?"

18

Spelling

"The other people that was involved in the Lincoln assination later exequded or killed themselves. Mary Tood Lincoln locked herself up in a closet and went crazy. She was declared mentally insane and put in a insane silome.

One day a long time later a man walked into Lincoln's office and found his son, Robert Tood, burning some of his daddy's old pappers. The man asked him why he was burning the pappers and Robert Tood said, 'Maybe they will criminate one of the members of the government,' which his daddy was in."

Bill Lawrence, Editor
Then Some Other Stuff Happened

A Word With You . . .

It isn't easy to become a good speller; in fact, many people never master the art. The high school student whose work is quoted above proves our point.

One famous English writer, George Bernard Shaw, was critical of our many spelling rules and the strange appearance of many of our words. He invested a large sum of money in a campaign to reform certain spelling practices. Shaw, however, was an excellent speller, regardless of his complaints.

There is no magic formula for learning how to spell. The ability to spell correctly results from persistent study. Here are some useful suggestions for studying spelling:

1. Use a small notebook exclusively for recording your personal spelling problem words.
2. Each time that you discover a problem word, enter it in your notebook. Check a dictionary for the correct syllabification and pronunciation.

3. Look at the word and say it in syllables.
4. Try to apply a rule that will help you to understand *why* the word is spelled as it is.
5. Close your eyes and picture the way the word looks.
6. Write the word. Check it. Rewrite it if necessary.
7. Review words you have already studied until you are absolutely sure that you know how to spell them.

Some words are correctly spelled in more than one way. For example, the word *catalogue* appears in one dictionary in the following way:

cat-a-logue, n. Also **catalog** . . .

In another dictionary, the entry says:

catalogue or **catalog**, n . . .

In the examples above, the use of the words *also* and *or* is important. For example, while *or* means that both spellings are equally common, *also* means that the first spelling is more common. How do you know for sure what policy a dictionary follows? Look at the front of the dictionary where all the rules and standards for that dictionary are explained. When in doubt, choose the first spelling unless the dictionary entry explains that there is a special reason for choosing the second.

There are many commonly misspelled words. Careful study of the list beginning on page 240 of this chapter will improve your spelling. There are also a number of hints and rules that are helpful in learning to spell.

Building Blocks of Words: Consonants, Vowels, Syllables

Of the twenty-six letters in the alphabet, twenty-one are consonants: b, c, d, f, g, h, j, k, l, m, n, p, q, r, s, t, v, w, x, y, z. The other five letters of the alphabet are vowels: a, e, i, o, u. Sometimes the consonant y is used as a vowel. When a consonant or consonants are combined with at least one vowel, a word or syllable results.

Example: let

A syllable is a word or part of a word pronounced with a single uninterrupted sound.

Nonsense syllable: ki

Meaningful syllable: sat

Learning to spell a long word is a much easier task if you divide the word into syllables.

Example: complacency = com • pla • cen • cy

You can learn to spell each syllable and, finally, to put the word together.

Adding to Words

Many words are formed by adding to the root (basic part) of the word. Prefixes are added to the beginning of a word, whereas suffixes are added to the end of a word. *For example:*

prefix	root	suffix
\	/	\
*dis*quiet	quiet	quiet*ly*

Rules Concerning Spelling

Rule 1: In most cases, a prefix can be added to a word without changing the spelling of that word.

PREFIX	(MEANING)	WORD COMBINATION
il	(not)	literate = illiterate
ir	(not)	regular = irregular

PRACTICE I

Directions: Add the correct prefix from the list below to each of the following words.

ac-	il-	in-	mis-	over-	mal-
dis-	ir-	un-	re-	im-	co-

1. ________instate
2. ________illusion
3. ________necessary
4. ________operate
5. ________mortal
6. ________spell
7. ________reverent
8. ________legal
9. ________climate
10. ________rate
11. ________content
12. ________accurate

Rule 2: When adding a suffix that begins with a consonant, the spelling of most words does not change.

	WORD	SUFFIX		WORD COMBINATION
	careless	ness	=	carelessness
	active	ly	=	actively
Exceptions:	true	ly	=	truly
	due	ly	=	duly

Rule 3: Suffixes do change the spelling of words that end in *y*.

WORD	SUFFIX		WORD COMBINATION
happy	ness	=	happiness
hearty	ly	=	heartily

Rule 4: When adding a suffix that begins with a vowel to a word that ends in *e*, drop the final *e*.

WORD	SUFFIX		WORD COMBINATION
fame	ous	=	famous
continue	ous	=	continuous

Exceptions: Words that end in *-ge* or *-ce* must retain the final *e* to maintain the soft sound of the *g* or *c*.

WORD	SUFFIX		WORD COMBINATION
courage	ous	=	courageous
notice	able	=	noticeable

Another exception is the word *dye*.

dye	ing	=	dyeing

PRACTICE II

Directions: Opposite each word below is a suffix that, when combined with the word, forms a new word. In the space provided, write the new word, making sure to spell it correctly.

	WORD	SUFFIX		WORD COMBINATION
1.	announce	ment	=	
2.	dye	ing	=	
3.	snappy	ness	=	
4.	associate	ion	=	
5.	dispense	able	=	
6.	definite	ly	=	
7.	economic	al	=	
8.	courage	ous	=	
9.	move	able	=	
10.	necessary	y	=	
11.	practical	ly	=	
12.	port	able	=	
13.	rude	ness	=	
14.	guide	ance	=	
15.	true	ly	=	

PRACTICE III

Directions: Blacken the circle containing the number that corresponds to the number of the incorrectly spelled word in each group. If there is no error, blacken circle number 5.

1. (1) unimportant (2) revelation (3) cumulative (4) irational (5) no error ① ② ③ ④ ⑤

2. (1) brighter (2) happyness (3) unaccustomed (4) berate (5) no error ① ② ③ ④ ⑤

3. (1) impossible (2) cooperation (3) inactive (4) mispell (5) no error ① ② ③ ④ ⑤

4. (1) commencement (2) coverage (3) practically (4) extraction (5) no error ① ② ③ ④ ⑤

5. (1) safty (2) forgiveness (3) shining (4) amusement (5) no error ① ② ③ ④ ⑤

6. (1) becoming (2) truly (3) plainness (4) actually (5) no error ① ② ③ ④ ⑤

7. (1) adorable (2) contagious (3) acumulate (4) supervise (5) no error ① ② ③ ④ ⑤

8. (1) lonliness (2) personal (3) barely (4) noticable (5) no error ① ② ③ ④ ⑤

9. (1) continuation (2) arguement (3) ridiculous (4) usage (5) no error ① ② ③ ④ ⑤

10. (1) surprised (2) acquisitiveness (3) carefully (4) virtuous (5) no error ① ② ③ ④ ⑤

The Role of Accent Marks

A word that contains more than one syllable has an accent on one of those syllables. Say this word in syllables: punc • tu • ate. Which syllable is stressed? Yes, the first syllable is stressed or accented, and its accent is marked in this way:

punc´ • tu • ate

PRACTICE IV

Directions: The following words have been divided into syllables. In each word, place an accent mark to show which syllable is stressed. The first word is done for you.

1. paint´ • er
2. pri • vate
3. of • fice
4. e • on • o • my
5. ad • vise
6. bal • ance
7. dis • sat • is • fy
8. de • vel • op • ment
9. in • di • vid • u • al
10. pre • fer
11. pref • er • ence
12. psy • chol • o •gy
13. vac • il •late
14. u • nan • i • mous
15. wretch • ed

Rule 5: **When changing the form of a one-syllable action word that ends in a consonant preceded by a vowel, double the final consonant.**

plan	planned
sun	sunning
run	runner

Rule 6: Double the final consonant when changing the form of a two-syllable word that ends in a consonant preceded by a vowel *and* which is accented on the second syllable.

refer	referred
occur	occurred
occur	occurrence

Rule 7: In a two- or three-syllable word, if the accent changes from the final syllable to a preceding one when a suffix is added (prefer′ pref′erence), do not double the final consonant.

refer	reference
confer	conference

PRACTICE V

Directions: Blacken the circle containing the number that corresponds to the number of the incorrectly spelled word in each group. If there is no error, blacken circle number 5.

1. (1) referred (2) preferrence (3) stunning (4) winding (5) no error ① ② ③ ④ ⑤
2. (1) thinner (2) conferred (3) reference (4) detered (5) no error ① ② ③ ④ ⑤
3. (1) binder (2) funnier (3) pictured (4) reared (5) no error ① ② ③ ④ ⑤
4. (1) cunning (2) preferable (3) deterent (4) banning (5) no error ① ② ③ ④ ⑤
5. (1) preferred (2) canning (3) fanned (4) occurence (5) no error ① ② ③ ④ ⑤

Rule 8: Use *i* before *e* except after *c*. For example relief, receipt.

Exception: Use *e* before *i* in words that sound like ā. For example neighbor, weigh.

Other exceptions: weird, seize, either, leisure, neither.

PRACTICE VI

Directions: Complete the following words with *ei* or *ie*.

1. n____ce
2. dec____ve
3. th____f
4. rel____ve
5. n____gh
6. rec____ve
7. conc____ve
8. bel____f
9. n____ther
10. s____ze

Rule 9: There are rules for forming the plurals of words. Following are the rules and a few examples of each.

A Most words form plurals by adding *s*.

radio	radios
towel	towels
chair	chairs
tray	trays

B Words ending in *y* preceded by a consonant form plurals by changing *y* to *i* and adding *es*.

sky	skies
story	stories

C Words ending in *o* preceded by a consonant form plurals by adding *es*.

tomato	tomatoes
hero	heroes

Exception: words ending in *o*, preceded by a consonant, but referring to music, form their plurals by adding only *s*.

alto	altos
piano	pianos

D Words ending in *s*, *sh*, *ch*, and *x* form plurals by adding *es*.

bunch	bunches
sex	sexes
boss	bosses
crush	crushes

E A compound word forms its plural by adding *s* to the principal word.

fathers-in-law
baby*sitters*

F Words ending in *-ful* form their plurals by adding *s*.

mouthfuls
cupfuls

G Some words have one spelling for singular and plural.

deer
trout
Chinese
sheep

H Numbers and letters form plurals by adding *'s*.

5's   h's

I Some words form their plurals by irregular changes.

thief	thieves
knife	knives
leaf	leaves
woman	women
child	children
tooth	teeth
louse	lice
crisis	crises
alumnus	alumni
datum	data
appendix	appendices

PRACTICE VII

Directions: Blacken the circle containing the number that corresponds to the number of the incorrectly spelled word in each group. If there is no error, blacken circle number 5.

1. (1) geese (2) mouthsful (3) commanders-in-chief (4) firemen (5) no error ① ② ③ ④ ⑤
2. (1) Chinese's (2) bases (3) workmen (4) ?'s (5) no error ① ② ③ ④ ⑤
3. (1) bacilli (2) son-in-laws (3) series (4) handkerchiefs (5) no error ① ② ③ ④ ⑤
4. (1) women (2) alumni (3) passerby (4) mice (5) no error ① ② ③ ④ ⑤
5. (1) 8s (2) Frenchmen (3) alumni (4) men-of-war (5) no error ① ② ③ ④ ⑤

Rule 10: Following are rules regarding *sede, ceed,* and *cede.*

A Only one word is spelled with an *sede* ending:

supersede

B Only three words are spelled with a *ceed* ending:

succeed exceed proceed

C All other words of this type are spelled with a *cede* ending:

secede precede recede concede

PRACTICE VIII

Directions: To complete each sentence, choose a word from the list below. Look up the definition of any word you don't know.

secede	supersede	precede	succeed
recede	exceed	concede	proceed

1. I know that you will not fail; you will succeed .

2. It was a sad time in our history when states threatened to ____________ from the union.
3. The flooded town waited for the water to ____________ .
4. I expect to ____________ the amount of business I said I would do.
5. ____________ with your work; I didn't mean to interrupt.
6. My new decision will ____________, or replace, the old one.
7. When they left the office, Ben ____________d Manuel.
8. At the end of election day, we don't expect our candidate to have to ____________ .

Spelling Review

PRACTICE IX

Directions: Blacken the circle containing the number that corresponds to the number of the incorrectly spelled word in each group. If there is no error, blacken circle number 5.

1. (1) overrate (2) misapprehend (3) habitualy (4) greenness (5) no error ① ② ③ ④ ⑤

2. (1) deferred (2) hoping (3) approval (4) defference (5) no error ① ② ③ ④ ⑤

3. (1) candys (2) valleys (3) torches (4) files (5) no error ① ② ③ ④ ⑤

4. (1) immaterial (2) dissapoint (3) practically (4) unabated (5) no error ① ② ③ ④ ⑤

5. (1) potatos (2) teeth (3) radios (4) sopranos (5) no error ① ② ③ ④ ⑤

6. (1) preparing (2) writing (3) propeling (4) controlled (5) no error ① ② ③ ④ ⑤

7. (1) crises (2) geese (3) concertos (4) trucksful (5) no error ① ② ③ ④ ⑤

8. (1) truely (2) moving (3) running (4) famous (5) no error ① ② ③ ④ ⑤

9. (1) shelves (2) benches (3) knives (4) churches (5) no error ① ② ③ ④ ⑤

10. (1) salarys (2) basketfuls (3) reddest (4) nameless (5) no error ① ② ③ ④ ⑤

11. (1) disagree (2) benefited (3) gases (4) casually (5) no error ① ② ③ ④ ⑤

12. (1) oxen (2) desirable (3) data (4) solves (5) no error ① ② ③ ④ ⑤

PRACTICE X

Directions: Blacken the circle containing the number that corresponds to the number of the incorrectly spelled word in each group. If there is no error, blacken circle number 5.

1. (1) belief (2) achieve (3) neice (4) weigh (5) no error ① ② ③ ④ ⑤

2. (1) yield (2) neighbor (3) deceive (4) releif (5) no error ① ② ③ ④ ⑤

3. (1) benefited (2) appealed (3) refered (4) equipped (5) no error ① ② ③ ④ ⑤

4. (1) preference (2) reference (3) asessment (4) colonel (5) no error ① ② ③ ④ ⑤

5. (1) stationery (2) stationary (3) sophomore (4) similar (5) no error ① ② ③ ④ ⑤

6. (1) primarily (2) principal (3) principle (4) receit (5) no error ① ② ③ ④ ⑤

7. (1) acquired (2) brief (3) contemptible (4) height (5) no error ① ② ③ ④ ⑤

8. (1) erred (2) millionaire (3) misanthrope (4) lieutenant (5) no error ① ② ③ ④ ⑤

9. (1) adjournament (2) caucus (3) contagious (4) digestible (5) no error ① ② ③ ④ ⑤

10. (1) cheff (2) calendar (3) macaroni (4) preceding (5) no error ① ② ③ ④ ⑤

PRACTICE XI

Directions: Blacken the circle containing the number that corresponds to the number of the incorrectly spelled word in each group. If there is no error, blacken circle number 5.

1. (1) changeable (2) atheletic (3) grammar (4) fortissimo (5) no error ① ② ③ ④ ⑤

2. (1) filial (2) leisure (3) temperature (4) treachery (5) no error ① ② ③ ④ ⑤

3. (1) bulletin (2) amendment (3) incessent (4) kindergarten (5) no error ① ② ③ ④ ⑤

4. (1) legitiment (2) vivisection (3) pervade (4) courtesies (5) no error ① ② ③ ④ ⑤

5. (1) prefer (2) preferred (3) preference (4) patrolled (5) no error ① ② ③ ④ ⑤

6. (1) ninth (2) correspondent (3) canon (4) hideous (5) no error ① ② ③ ④ ⑤

7. (1) apparently (2) foreign (3) carriage (4) forfeit (5) no error ① ② ③ ④ ⑤

8. (1) aggregate (2) massacre (3) omissions (4) tetnus (5) no error ① ② ③ ④ ⑤

9. (1) exceed (2) intercede (3) proceed (4) procedure (5) no error ① ② ③ ④ ⑤

10. (1) fundimental (2) misspell (3) odyssey (4) penitentiary (5) no error ① ② ③ ④ ⑤

PRACTICE XII

Directions: Blacken the circle containing the number that corresponds to the number of the incorrectly spelled word in each group. If there is no error, blacken circle number 5.

1. (1) torches (2) salaries (3) valleys (4) shelves (5) no error ① ② ③ ④ ⑤
2. (1) absense (2) gases (3) accident (4) citizen (5) no error ① ② ③ ④ ⑤
3. (1) executive (2) divide (3) discusion (4) eager (5) no error ① ② ③ ④ ⑤
4. (1) contrary (2) impecable (3) critical (4) banquet (5) no error ① ② ③ ④ ⑤
5. (1) association (2) character (3) earliest (4) decide (5) no error ① ② ③ ④ ⑤
6. (1) Wenesday (2) knives (3) concerning (4) executive (5) no error ① ② ③ ④ ⑤
7. (1) appreciate (2) except (3) scene (4) numerous (5) no error ① ② ③ ④ ⑤
8. (1) national (2) posession (3) industrious (4) volume (5) no error ① ② ③ ④ ⑤
9. (1) patient (2) quantity (3) boundary (4) probably (5) no error ① ② ③ ④ ⑤
10. (1) warrant (2) laboratory (3) interesting (4) library (5) no error ① ② ③ ④ ⑤

PRACTICE XIII

Directions: Blacken the circle containing the number that corresponds to the number of the incorrectly spelled word in each group. If there is no error, blacken circle number 5.

1. (1) derogatory (2) neglagible (3) rehearsal (4) yacht (5) no error ① ② ③ ④ ⑤
2. (1) queue (2) jeopardy (3) forfeit (4) gelatin (5) no error ① ② ③ ④ ⑤

3. (1) bureau (2) blamable (3) desecration (4) harass (5) no error ① ② ③ ④ ⑤

4. (1) falibility (2) heinous (3) myriad (4) remnant (5) no error ① ② ③ ④ ⑤

5. (1) hygienic (2) medallion (3) midget (4) prommisory (5) no error ① ② ③ ④ ⑤

6. (1) complacency (2) efemeral (3) exaggerate (4) realize (5) no error ① ② ③ ④ ⑤

7. (1) lacquer (2) currency (3) exortation (4) emolument (5) no error ① ② ③ ④ ⑤

8. (1) apologetic (2) coroner (3) clique (4) exzema (5) no error ① ② ③ ④ ⑤

9. (1) disatisfied (2) moribund (3) warrant (4) surgeon (5) no error ① ② ③ ④ ⑤

10. (1) defered (2) extraordinary (3) journal (4) intercede (5) no error ① ② ③ ④ ⑤

PRACTICE XIV

Directions: Blacken the circle containing the number that corresponds to the number of the incorrectly spelled word in each group. If there is no error, blacken circle number 5.

1. (1) responsibility (2) resonence (3) rheostat (4) rhetoric (5) no error ① ② ③ ④ ⑤

2. (1) salient (2) patronize (3) pateint (4) parliament (5) no error ① ② ③ ④ ⑤

3. (1) secretery (2) piquancy (3) integrity (4) innocuous (5) no error ① ② ③ ④ ⑤

4. (1) diphtheria (2) distinguished (3) category (4) cemetery (5) no error ① ② ③ ④ ⑤

5. (1) abscess (2) chamois (3) effects (4) ingenuous (5) no error ① ② ③ ④ ⑤

6. (1) accessible (2) chauffur (3) elaborate (4) inimitable (5) no error ① ② ③ ④ ⑤

7. (1) impromptu (2) incongruity (3) permissable (4) precede (5) no error ① ② ③ ④ ⑤

8. (1) tremendous (2) punctilious (3) recognizible (4) tariff (5) no error ① ② ③ ④ ⑤

9. (1) reasonable (2) mischivous (3) picnicking (4) repetitious (5) no error ① ② ③ ④ ⑤

10. (1) sobriquet (2) soveriegn (3) staunch (4) stretch (5) no error ① ② ③ ④ ⑤

PRACTICE XV

Directions: Blacken the circle containing the number that corresponds to the number of the incorrectly spelled word in each group. If there is no error, blacken circle number 5.

1. (1) addressee (2) carburator (3) intercede (4) murmuring (5) no error ① ② ③ ④ ⑤

2. (1) biscut (2) financier (3) previous (4) preceding (5) no error ① ② ③ ④ ⑤

3. (1) hearth (2) bounteous (3) judgment (4) heritage (5) no error ① ② ③ ④ ⑤

4. (1) aversion (2) aquatic (3) facilitation (4) bookkeeping (5) no error ① ② ③ ④ ⑤

5. (1) dilapidated (2) function (3) relevent (4) regrettable (5) no error ① ② ③ ④ ⑤

6. (1) dearth (2) deceive (3) proceed (4) wethar (5) no error ① ② ③ ④ ⑤

7. (1) excede (2) feudal (3) grandeur (4) vacuum (5) no error ① ② ③ ④ ⑤

8. (1) realize (2) foriegn (3) nevertheless (4) matinee (5) no error ① ② ③ ④ ⑤

9. (1) criticism (2) plagiarism (3) equiped (4) preferably (5) no error ① ② ③ ④ ⑤

10. (1) beatitude (2) corruggated (3) existence (4) succeed (5) no error ① ② ③ ④ ⑤

PRACTICE XVI

Directions: Blacken the circle containing the number that corresponds to the number of the incorrectly spelled word in each group. If there is no error, blacken circle number 5.

1. (1) angle (2) conciliatory (3) exersise (4) compel (5) no error ① ② ③ ④ ⑤
2. (1) description (2) hindrence (3) memoir (4) publicity (5) no error ① ② ③ ④ ⑤
3. (1) belligerent (2) dearth (3) equator (4) decieve (5) no error ① ② ③ ④ ⑤
4. (1) bankruptcy (2) deliberate (3) histrionic (4) demurrer (5) no error ① ② ③ ④ ⑤
5. (1) crystallized (2) mackeral (3) maintenance (4) masquerade (5) no error ① ② ③ ④ ⑤
6. (1) sandwich (2) peculiar (3) neumonia (4) scissors (5) no error ① ② ③ ④ ⑤
7. (1) temperment (2) summarize (3) scripture (4) occur (5) no error ① ② ③ ④ ⑤
8. (1) abundence (2) citation (3) clamorous (4) colossal (5) no error ① ② ③ ④ ⑤
9. (1) acumulation (2) circumstantial (3) adoption (4) adage (5) no error ① ② ③ ④ ⑤
10. (1) apparatus (2) ancient (3) amplify (4) allege (5) no error ① ② ③ ④ ⑤

PRACTICE XVII

Directions: Each of the following paragraphs has five underlined words, one of which is misspelled. Select the incorrectly spelled word and blacken the circle containing the number that corresponds to that word. Then write the word correctly on the line provided below.

Paragraph 1: Each year, the Township Comittee (1) sponsors a dinner to acknowledge (2) the fine performance (3) of our local police department (4). All policemen (5) are invited.

① ② ③ ④ ⑤

____

Paragraph 2: The angry passengers (1) stormed the ticket counter. The attendant tried to pacify (2) the crowd (3) but could not. Courtesy (4) was forgotten as the mob protested the third cancelation (5) of the California flight.

① ② ③ ④ ⑤

____

Paragraph 3: When Smith and Jones agreed to dissolve (1) their partnership, they wrote (2) an agreement. They believed (3) that attorneys were not necessary (4) because both Smith and Jones were honest men. They both remain honest men, but they are no longer freinds (5).

① ② ③ ④ ⑤

____

Paragraph 4: Because of declining enrollment (1) during the 1970's, many schools closed. Now many of these neighborhoods (2) have increasing numbers of children. School superintendants (3) are requesting (4) additional space, but the closed schools have been converted (5) to other uses. ① ② ③ ④ ⑤

____

Paragraph 5: Officials (1) are seeking to relieve (2) the acumulation (3) of garbage in our towns. The abundance (4) of waste in local landfills far exceeds (5) the capacity to store it. ① ② ③ ④ ⑤

____

Paragraph 6: One way to address (1) the problem is known as source reduction. (2) Some states have returned to the practice (3) of returning bottles. Some consumers have eliminated extravagent (4) purchases such as disposable (5) razors and other plastic products. ① ② ③ ④ ⑤

____

Commonly Misspelled Words

Give special review to all those words that have given you trouble. Do not try to learn more than 10 new words at a time.

abandoned
aberration
abeyance
ability
abscess
absence
absurd
abundance
abutting
academy
accent
accede
accessible
acclimate
accommodate
accumulation
accusation
achievement
acknowledge
acquaint
acquired
acquisition
across
actually
acutely
adage
addressee
adequate
adieu
adjournment
adjunct
adopted
adoption
advertisement
advice
advise
advisable
advising
aerial
affirmative
aggravate
aggregate
agitation
agreeable
agreement
aisle
alcohol
allege
allies
all right
a lot
amateur
ambassador
amendment
America
amplify
analysis
analyze
ancient
anecdote
anemia
angle
annoyance
annum
anticipate
antipathy
antique
anxious
apologetic
apparatus
apparently
appellate
appetite
appreciation
appropriation
apricot
aquatic
architecture
arduous
arguing
arouse
arraignment
arrest
article
artificial
ascertain
aspirations
assassination
assessment
assigned
association
assurance
athletic
attach
attempt
attendance
attendants
attorneys
authentic
aversion
awkward
axle

baccalaureate
bachelor
bacteria
balance
banana
bankruptcy
barely
beaker
beatitude
beleaguered
belligerent
benefit
biased
bigamy
bimonthly
biscuit
blamable
blight
bookkeeping
border
bored
bounteous
breeding
brief
bulletin
bungalow
bureau
burglaries
business
cafeteria
calendar
cameos
campaign
cancel
candidacy
candle
cannon
canon
capital
capitol
(a building)
carburetor
carnage
carriage
category
caucus
cauldron
cavalier
cavalry
cease
ceiling
cemetery
certain
certified
chagrined
chamois
chancellor
changeable
character
charitable
chauffeur
chef
chisel
Christian
circumstantial
citation
clamorous
classified
clique
clothe
colonel
colossal
column

comedian
commandant
commemorate
commenced
committal
committee
community
comparative
compel
competition
competitors
complacency
conciliatory
conclusively
condemned
confectionery
congenial
congestion
conjunction
connoisseur
conquer
conscript
consequently
conservatory
consistent
consummation
contagious
contemptible
continually
control
controller
convenient
conversant
cooperate
coronation
coroncr
corporal
corral
(an enclosure)
correlation
correspondence
correspondent
corrugated
corset
countenance
courtesies
courtesy
criticism
criticize
crochet
cronies
crowded
crucial
crystallized
currency
cylinder

death
deceive
decision
declaration
deferred
definite
delegate
deliberate
delicious
delinquent
democrat
demurrage
denunciatory
deodorize
derogatory
description
desecration
desert
desirable
despair
dessert (food)
destruction
detrimental
development
digestible
dilapidated
dining room
diocese
diphtheria
dirigible
disappear
disappearance
disapprove
discipline
discretion
diseases
disgust
dispatch
dispensable
dissatisfied
dissatisfy
dissolution
distillery
distinguished
distributor
dizzy
doctor
dormitory
drastically
dual
duchess
duly
dungarees
duped
dyeing

economical
economy
ecstasy
eczema
effects
efficient
elaborate
electrolysis
embarrass
embassies
emergency
eminently
emolument
emphasis
emphasize
emphatically
endurance
enlargement
enormous
enthusiastic
ephemeral
equilibrium
equinoctial
equipped
error
essential
everlasting
exaggerate
exceed
excel
exercise
exhibition
exhortation
existence
extradite
extraordinary
extravagant

facilitation
faculties
fallibility
falsify
falsity
fascinated
fatal
feudal
filial
finally
financial
financier
finely
fireman
flexible
foggy
foliage
forcible
foreign
foretell
forfeit
fortissimo
forty
fragrance
fraternally
freshman
frightfully
frostbitten
function
fundamental
furl

gallery
galvanized
gelatin
glimpse
guaranteed
guardian
gout
government
grammar
grandeur
grapevines
grease
grieve

guidance
guild
guitar

handicapped
handkerchief
harass
hearth
height
heinous
hence
herald
heritage
hideous
hindrance
histrionic
holly
hosiery
humorists
hybrid
hygienic
hysterics

idiomatic
ignoramus
ignorant
illegitimate
illuminate
illustrative
imminent
impartiality
impeccable
impromptu
incongruity
indecent
indictment
individual
ingenuity
ingenuous
inimitable
innocent
innocuous
inoculate
insulation
insurance
integrity
intelligence
intercede
interruption
irreparably
itemized

jealous
jeopardy
journal
jovial
judgment
judiciary
jurisdiction

kindergarten
kinsman

label
laboratory
labyrinth
laceration
lacquer
ladies
larceny
latter
leased
legend
leggings
legitimate
leisure
libel
lieutenant
ligament
lightning
likeness
likewise
liquidate
literally
logical
loose
loot
lose
losing
lovable
loveliness
loyalty
lucrative
luxury
lynch

macaroni
mackerel
magnificent
maintain
maintenance
malice
maneuver
mania
manual
marital
marmalade
masquerade
massacre
matinee
matrimony
mattress
maturity
mayonnaise
mechanical
medal
medallion
medicine
medieval
mediocrity
melancholy
memoir
mercantile
mercury
merely
midget
midriff
military
millinery
millionaire
misanthrope
miscellaneous
mischievous
misdemeanor
mislaid
misspell
misstep
monarchial
monkeys
morale
moribund
mortgage
movable
murmuring
muscle
museum
myriad
necessity
negligible
negotiate
nervous
nevertheless
nickel
niece
ninety
ninth
notary
notoriety
nowadays
nuisance

obedient
obliged
obstacles
occasionally
occur
occurrence
odyssey
official
omissions
omitted
operated
opportunity
option
ordinance
overwhelming

pacifist
pageant
pamphlet
panel
panicky
papal
parachute
paradoxical
parasite
parliament
parole
partisan
partner
patient
patronize
pattern
peculiar
penitentiary
people's

perilous
perjury
permanent
permissible
persevere
pervade
phrenologist
physical
physician
picnicking
piquancy
pitiful
plagiarism
plague
planned
playwright
pneumonia
policy
politician
portable
portend
portiere
possession
possibilities
post office
postpone
potato
poultry
prairie
preceding
precious
predatory
predilection
preferably
preference
premises
preparation
prestige
presume
presumptuous
previous
primarily
primitive
principal
principalship
prisoner
privilege
probably
proffer

profit
proletarian
promissory
promptness
propaganda
proprietor
psychology
publicity
publicly
punctilious

quantities
quartet
questionnaire
queue
quinine

rabid
raisin
realize
reasonable
receipted
receipts
receptacle
recognizable
recommend
recompense
reconcile
recruit
refrigerator
regrettable
regretted
rehearsal
relevant
relieve
religious
remodel
renaissance
renascence
repetitious
requisition
resemblance
reservoir
resilience
resonance
resources
response
responsibility
responsible

restaurant
rheostat
rhetorical
rheumatism
rhubarb
rhythm
rickety
ridiculous
righteous
roommate
routine

Sabbath
sacrilegious
salable
salaries
salient
sandwiches
Saturn
saucy
scenes
scissors
screech
scripture
scrutiny
secretary
seize
senior
serenity
series
session
sieges
significant
silhouette
similar
sincerely
sitting
sobriquet
society
solemn
soliciting
sophomore
soporific
source
sovereign
specialized
specific
specifically
speech

spiritualist
squalor
squirrels
staid
staunch
standard
stationary (fixed)
statistics
statutes
steak
strengthen
strenuous
stretch
studying
subsidy
suburb
subversive
succeed
successor
suffrage
summarize
superb
superintendent
surfeit
surgeon
symmetrical
sympathy
systematic

tableaux
(or tableaus)
taciturn
talcum
tantalizing
tariff
taunt
technical
temperament
temperature
temporarily
tenet
tennis
terse
tetanus
thermometer
thesis
thorough
thought
together

tournament
tragedy
traitor
transaction
transient
transparent
treachery
tremendous
triumph
troupe (theatrical)
truce
tuition
turkeys
twelfth
twins
typewriting
typhoid
tyranny

unanimous
unauthorized
unbearable
unconscious
undecided
undoubtedly
undulate
unfortunately
uniform
unify
universe
unnecessary
utilize

vacancy
vacillate
vacuum
vague
valuing
vegetable
velvet
vengeance
verbal
villain
visible
vivisection
voluntary
voucher

warrant
warranted
weather
Wednesday
weird
welfare
we're
whether
wholly
width
wield
wiring
witnesses
woman's
women's
worlds
wrapped
wretched

yacht
yoke

zephyr

ANSWER KEY

Chapter 18

Spelling

Practice I *Page 223.*

1. reinstate
2. disillusion
3. unnecessary
4. cooperate
5. immortal
6. misspell
7. irreverent
8. illegal
9. acclimate
10. overrate
11. malcontent
12. inaccurate

Practice II *Page 224.*

1. announcement
2. dyeing
3. snappiness
4. association
5. dispensable
6. definitely
7. economical
8. courageous
9. movable
10. necessarily
11. practically
12. portable
13. rudeness
14. guidance
15. truly

Practice III *Page 225.*

1. (4) irrational
2. (2) happiness
3. (4) misspell
4. (5) no error
5. (1) safety
6. (5) no error
7. (3) accumulate
8. (4) noticeable
9. (2) argument
10. (5) no error

Practice IV *Page 226.*

1. paint´• er
2. pri´• vate
3. of´• fice
4. e •con´• o • my
5. ad • vise´
6. bal´• ance
7. dis • sat´• is • fy
8. de • vel´• op • ment
9. in • di • vid´• u • al
10. pre • fer´
11. pref´• er • ence
12. psy • chol´ • o • gy
13. vac´• il • late
14. u • nan´• i • mous
15. wretch´• ed

Practice V *Page 227.*

1. (2) preference
2. (4) deterred
3. (5) no error
4. (3) deterrent
5. (4) occurrence

Practice VI *Page 228.*

1. niece
2. deceive
3. thief
4. relieve
5. neigh
6. receive
7. conceive
8. belief
9. neither
10. seize

Practice VII *Page 229.*

1. (2) mouthfuls
2. (1) Chinese
3. (2) sons-in-law
4. (5) no error
5. (1) 8's

Practice VIII *Page 230.*

1. succeed
2. secede
3. recede
4. exceed
5. Proceed
6. supersede
7. preceded
8. concede

Practice IX *Page 231.*

1. (3) habitually
2. (4) deference
3. (1) candies
4. (2) disappoint
5. (1) potatoes
6. (3) propelling
7. (4) truckfuls
8. (1) truly
9. (5) no error
10. (1) salaries
11. (5) no error
12. (5) no error

Practice X *Page 232.*

1. (3) niece
2. (4) relief
3. (3) referred
4. (3) assessment
5. (5) no error
6. (4) receipt
7. (1) acquired
8. (5) no error
9. (1) adjournment
10. (1) chef

Practice XI *Page 233.*

1. (2) athletic
2. (3) temperature
3. (3) incessant
4. (1) legitimate
5. (5) no error
6. (5) no error
7. (5) no error
8. (4) tetanus
9. (5) no error
10. (1) fundamental

Practice XII *Page 234.*

1. (5) no error
2. (1) absence
3. (3) discussion
4. (2) impeccable
5. (5) no error
6. (1) Wednesday
7. (5) no error
8. (2) possession
9. (5) no error
10. (5) no error

Practice XIII *Page 235.*

1. (2) negligible
2. (5) no error
3. (5) no error
4. (1) fallibility
5. (4) promissory
6. (2) ephemeral
7. (3) exhortation
8. (4) eczema
9. (1) dissatisfied
10. (1) deferred

Practice XIV *Page 236.*

1. (2) resonance
2. (3) patient
3. (1) secretary
4. (5) no error
5. (5) no error
6. (2) chauffeur
7. (3) permissible
8. (3) recognizable
9. (2) mischievous
10. (2) sovereign

Practice XV *Page 237.*

1. (2) carburetor
2. (1) biscuit
3. (5) no error
4. (5) no error
5. (3) relevant
6. (4) weather
7. (1) exceed
8. (2) foreign
9. (3) equipped
10. (2) corrugated

Practice XVI *Page 238.*

1. (3) exercise
2. (2) hindrance
3. (4) deceive
4. (5) no error
5. (2) mackerel
6. (3) pneumonia
7. (1) temperament
8. (1) abundance
9. (1) accumulation
10. (2) ancient

Practice XVII *Page 239.*

Paragraph 1:	(1)	Committee
Paragraph 2:	(5)	cancellation
Paragraph 3:	(5)	friends
Paragraph 4:	(3)	superintendents
Paragraph 5:	(3)	accumulation
Paragraph 6:	(4)	extravagant

19.
Word Usage

I was a pretty good student back in Wilberforce in the 1930's but there were a few things that always gave me trouble. I never felt comfortable with *affect* and *effect, capital* and *capitol, beside* and *besides*—and hundreds of others like that with which Miss Conway used to torture us every Friday.

"Now we come to words frequently confused," she would drool, adjusting wig and lorgnette, her eyes brightening with anticipation.

I think what really turned me off on that subject was when old Mr. Wentworth tried to show me the difference between *principal* and *principle*, pontificating that "Your princi*pal* is your *pal*," and spraying me with tobacco juice in the process.

I didn't believe him then, and I still have trouble with those words, forty years later. Traumatic, I guess.

—Oliver L. Kenworthy
Bluegrass Lawyer

A Word With You . . .

English seems to have so many words that sound alike and more words that are frequently confused than any other language. The same problems which young Oliver Kenworthy found in Wilberforce, Kentucky may have plagued you, too.

In the following pages, you will find some of the more troublesome sets of words. See how well you can handle them.

Many words are easily confused. Some words sound the same but are spelled differently and have different meanings. These are *homonyms*. *For example:*

1. A full moon *shone* brightly last night.

   The film was *shown* on TV.

2. Once we nail up this *board*, the tool shed will be finished.

   I was very *bored* during that long, rainy week.

3. The *pain* in my lower back increases during rainy weather.

   Could you please replace the cracked *pane* of glass?

Other words are confusing because they sound almost the same.

For example:

1. The legislators had an angry debate before *adopting* a policy on school funding.

   Since we moved from the West Coast to the Midwest, we've had to *adapt* to colder weather.

2. The politician's *allusions* to his opponent's past errors in judgment were unnecessary.

   In the story *The Christmas Carol*, Scrooge's visitors were *illusions*.

3. How do you think the current job action will *affect* management?

   I think the *effect* will be that management will meet labor's demands.

In order to improve your understanding of easily confused words, study the following list. An example of correct usage is given for each commonly confused word.

Commonly Misused Words

1. accept—except

   I *accept* your apology.

   Everyone *except* John may leave.

2. adapt—adopt

   When visiting a foreign country, you must *adapt* yourself to the customs practiced there.

   The Grays plan to *adopt* several hard-to-place children.

3. advice—advise

   Because of Michael's excellent *advice*, Bob completed a successful deal.

   Michael will *advise* Bob to be daring.

4. affect—effect

   The accident did not *affect* Thomas.

   The *effect* on his brother, however, was great.

5. aggravate—annoy

   When you forget your medication, you *aggravate* your medical condition.

   Your forgetting *annoys* me.

6. all ready—already

   Call me when you are *all ready* to go.

   By the time Sue arrived, we had *already* finished dinner.

7. all right (*Alright* is not an acceptable word.)

   Is it *all right* to leave this window open?

8. all together—altogether

   The four of us were *all together* at the coffee shop.

   This book is *altogether* too long.

9. allude—refer

   At some point, the speaker *alluded* to the new opportunities in business.

   The speaker *referred* to statistics that demonstrated the increased number of small businesses.

10. allusion—illusion

    I resent your *allusion* to my cooking as comparable with McDonald's

    You have the *illusion* that I enjoy classical music—I don't.

11. altar—alter

Many a would-be bride has been left at the *altar*.

Would it be inconvenient for you to *alter* your plans for this weekend?

12. among—between

The campaign director divided the state *among* his *three* most competent assistants.

In many of today's homes, the care of the children is divided *between* the *two* parents.

13. amount—number

You would not believe the *amount* of time I have spent on this project.

I wish I could reuse the *number* of hours I have spent on this project.

14. angry at—angry with

Ira was *angry at* the thought of working overtime.

Ira was *angry with* his boss for insisting that Ira work overtime.

15. anxious—eager

I am *anxious* about the diagnosis.

I am *eager* to see your new car.

16. anywhere (There is no such word as *anywheres*.)

Marlene cannot find her glasses *anywhere*.

17. as—like

Paula looks very much *like* her sister.

Rosemary swims *as* well as Pam does.

Carl looks as if he needs a nap.

18. **ascent—assent**

    The *ascent* to the tower was frighteningly steep.

    Because I value his opinion, I will not go ahead with the project without his *assent*.

19. **awful—very—real**

    This milk tastes *awful.*

    This milk tastes *very* sour.

    She wore *real* pearls.

20. **beside—besides**

    Linda likes to sit *beside* Ellen at the table.

    Who, *besides* Pam, is taking swimming lessons?

21. **born—borne**

    Our youngest child was *born* last month.

    John has *borne* the burden by himself for long enough.

22. **borrow from** (*borrow off* is unacceptable)

    Mickey borrowed the soldering iron *from* Allen.

23. **borrow—lend—loan**

    Can I *borrow* your car?

    I can *lend* you some money.

    I took a *loan* from the bank.

24. **brake—break**

    I prefer a bicycle with a foot *brake.*

    Because he did not *brake* in time, Herman crashed into the tree.

    If you are not careful, you will *break* that dish.

25. **can—may**

    Some fortunate people *can* arrange their time to include work and pleasure.

You *may* hunt deer only during certain seasons.

26. capital—capitol—Capitol

Ricardo has 90% of the necessary *capital* for his new business venture.

Trenton is the *capital* of New Jersey.

New Jersey's *capitol* building is in Trenton.

Did you visit the *Capitol* when you were in Washington, D.C.?

27. cite—sight—site

An attorney often *cites* previous cases that support his argument.

One of the most beautiful *sights* in the country is the Grand Canyon.

The alternative school will be built on this *site*.

28. coarse—course

I find this *coarse* fabric to be abrasive.

That is an acceptable *course* of action.

29. complement—compliment

Rice nicely *complements* a chicken dinner.

I'd like to *compliment* you for doing such a thorough job.

30. communicate with—contact

I will *communicate with* (call, write, speak) you in the morning.

Superglue adheres on *contact* (touch).

31. continually—continuously

Tom is *continually* late.

The river runs *continuously* through several towns.

32. council—counsel

Our neighbor has just been elected to the town *council*.

The troubled man sought his friend's *counsel*.

33. credible—creditable—credulous

Because the defendant had a good alibi, his story seemed *credible.*

As a result of many hours of hard work, Joe presented a *creditable* report.

Sally is so *credulous* that one could sell her the Brooklyn Bridge.

34. currant—current

His unusual recipe called for *currant* jelly.

Because the *current* was swift, the canoe was difficult to maneuver.

35. desert—dessert

The *desert* is very hot and dry.

More and more young soldiers have been *deserting* the army.

Apple pie is America's favorite *dessert.*

36. die—dye

Eventually, every living thing *dies.*

I'll never *dye* my hair.

37. discover—invent

The builders *discovered* oil on our land.

Whitney *invented* the cotton gin.

38. draw—drawer

Marlene *draws* very well.

She keeps her pads and pencils in the top *drawer* of her desk.

39. emigration—immigration

The Harlows *emigrated* from England.

After *immigrating* to the United States, the Harlows settled in Kansas.

40. famous—infamous

John Simpson is a *famous* pianist.

Arthur Jones is an *infamous* car thief.

41. farther—further

My car can run *farther* on this other brand of gasoline.

I cannot continue this discussion any *further*.

42. fewer—less

Gerry invited *fewer* people to her office party this year.

Since she moved from a house to an apartment, she has *less* space.

43. formally—formerly

Please dress *formally* for the wedding.

I was *formerly* employed by a jewelry company, but I am now working in a bank.

44. good—well

Anna performed a *good* job.

Anna performed the job *well*.

Anna feels *good* about herself. (not *bad*)

Anna feels *well* today. (not *sick*)

45. grate—great

The continuous, harsh, and rasping sound *grated* on my nerves.

A *grate* in the sidewalk covered the opening to the sewer.

Ernest Hemingway was considered a *great* writer in his own lifetime.

46. healthful—healthy

Orange juice is *healthful*.

If you eat properly and exercise sufficiently, you will be *healthy*.

47. imply—infer

Although he did not state it directly, the candidate *implied* that his opponent was dishonest.

From the mayor's constructive suggestions, the townsfolk *inferred* that he was trying his best to do a good job.

48. in—into

Marlene stood *in* her living room.

Wayne came rushing *into* the room.

49. it's—its

I think *it's* a fine idea!

The dog wagged *its* tail.

50. kind of—sort of—type of (These expressions can be used interchangeably. They should never be followed by "a.")

Mrs. Peterson always buys that *kind of* meat.

I like that *sort of* book.

This is my favorite *type of* music.

51. lead—led

I'll need one more *lead* pipe to complete this plumbing job.

I only enjoy a race when I am in the *lead*.

John was unfamiliar with that route, so Jules *led* the way.

52. learn—teach

Tim needs to *learn* how to communicate with people.

Leslie is patiently trying to *teach* me how to type.

53. leave—let

If the customs officer finds nothing wrong with a traveler's baggage, the officer *lets* the traveler *leave* the area.

54. loose—lose

Eric was excited about his first *loose* tooth.

55. If you step out of line, you will *lose* your place.

manor—manner

The *manor*, or landed estate, dates back to feudal times in England.

They don't like the *manner* in which you responded to my sincere question.

56. miner—minor

The coal *miners* were trapped during the cave-in.

The young man was not allowed to enter the bar because he was a *minor*.

57. moral—morale

Because of Ed's high *moral* standards, he returned the wallet to its owner.

The story of *The Boy Who Cried Wolf* has a *moral* that applies to everyone.

Because the war was immoral, the *morale* of the troops was low.

58. nauseated—nauseous

When we drove past the skunk, the car was filled with a *nauseous* odor.

The odor of the skunk *nauseated* Sara.

59. pail—pale

The amount of paint needed to finish the job would fill a one-gallon *pail*.

Because of her long illness, Maria's complexion was very *pale*.

60. passed—past

We *passed* the Model T on the parkway.

You cannot always try to recapture the *past*.

61. **peace—piece**

If we work together, perhaps we can end the war and achieve a truly lasting *peace*.

In time, we will be paying an extremely high price for a *piece* of paper.

62. **persecute—prosecute**

Older children frequently *persecute* their younger siblings.

If you do not return the stolen money, you will be *prosecuted*.

63. **personal—personnel**

The items written in a young girl's diary are very *personal*.

When applying for a job at a large company, you must go to the *personnel* office.

64. **plain—plane**

The meaning is quite *plain* and requires no further explanation.

We rode for miles across the open *plains* of Kansas.

The *plane* landed smoothly.

Please *plane* that wood so that I can build a birdhouse from it.

65. **practicable—practical**

Studying computer programming is a *practicable* plan in today's job market.

Computerizing payroll is a *practical* business decision.

66. **precede—proceed**

A preface always *precedes* the body of a book.

Don't let me interrupt you; *proceed* with your work.

67. **principal—principle**

A school is as good as the teachers and *principal*.

The *principal* actors in the play remained for a final rehearsal of the second act.

The *principle* upon which many simple machines are based is frequently the lever.

68. quiet—quite

As the campers lay down for the night, *quiet* settled over the campsite.

That is *quite* a strong accusation.

69. raise—rise

When we *raise* the flag at the game, everyone will *rise.*

70. sit—set

The chairman requested committee members to *sit* down.

The artist *set* his clay on the workbench and began to create a sculpture.

71. stationary—stationery

Theater seats are most often *stationary*.

At work, I use the company's business *stationery.*

72. sure—surely

Ms Sanchez was *sure* the meeting would start on time.

Surely, I can rely on your being there on time.

73. teach—learn

Miss Smith *teaches* math every Thursday.

Ron Jonas, a student, *learns* math from Miss Smith.

74. than—then

New York is smaller *than* Wyoming, but Wyoming has a much smaller population *than* New York.

First the eastern seaboard was colonized, *then* settlers moved westward.

75. their—there—they're

When leaving *their* war-torn country, most of the refugees left all their possessions behind.

There are no easy answers to the problem of world-wide hunger.

As for the members of Congress, *they're* not always responsible for the wisest decisions.

76. through—threw

The special crew worked *through* the night to repair the damaged wires.

When the Little League pitcher *threw* the ball, her teammates cheered.

77. to—too—two

United States presidents often travel *to* foreign countries.

Many foreign heads of state visit the United States, *too*.

Two visitors were Mugabe and Yeltsin.

78. vain—vane—vein

The *vain* man peered at his reflection in every window as he strolled down the street.

A rooster is the traditional weather *vane* symbol.

Veins are passageways that carry deoxygenated blood to the heart.

79. vale—veil

Vale is an uncommonly used synonym for valley.

The mourning woman hid her grief behind her *veil*.

80. wade—weighed

The smaller children were told to *wade* near the shore.

The clerk *weighed* and priced the fresh vegetables.

81. waist—waste

If you measure your *waist* before you go to buy a pattern, you will avoid much confusion.

Don't *waste* precious time gossiping on the phone.

82. weather—whether

Tomorrow morning the general *weather* conditions will determine the distance of our first day's hike.

Whether or not you wish to pay taxes, you must.

83. who's—whose

The teacher asked, "*Who's* responsible for clean-up today?

We must determine *whose* turn it is.

84. writes—rights—rites

Kurt Vonnegut *writes* excellent fiction.

Their attorney explained the family's *rights* in the lawsuit.

The religious *rites* of many an Indian tribe are an impressive part of their culture.

85. your—you're

Where is *your* car parked?

You're attempting something that's too difficult for you.

PRACTICE I

Directions: In each of the following groups of sentences, find the sentence that has an error in word usage. If there is no error, choose option (5).

1. (1) The jewel was shown to thc prospective buyer. ① ② ③ ④ ⑤
(2) Her hair shown in the bright sunlight.
(3) The sun shone brightly this morning.
(4) I have never been shown how to use this machine.
(5) No error

2. (1) I would like you to cite at least three examples. ① ② ③ ④ ⑤
(2) Her husband was cited for contempt.
(3) For that sight, we're planning a municipal parking lot.

(4) When the bridge is within your sight, start looking for our street.
(5) No error

3. (1) The some total of these facts spells disaster. ① ② ③ ④ ⑤
(2) Take some cake with you to the picnic.
(3) I have some clothes that are no longer useful to me.
(4) That sum of money is to be labeled petty cash.
(5) No error

4. (1) Since the development of the tape recorder, Braille is no longer the sole method of communicating fine literature to sightless people. ① ② ③ ④ ⑤
(2) Lemon sole is one of the many varieties of fish that can enhance a meatless diet.
(3) Sole music is very popular among people of all ages.
(4) The concept of the soul does not have the same meaning in all religions.
(5) No error

5. (1) Napoleon had a great deal at steak when he decided to invade Russia. ① ② ③ ④ ⑤
(2) Finally, William hammered the last stake into the ground.
(3) I would enjoy a steak dinner tonight.
(4) Sue was upset because her job was at stake.
(5) No error

6. (1) Please, remain stationary while I draw your picture. ① ② ③ ④ ⑤
(2) Irene wrote the letter on her finest stationary.
(3) I believe you can buy staples at the stationery store.
(4) This appliance cannot be moved; it is stationary.
(5) No error

7. (1) Ilene attended a conference there. ① ② ③ ④ ⑤
(2) There is the book I've been wanting to read.

(3) There's is a truly open relationship.
(4) I have never been to their summer home.
(5) No error.

8. (1) Those two stairs make this house bi-level. ① ② ③ ④ ⑤
(2) Hers was hardly a friendly stair.
(3) We've already swept the stairs today.
(4) Don't stare at me!
(5) No error

9. (1) I think it's time that he buys a new suite of furniture. ① ② ③ ④ ⑤
(2) We've already eaten our portion of sweets for this day.
(3) The visiting lecturer's hotel suite was paid for by the university.
(4) Don't make the chocolate pudding overly sweet.
(5) No error

10. (1) The boat was taken in toe after its motor failed. ① ② ③ ④ ⑤
(2) We were towed all the way to the shore.
(3) At the football game we had a bad case of frozen toes.
(4) When you go beyond your own authority, you must step on somebody's toes.
(5) No error

PRACTICE II

Directions: Each of the following sentences has an error in word usage. For each item, choose the one best answer that would result in the correct writing of the sentence.

1. The guide led us on a straight ascent up through the woods and to a lovely veil.

What correction should be made to this sentence?

(1) replace led with lead ① ② ③ ④ ⑤
(2) replace straight with strait
(3) replace ascent with assent
(4) replace through with threw
(5) replace veil with vale

2. My neighbor dies her hair two times every month.

What correction should be made to this sentence?

(1) replace dies with dyes ① ② ③ ④ ⑤
(2) replace hair with hare
(3) replace two with to
(4) replace two with too
(5) replace week with weak

3. We had already planned our vacation to a quiet isle when our friends said that they were all ready to come along to.

What correction should be made to this question?

(1) replace already with all ready ① ② ③ ④ ⑤
(2) replace quiet with quite
(3) replace isle with aisle
(4) replace all ready with already
(5) replace along to with along too

4. You are all together mistaken about their decision to write to the newspaper.

What correction should be made to this sentence?

(1) replace all together with altogether ① ② ③ ④ ⑤
(2) replace their with there

(3) replace their with they're
(4) replace to write with too write
(5) replace write with right

5. Ina Swanson writes about the religious rights of the Indians who inhabit the island right off the coast of Japan.

What correction should be made to this sentence?

(1) replace writes with rights ① ② ③ ④ ⑤
(2) replace writes with rites
(3) replace rights with rites
(4) replace rights with writes
(5) replace right with rite

6. The capital of each state is the cite of the capitol building and the main attraction for sightseers.
What correction should be made to this sentence?

(1) replace capital with capitol ① ② ③ ④ ⑤
(2) replace cite with sight
(3) replace cite with site
(4) replace capitol with capital
(5) replace sightseers with siteseers

7. The effect of the currant there was so strong, we had great difficulty reaching shore.

What correction should be made to this sentence?

(1) replace effect with affect ① ② ③ ④ ⑤
(2) replace currant with current
(3) replace there with their

(4) replace so with sew
(5) replace great with grate

PRACTICE III

Directions: The following items are based on paragraphs that contain numbered sentences. Some of the sentences may contain errors in word usage. Other sentences are correct as they appear in the paragraphs. Read each paragraph and then answer the item based on it. For each item, choose the one best answer that would result in the correct word usage in the sentence.

(1) Because I was anxious to avoid another argument, I accepted Roy's apology. (2) His story seemed credible so there was no point in carrying the argument any further.

1. Sentence 1: **Because I was anxious to avoid another argument I accepted Roy's apology.**

   Which of the following is the best way to write the underlined portion of this sentence? If you think the original is the best way, choose option (1).

   (1) I was anxious to avoid ① ② ③ ④ ⑤
   (2) I was anxious too avoid
   (3) I was anxious to avert
   (4) I was eager to avoid
   (5) I was eager too avert

(1) Sue left the elevator and proceeded to the personal office. (2) The cold, efficient interviewer lowered Sue's morale, but nevertheless, Sue was eager to obtain the job.

2. Sentence 1: **Sue left the elevator and proceeded to the personal office.**

   Which of the following is the best way to write the underlined portion of this sentence? If you think the original is the best way, choose option (1).

(1) proceeded to the personal office. ① ② ③ ④ ⑤
(2) preceded to the personal office.
(3) proceeded to the personnel office.
(4) proceeded too the personal office.
(5) preceded to the personnel office.

(1) The effect of the unusual visitor on the family was startling. (2) Mother adopted Mrs. Chuggley's speech habits. (3) Father altered his smoking habits to suit Mrs. Chuggley's allergy. (4) I found myself continuously saying, "Yes, Ma'am."

3. Sentence 4: **I found myself continuously saying, "Yes, Ma'am."**

Which of the following is the best way to write the underlined portion of this sentence? If you think the original is the best way, choose option (1).

(1) found myself continuously saying, ① ② ③ ④ ⑤
(2) continuously found myself saying,
(3) found me continuously saying,
(4) found myself continually saying,
(5) found myself saying,

(1) The course of action determined by the city counsel at its last meeting has already begun to affect us. (2) The exorbitant expenditure for a parking garage is a waste.

4. Sentence 1: **The course of action determined by the city counsel at its last meeting has already begun to affect us.**

Which of the following is the best way to write the underlined portion of this sentence? If you think the original is the best way, choose option (1).

(1) course of action determined by the city counsel ① ② ③ ④ ⑤
(2) course of action determined by the city council

(3) coarse of action determined by the city counsel
(4) coarse of action determined by the city council
(5) Course of action determined buy the city council

(1) Family gatherings are always interesting. (2) Grandpa is usually angry with Aunt Jean. (3) Rhoda insists upon sitting besides Grandma. (4) Mother tries to divide her attention equally among all of the guests.

5. Sentence 3: **Rhoda insists upon sitting besides Grandma.**

Which of the following is the best way to write the underlined portion of the sentence? If you think the original is the best way, choose option (1).

(1) insists upon sitting besides ① ② ③ ④ ⑤
(2) insists upon setting besides
(3) insists upon sitting beside
(4) insists upon setting beside
(5) insists on setting besides

PRACTICE IV

Directions: In each of the following groups of sentences, find the sentence that has an error in word usage. If there is no error, choose option (5).

1. (1) The damage has all ready been done. ① ② ③ ④ ⑤
(2) Father was altogether too surprised to speak.
(3) Events have borne out my prediction.
(4) Perry is an altar boy at Queen of Peace Church.
(5) No error

2. (1) The family was all together for the annual picnic. ① ② ③ ④ ⑤
(2) Terry's mother cautioned, "If you break a window, you will have to pay for it."
(3) Paris is the capital of France.
(4) My mother was borne in Canada.
(5) No error

3. (1) Was his work all right? ① ② ③ ④ ⑤
(2) I use old shirts for cleaning cloths.
(3) The dome on the capital is lighted each night.
(4) Everyone was wearing his best clothes.
(5) No error

4. (1) I applied the brakes immediately. ① ② ③ ④ ⑤
(2) Cars are borne across the river on a ferry.
(3) Are you feeling all right?
(4) When you are all ready, I will pick you up.
(5) No error

5. (1) John is considered an imminent member of Congress. ① ② ③ ④ ⑤
(2) The duke was received formally at the ambassador's home.
(3) Out of deference to her loss, we did not resume the music.
(4) We could hear a vigorous discussion of current problems.
(5) No error

6. (1) When you give your report, be sure to cite as many concrete examples as possible. ① ② ③ ④ ⑤
(2) "I am surely not guilty of excessive spending!" he shouted.
(3) We are not likely to meet again in the near future.
(4) Because of several miner disagreements, the discussion came to a halt.
(5) No error

7. (1) The politician was asked to accede to the council's wishes. ① ② ③ ④ ⑤
(2) I am opposed to the construction of the bridge for two good reasons.
(3) Do not hire anyone whose personality doesn't complement the rest of the staff.

(4) Prospective homeowners are eager for reduction of the mortgage interest rate.
(5) No error

8. (1) The attorney set fourth his ideas and told us all of the angles of his case. ① ② ③ ④ ⑤
(2) Will you sign this Senior Citizen petition?
(3) The beauty of the mountains exceeded all our expectations.
(4) Mike is quite an athlete.
(5) No error

9. (1) Wayne is likely to be defeated. ① ② ③ ④ ⑤
(2) There was nothing to do but accept his plan.
(3) I am opposed too airing family matters in public.
(4) The crowd was quiet until the rocket ascended.
(5) No error

10. (1) After listening with great patience, the diplomat listed his objectives. ① ② ③ ④ ⑤
(2) No one knew him as well as I.
(3) Choose your coarse of action and stick to it.
(4) I think the skirt is too loose on you.
(5) No error

PRACTICE V

Directions: Each of the following items has an error in word usage. For each item, choose the one best answer that would result in the correct writing of the sentence.

1. The principal members of the committee led a discussion about the peace movement and the type of a person attracted to it.

What correction should be made to this sentence?

(1) replace principal with principle ① ② ③ ④ ⑤
(2) replace led with lead

(3) replace discussion with talk
(4) replace peace with piece
(5) remove a after type of

2. Many of the minors in the audience began to lose there tempers because the discussion seemed partisan.

What correction should be made to this sentence?

(1) replace minors with miners ① ② ③ ④ ⑤
(2) replace lose with loose
(3) replace there with they're
(4) replace there with their
(5) replace seemed with seamed

3. The chairman tried to explain that the principle of freedom to pursue yore beliefs was not the main issue.

What correction should be made to this sentence?

(1) replace tried with triad ① ② ③ ④ ⑤
(2) replace principle with principal
(3) replace yore with your
(4) insert only before main
(5) replace main with mane

4. It was not the committee's intention to persecute anyone but rather to make plain the already divergent viewpoints and to precede to bring them together.

What correction should be made to this sentence?

(1) replace persecute with prosecute ① ② ③ ④ ⑤
(2) replace plain with plane
(3) insert very before plain
(4) replace already with all ready
(5) replace precede with proceed

5. The main effect of the chairman's speech was to quiet the audience so that the discussion could continue farther.

What correction should be made to this sentence?

(1) replace main with mane ① ② ③ ④ ⑤
(2) replace effect with affect
(3) replace to quiet with too quiet
(4) replace farther with father
(5) replace farther with further

6. The next speaker waisted more time by expressing anger with the young people present rather than by formally addressing the current issues.

What correction should be made to this sentence?

(1) replace waisted with wasted ① ② ③ ④ ⑤
(2) replace with with at
(3) replace than with then
(4) replace formally with formerly
(5) replace current with currant

7. I am quite certain that the committee learned a lesson about discussing volatile issues. Next time, it will altar its presentation so that speakers will be more to the point.

What correction should be made to these sentences?

(1) replace quite with quiet ① ② ③ ④ ⑤
(2) replace certain with positive
(3) insert such before volatile
(4) replace altar with alter
(5) replace its with it's

8. That way, less misunderstandings will occur. The Lakeview Town Council had weighed having a similar discussion, but changed its program.

What correction should be made to these sentences?

(1) replace less with fewer ① ② ③ ④ ⑤
(2) replace Council with Counsel
(3) replace weighed with wade
(4) replace but with butt
(5) replace its with it's

ANSWER KEY

Chapter 19

Word Usage

Practice I *Page 261.*

1. (2) shone
2. (3) site
3. (1) sum
4. (3) Soul
5. (1) stake
6. (2) stationery
7. (3) Theirs
8. (2) stare
9. (5) No error
10. (1) tow

Practice II *Page 263.*

1. (5) vale
2. (1) dyes
3. (5) too
4. (1) altogether
5. (3) rites
6. (3) site
7. (2) current

Practice III *Page 266.*

1. (4) I was eager to avoid
2. (3) proceeded to the personnel office
3. (4) found myself continually saying,
4. (2) course of action determined by the city council
5. (3) insists upon sitting beside

Practice IV *Page 268.*

1. (1) already
2. (4) born
3. (3) Capitol
4. (5) No error
5. (1) eminent
6. (4) minor
7. (5) No error
8. (1) forth
9. (3) to
10. (3) course

Practice V *Page 270.*

1. (5) type of
2. (4) their
3. (3) your
4. (5) proceed
5. (5) further
6. (1) wasted
7. (4) alter
8. (1) fewer

20.
Cumulative Review

This review covers the following concepts that have been included in the preceding chapters.

- Effective Expression
- Punctuation
- Capitalization
- Spelling
- Word Usage

After completing the Cumulative Review exercises and checking your answers against the ANSWER KEY, evaluate your ability on the SUMMARY OF RESULTS chart on page 290. Acceptable scores for each practice section are given.

To identify your areas for skill improvement, find the question numbers you answered incorrectly on the SKILLS ANALYSIS table. The table will show which of your skills need improvement and the necessary chapters to review.

PRACTICE I

Directions: In each of the following groups of sentences, find the sentence that is incorrect. If there is no error, choose option (5).

1. (1) Doctor Smith ordered a mahogany, octagonal-shaped table for his office. ① ② ③ ④ ⑤
(2) I wasn't never told to take this highway to your house.
(3) My aunt baked that cake for me because I'm giving a party for my friend Joan.
(4) The plumber left the job almost immediately because he did not have the parts he needed.
(5) No error

2. (1) After the clerk gave the customer the change, he heard the store's closing bell. ① ② ③ ④ ⑤
(2) We went to a concert at City Center and heard an especially fine pianist, Peter Serkin.
(3) The best part of our day occurred when we realized we were seated behind Woody Allen.
(4) The traveling lecturer hardly ever has time for lunch.
(5) No error

3. (1) The lecturer prepared slides to accompany his talk. ① ② ③ ④ ⑤
(2) Since the hour was late, the Senate adjourned its session.
(3) Commenting on his theory, the book was discussed by its author.
(4) Although our building was painted last year, it looks as if it needs to be painted again.
(5) No error

4. (1) Our group, we visited the museum to see a display of mobiles. ① ② ③ ④ ⑤
(2) The supplies included pencils, papers, rulers, and blackboards.
(3) I have never seen a neater room!
(4) The president meets with his aides at 11:55 A.M.
(5) No error

5. (1) I cancelled the meeting; because I expected to be too busy to attend. ① ② ③ ④ ⑤

(2) Do you ever feel pressured by a too-full schedule?
(3) Because the plane arrived late, we missed our connecting flight.
(4) The resettled refugees finally got jobs.
(5) No error

6. (1) The best part of the book occurs when the brothers meet after a 25-year separation. ① ② ③ ④ ⑤
(2) The most exciting event in the movie is the auto race.
(3) The reason for his absence is because he has the flu.
(4) Richard Robinson hasn't been seen for weeks.
(5) No error

7. (1) What the sergeant wanted to know was what supplies the unit needed. ① ② ③ ④ ⑤
(2) Because it's Monday, the stores are open late.
(3) The reason for my confusion is that my notes are incomplete.
(4) My children left for day camp at 9:00 A.M.
(5) No error

8. (1) Because the power steering fluid had evaporated, the wheel would not turn. ① ② ③ ④ ⑤
(2) Having established itself in an area, it's difficult to eliminate an insect.
(3) William the Conqueror and the barons of Normandy were not in agreement about the invasion of England.
(4) His parents said that John was neither too young nor too busy to hold a part-time job.
(5) No error

9. (1) If history doesn't repeat itself, why is there never an end to war? ① ② ③ ④ ⑤
   (2) Why is it that nothing never goes smoothly?
   (3) On the subject of the dangerous effects of spray cans, one cannot hope for scientists' accord.
   (4) An automobile accident occurred when two drivers proceeded into the intersection at the same time.
   (5) No error

10. (1) More and more people are buying cars even though the prices are very high. ① ② ③ ④ ⑤
   (2) There are many solutions to the energy crisis.
   (3) Carrying a fishing pole and wearing hip boots, a man stood knee-deep in water in the flooded street.
   (4) None of Albert Schweitzer's expenses was borne by the Evangelical Mission which had sent him to Lambaréné.
   (5) No error

11. (1) The football team played football well yesterday at the football game. ① ② ③ ④ ⑤
   (2) Mark's hockey team is the best in the league.
   (3) None of the basketball players was at the victory party.
   (4) Monica Seles rarely plays tennis with a player who isn't a pro.
   (5) No error

12. (1) Sylvester Stallone's latest movie seems to be a variation on his famous *Rocky* movies. ① ② ③ ④ ⑤

(2) The novel which the customer requested was out of print.
(3) Herbert Hoover a man of humble beginnings, was the son of a blacksmith.
(4) Because the restriction on misleading food labels is vague, the consumer must be vigilent.
(5) no error

13. (1) The reason the ERA was defeated was a lack of understanding of the benefits. ① ② ③ ④ ⑤
(2) The reason that primitive people relied on witch doctors was because these people feared attack by evil spirits.
(3) Our specialty is good service.
(4) We feature the finest service in the field.
(5) No error

14. (1) Although I am exhausted, I plan to rest this afternoon. ① ② ③ ④ ⑤
(2) Please don't leave early; we are enjoying your company.
(3) The world's future population is hardly ever discussed without mention of food and other resources.
(4) If you continue to smoke, I'll continue to ask you to stop.
(5) No error

15. (1) Don't you find talk shows boring? ① ② ③ ④ ⑤
(2) Are you not Mary Smith's aunt?
(3) The business manager, who was ranting uncontrollably, lost the respect of his colleagues.
(4) Although it isn't none of my business, I'm concerned about your health.
(5) No error

PRACTICE II

Directions: Choose the one best sentence completion for each of the following items.

1. The mailman slipped on the steps
(1) because he was wearing boots. ① ② ③ ④
(2) even though they were icy.
(3) because the steps, they were icy.
(4) because they were icy.

2. Jules continues to smoke
(1) because he cannot read the warning. ① ② ③ ④
(2) since smoking is hazardous to his health.
(3) although smoking is hazardous to his health.
(4) when it's hazardous to his health.

3. The camping trip was uncomfortable
(1) in spite of the heat and the bugs. ① ② ③ ④
(2) although it was hot and buggy.
(3) even though it was hot and buggy.
(4) because of the heat and the bugs.

4. The Giants played well
(1) because they feared the fans. ① ② ③ ④
(2) because the day was unseasonably hot.
(3) even though the day was unseasonably hot.
(4) even though the weather was perfect.

5. That man, who speaks at every public meeting,
(1) he is my uncle Joe. ① ② ③ ④
(2) he is a town nuisance.
(3) never offers a suggestion that we like.
(4) he hardly ever offers an acceptable suggestion.

6. I'd like draperies made of a transparent fabric
(1) that sees through and is durable. ① ② ③ ④
(2) that is durable.
(3) that I can see through and is durable.
(4) that is durable and I can see through.

7. My favorite scene in *Romeo and Juliet*
(1) is when Romeo kills himself. ① ② ③ ④
(2) is the one where Romeo kills himself.
(3) is because Romeo kills himself.
(4) is the one in which Romeo kills himself.

PRACTICE III

Directions: What correction in punctuation should be made to each of the following sentences?

1. "Would you like to record the song you wrote?", the conductor asked the singer.
(1) remove the quotation marks before Would and after wrote ① ② ③ ④ ⑤
(2) remove the question mark after wrote
(3) replace the question mark after wrote with a period
(4) remove the comma after wrote
(5) replace the period after singer with a question mark

2. If you wish, you may pick some flowers—but only those along the side of the house—for your centerpiece."

(1) remove the comma after wish ① ② ③ ④ ⑤
(2) replace the dash after flowers with a comma
(3) replace the dash after flowers with a semicolon
(4) replace the dash after house with a comma
(5) remove the quotation mark after centerpiece

3. "My favorite book," said Melissa "is *Animal Farm.*"

(1) remove the quotation mark before My ① ② ③ ④ ⑤
(2) remove the comma after book
(3) insert a comma after is
(4) insert a comma after Melissa
(5) insert a period after the quotation mark following Farm

4. The show (for which you have tickets) begins promptly at 7:45 P.M. and ends (believe it or not at 11:00 P.M.

(1) remove the parentheses before for and after tickets ① ② ③ ④ ⑤
(2) insert a comma after show
(3) remove the colon from 7:45
(4) insert a comma after ends
(5) insert a parenthesis mark after not

5. Last Sunday, I met my ex roommate (whom I haven't seen for twelve years) in the supermarket.

(1) replace the comma after Sunday with a dash ① ❷ ③ ④ ⑤
(2) insert a hyphen between ex and roommate
(3) insert a comma after years)
(4) remove the parentheses before whom and after years
(5) replace the period after supermarket with an exclamation point

6. "After you've practiced writing r's," said Miss Green, go right on to s's."

(1) remove the apostrophe in you've ① ② ③ ❹ ⑤
(2) change r's," to r's",
(3) remove the apostrophe in r's
(4) insert quotation marks before go
(5) replace the comma after Miss Green with a semicolon

7. The Brownies annual party was at the home of Jane Simpson on Friday, at 4:15 P.M.

(1) change Brownies to Brownies' ❶ ② ③ ④ ⑤
(2) insert a comma after party
(3) change Brownies to Brownie's
(4) remove the colon in 4:15
(5) insert a period after P.M.

8. Eighty four of the members voted—despite last year's increase—to increase the dues for the next fiscal year.
   (1) insert a hyphen between Eighty and four ➊ ② ③ ④ ⑤
   (2) remove the dashes after voted and increase
   (3) remove the apostrophe in year's
   (4) insert a comma after dues
   (5) change year's to years'

9. The painter called this morning to say "that he won't be able to begin working until next weekend."
   (1) insert a comma after that ① ② ➌ ④ ⑤
   (2) insert a comma after morning
   (3) remove the quotation marks before that and after weekend
   (4) remove the apostrophe from won't
   (5) insert a colon after say

PRACTICE IV

Directions: Some of the following sentences may contain an error in capitalization. Correct each error that you find.

1. Sue Anderson, the lead in *The Glass Menagerie*, is a really competent actress.

2. When you leave School today, take a bus and meet me in New York City.

3. Our course, history IA, will include discussion on the settlement of the American colonies.

4. Remember that Ellie said we should meet Her for lunch on Tuesday.

5. On Twenty-second Street, there's a charming restaurant called Lou's.

6. Mr. Goren reminded us, "all lights must be turned off in the laboratory at the end of the workday."

7. The lieutenant asked captain John Forbes to cut the ribbon at the ceremonies marking the opening of Fort Titan.

8. This October, halloween falls on a Tuesday.

9. "We can learn much," said Edith, "from the cultures of the east."

10. One of the earliest and most significant British documents is the magna carta.

PRACTICE V

Directions: Blacken the circle that corresponds to the number of the incorrectly spelled word in each group. If there is no error, blacken circle number 5.

1. (1) reinstitute (2) overated (3) happily (4) foxes (5) no error ① ② ③ ④ ⑤

2. (1) dyeing (2) dying (3) dies (4) dice (5) no error ① ② ③ ④ ⑤

3. (1) truly (2) noticable (3) famous (4) duly (5) no error ① ② ③ ④ ⑤

4. (1) guidance (2) necessarily (3) mispell (4) edibles (5) no error ① ② ③ ④ ⑤

5. (1) safely (2) proceed (3) preceed (4) recede (5) no error ① ② ③ ④ ⑤

6. (1) merrily (2) quickly (3) niece (4) theif (5) no error ① ② ③ ④ ⑤

7. (1) succeed (2) willingly (3) reference (4) wierd (5) no error ① ② ③ ④ ⑤

8. (1) canning (2) caning (3) confering (4) radios (5) no error ① ② ③ ④ ⑤

9. (1) seize (2) secede (3) skys (4) axes (5) no error ① ② ③ ④ ⑤

10. (1) recede (2) ilegal (3) disillusion (4) hunches (5) no error ① ② ③ ④ ⑤

11. (1) sheep (2) data (3) datum (4) exrays (5) no error ① ② ③ ④ ⑤

12. (1) sevens (2) courtisans (3) 9s (4) loosens (5) no error ① ② ③ ④ ⑤

13. (1) atheletic (2) exceed (3) supersede (4) mice (5) no error ① ② ③ ④ ⑤

14. (1) vaccinate (2) mouthsful (3) oxen (4) height (5) no error ① ② ③ ④ ⑤

15. (1) befitting (2) allegiance (3) tonage (4) leisure (5) no error ① ② ③ ④ ⑤

16. (1) deceive (2) relieve (3) ferret (4) heroes (5) no error ① ② ③ ④ ⑤

17. (1) contraltoes (2) trout (3) brothers-in-law (4) duly (5) no error ① ② ③ ④ ⑤

18. (1) crises (2) knifes (3) disappoint (4) seeing (5) no error ① ② ③ ④ ⑤

19. (1) colonel (2) interceed (3) release (4) concurred (5) no error ① ② ③ ④ ⑤

20. (1) rheostat (2) tariff (3) trafic (4) vacuum (5) no error ① ② ③ ④ ⑤

PRACTICE VI **Directions:** In each of the following groups of sentences, find the sentence that is incorrect. If there is no error, choose option (5).

1. (1) Once the bill was defeated, it was too late to argue its merits. ① ② ③ ④ ⑤
   (2) In this decade of shortages, the large-scale waist of paper is outrageous.
   (3) During the 1992 election, Bill Clinton led the Democrats to victory.
   (4) The doorbell interrupted the two women before they ended their dispute.
   (5) No error

2. (1) The headlights of a solitary car shone down the deserted country road. ① ② ③ ④ ⑤
   (2) All of the museum's newest paintings were shone at the recent exhibition.
   (3) The weather vane is broken again.
   (4) Beneath his unruffled exterior were the falsely arrested gentleman's true feelings of rage.
   (5) No error

3. (1) Napoleon would not settle for a small piece of Europe. ① ② ③ ④ ⑤
   (2) The judge carefully weighed both arguments.
   (3) Crew is a sport in which races with rowboats take place.
   (4) Former Sentor Bill Bradley was once a principal player on the New York Knicks.
   (5) No error

4. (1) During the summer of 1994, many American families traveled to England. ① ② ③ ④ ⑤
(2) Many immigrants have had difficulty adapting to living in America.
(3) If you plan to film the entire Thanksgiving Day Parade, you'll need more than one real of film.
(4) Even an expert fisherman has, on occasion, lost a rod and reel.
(5) No error

5. (1) The United States had overlooked many acts of aggression by Germany toward other nations, until the Germans sank the *Lusitania*. ① ② ③ ④ ⑤
(2) Mark lifts weights every morning.
(3) My wait has dropped considerably since I've been on that diet.
(4) Phil refuses to wait in line for a movie, a show, or dinner.
(5) No error

6. (1) Some people enjoy camping. ① ② ③ ④ ⑤
(2) The sum of my camping experience is two days.
(3) Martha is too vane to travel without a mirror.
(4) All of our efforts were in vain because the project failed.
(5) No error

7. (1) A bird flew past the window. ① ② ③ ④ ⑤
(2) Ira is home with the flu.
(3) A squirrel was trapped in the chimney flu.
(4) Who let in all the flys?
(5) No error

8. (1) A female pig is called a sow. ① ② ③ ④ ⑤
(2) Jeannette cannot sew well at all.
(3) That gift is so nice!
(4) The ball crashed through the pain of glass.
(5) No error

9. (1) The old man could not walk without his cane. ① ② ③ ④ ⑤
(2) Sugar comes from sugarcane and sugar beets.
(3) After her promotion, Mary ordered new stationary.
(4) That sprained ankle caused me great pain.
(5) No error

10. (1) The bough was full of blossoms. ① ② ③ ④ ⑤
(2) Everyone cheered when the pitcher through the third strike.
(3) I don't like to sit in the bow of the boat.
(4) Suzy enjoys wearing bows in her hair.
(5) No error

11. (1) Do you like to walk in the rain? ① ② ③ ④ ⑤
(2) Have you ever seen a ewe?
(3) The canoe floated silently down the strait.
(4) Please, straighten your tie.
(5) No error

12. (1) Some girls will not marry because they are waiting for nights in shining armor. ① ② ③ ④ ⑤

(2) My favorite fish dinner is baked fillet of sole.
(3) Many poems have been written about the journeys of the soul.
(4) Because I was the sole tennis player in the group, I played a great deal of golf.
(5) No error

13. (1) Do you grate potatoes into that recipe? ① ② ③ ④ ⑤
(2) No, but I beet the eggs thoroughly.
(3) Have you tried beet soup?
(4) Yes, it's delicious.
(5) No error

14. (1) I am not fond of that newscaster. ① ② ③ ④ ⑤
(2) His manor is very offensive.
(3) Did you visit the Manor House at Batsto?
(4) In what manner would you like the idea presented?
(5) No error

15. (1) Since the meat shortage began, I've been freezing a great deal of meat. ① ② ③ ④ ⑤
(2) The article discussed the affect of radiation on cells.
(3) Please meet me at the florist.
(4) Lately, loud noises wear on my nerves.
(5) No error

SUMMARY OF RESULTS

After reviewing the Answer Key on page 292, chart your scores below for each practice section.

Practice Number	Your Number Right	Your Number Wrong (Including Omissions)	Acceptable Score
I			11 correct
II			5 correct
III			7 correct
IV			7 correct
V			15 correct
VI			11 correct

SKILLS ANALYSIS

To discover your areas for skill improvement, locate the question numbers you got wrong and circle them on this Skills Analysis chart. Then, refer to the chapters listed in column 3.

Skill	Question Number	Chapter Reference
Practice I		*See Chapter*
Double Negative	1, 9, 15	15
Unclear Pronoun Reference	2	15
Repetition	4, 11	15
Logic	3, 8	15
Wordiness	6, 7, 13	15

Skill	Question Number	Chapter Reference
Punctuation	5, 12	16
Coordination of Ideas	14	15
Practice II		
Coordination of Ideas	1, 2, 3, 4	15
Repetition	5, 6	15
Style	7	15
Practice III		
Quotation Marks	1, 2, 3, 6, 9	16
Parenthesis	4	16
Hyphen	5, 8	16
Apostrophe	7	16
Practice IV		
Capitalization	1 to 10	17
Practice V		
Spelling	1 to 20	18
Practice VI		
Word Usage	1 to 15	19

ANSWER KEY

Chapter 20

Cumulative Review

Practice I *Page 274.*

1. (2) I wasn't *ever* told to take this highway to your house.
   Never use *not* (n't) and *never* together.
2. (1) After giving the customer the change, *the clerk* heard the store's closing bell.
   Substitute *the clerk* for *he* in order to clarify who *heard*.
3. (3) Commenting on his theory, *the author* discussed the book.
   Commenting on his theory describes the *author*, not the book.
4. (1) *Our group visited* the museum to see a display of mobiles.
   We refers to *our group* and is, therefore, repetitious.
5. (1) I cancelled the meeting because I expected to be too busy to attend.
   . . . *because I expected to be too busy to attend* is not a complete thought. Use a semicolon to connect two complete thoughts.
6. (3) *He is absent* because he has the flu.
   Is because is an unacceptable form. The sentence reads more smoothly as corrected.
7. (1) *The sergeant wanted* to know what supplies the unit needed.
   What . . . was is poor form. The sentence reads more smoothly as corrected.
8. (2) *An insect is difficult to eliminate* after it has established itself in an area. OR Having established itself in an area, an insect is difficult to eliminate.
   Having established itself in an area describes *insect.*
9. (2) Why is it that nothing *ever* goes smoothly?
   Never use *nothing* and *never* together.
10. (5) No error
11. (1) *The football team played well yesterday.*
    Football and *at the football game* add wordiness and are not necessary.
12. (3) Herbert Hoover, a man of humble beginnings, was the son of a blacksmith.
    Commas precede and follow a group of words that describe the performer.
13. (2) *Primitive people relied on witch doctors because* these people feared attack by evil spirits.
    Was because is unacceptable form. The sentence reads more smoothly as corrected.
14. (1) *Because* I am exhausted, I plan to rest this afternoon.
    Although contradicts the intended meaning of the sentence.
    Because clarifies the meaning.
15. (4) Although it isn't *any* of my business, I'm concerned about your health.
    Never use *not (n't)* and *none* together.

Practice II *Page 279.*

1. (4) The mailman slipped on the steps *because they were icy.*
   Because they were icy explains, simply, why the mailman slipped on the steps. The word *because* makes the connection between the mailman's slipping and the icy steps.
2. (3) Jules continues to smoke *although smoking is hazardous to his health.*
   Although smoking is hazardous to his health shows that Jules continues to smoke despite the hazards.
3. (4) The camping trip was uncomfortable *because of the heat and the bugs.*
   Because of the heat and the bugs explains, simply, why the camping trip was uncomfortable. The word *because* makes the connection between the discomfort and the heat and the bugs.
4. (3) The Giants played well *even though the day was unseasonably hot.*

Even though the day was unseasonably hot shows that the Giants played well despite the heat.

5. (3) That man, who speaks at every meeting, *never offers a suggestion that we like.*
   Never offers a suggestion that we like is the only grammatically correct completion for this sentence.
6. (2) I'd like draperies made of a transparent fabric *that is durable.*
   That is durable is the only possible completion for this sentence. All other choices are grammatically incorrect and repetitive.
7. (4) My favorite scene in *Romeo and Juliet is the one in which Romeo kills himself.*
   Is the one in which Romeo kills himself is the only completion which conforms to correct style.

Practice III *Page 280.*

Turn to Chapter 16 for the appropriate rule.

1. (4) "Would you like to record the song you wrote?" the conductor asked the singer. See Rule 4, Quotation Marks.
2. (5) If you wish, you may pick some flowers—but only those along the side of the house—for your centerpiece. See Rule 1, Quotation Marks.
3. (4) "My favorite book," said Melissa, "is *Animal Farm.*" See Rules 1 and 2, Quotation Marks.
4. (5) The show (for which you have tickets) begins promptly at 7:45 P.M. and ends (believe it or not) at 11:00 P.M.. See Rule 12, Other Marks of Punctuation.
5. (2) Last Sunday, I met my ex-roommate (whom I haven't seen for twelve years) in the supermarket. See Rule 7, Other Marks of Punctuation.
6. (4) "After you've practiced writing r's," said Miss Green, "go right to the s's." See Rule 2, Quotation Marks.
7. (1) The Brownies' annual party was at the home of Jane Simpson on Friday, at 4:15 P.M. See Rule 9, Other Marks of Punctuation.
8. (1) Eighty-four of the members voted—despite last year's increase—to increase the dues for the next fiscal year. See Rule 5, Other Marks of Punctuation.
9. (3) The painter called this morning to say that he won't be able to begin working until next weekend. See Rule 1, Quotation Marks.

Practice IV *Page 283.*

1. Sue Anderson, the lead in *The Glass Menagerie*, is really a competent actress.
   Capitalize the complete title of a play, book, or long poem.
2. When you leave *school* today, take a bus and meet me in New York City.
   School is not capitalized, because it does not refer to a particular school.
3. Our course, *History IA*, will include discussion of the settlement of the American colonies.
   History IA is the name of a particular course and, therefore, should be capitalized.
4. Remember that Ellie said we should meet *her* for lunch on Tuesday.
   Never capitalize a pronoun unless it is the first word of a sentence or a quotation, or refers to the Deity.
5. No error
6. Mr. Goren reminded us, "*All* lights must be turned off in the laboratory at the end of the workday."
   All is the first word of the quotation and must be capitalized.
7. The lieutenant asked *Captain* John Forbes to cut the ribbon at the ceremonies marking the opening of Fort Titan.
   Captain refers to a particular captain, *Captain John Forbes*, and must be capitalized.
8. This October, *Halloween* falls on a Tuesday.
   Halloween is the name of a holiday and, therefore, must be capitalized.
9. "We can learn much," said Edith, "from the cultures of the *East*."
   East refers to a particular section of the world and, therefore, must be capitalized.

10. One of the earliest and most significant British documents is the *Magna Carta*. *Magna Carta* is the title of a document and, therefore, must be capitalized.

Practice V *Page 284.*

For explanations of the following answers, see the spelling rules in Chapter 18.

1. (2) overrated
2. (5) No error
3. (2) noticeable
4. (3) misspell
5. (3) precede
6. (4) thief
7. (4) weird
8. (3) conferring
9. (3) skies
10. (2) illegal
11. (4) x-rays
12. (3) 9's
13. (1) athletic
14. (2) mouthfuls
15. (3) tonnage
16. (5) no error
17. (1) contraltos
18. (2) knives
19. (2) intercede
20. (3) traffic

Practice VI *Page 286.*

For explanations of the following answers, see the list of commonly misused words (and examples) in Chapter 19.

1. (2) In this decade of shortages, the large-scale *waste* of paper is outrageous.
2. (2) All of the museum's newest paintings were *shown* at the recent exhibition.
3. (4) Former Senator Bill Bradley was once a *principal* player on the New York Knicks.
4. (3) If you plan to film the entire Thanksgiving Day Parade, you'll need more than one *reel* of film.
5. (3) My *weight* has dropped considerably since I've been on that diet.
6. (3) Martha is too *vain* to travel without a mirror.
7. (4) Who let in all the *flies*?
8. (4) The ball crashed through the *pane* of glass.
9. (3) After her promotion, Mary ordered new *stationery*.
10. (2) Everyone cheered when the pitcher *threw* the third strike.
11. (3) No error
12. (1) Some girls will not marry because they are waiting for *knights* in shining armor.
13. (2) No, but I *beat* the eggs thoroughly.
14. (2) His *manner* is very offensive.
15. (2) The article discussed the *effect* of radiation on cells.

21.
Writing Skills: Essays

"Your plan is brilliant, Von Rysbroeck!" I admitted, calmly aware of the whitening knuckle on his gun hand. "But I'm afraid you have overlooked one thing—namely, that where all beneficiaries of a trust established before 1949 reside, during a taxation year, in one country other than Canada and all amounts included in computing income of the trust for the taxation year were received from persons resident in that country, no tax is payable to a beneficiary as income of or from the trust; anyway, there is no eighth metatarsal bone, and furthermore, you have no gun."

—Patrick S. Finnegan
Victoria, British Columbia, Canada
from *Bride of Dark and Stormy*
compiled by Scott Rice

A Word With You . . .

The Bulwer-Lytton Fiction Contest, sponsored by San Jose University's English Department, is an annual event that asks entrants to write "the worst possible opening sentence to a novel." *Bride of Dark and Stormy* is a compilation of contest entries. We chose to share an entry with you to give you a chuckle and to emphasize the importance of the opposite style of writing—clear and concise.

No matter what your writing requirements are, whether for your job, a school assignment, a social occasion, or the essay part of the GED Writing Skills test, you need to know certain basic writing skills:

- how to write strong sentences
- how to prepare a well-developed paragraph
- how to plan a successful piece of writing

The discussions that follow on strong sentences and well-developed paragraphs will apply to many of your writing tasks. The last part of this chapter focuses on the essay, particularly as it occurs in the GED Writing Skills test.

Strong Sentences

We'll start with ways you can make some important improvements in the style of your sentences.

Strong Sentences Stress Important Ideas

Where you place an idea in a sentence determines its emphasis. One way to achieve emphasis is to place the key idea at the end of the sentence.

For example, look at the following two versions of a sentence that appeared in an article on especially livable cities in the United States. This particular section of the article emphasized the different kinds of people who occupy different sections of the city. Which sentence emphasizes the writer's main point?

1. The yuppiest part of town is Shadyview, a neighborhood at the northwestern corner of the city.
2. Shadyview, a neighborhood at the northwestern corner of the city, is the yuppiest part of town.

Sentence 2 clearly emphasizes that "yuppies" occupy this section of the city.

Now look at another example, this time from an essay that opens with a discussion of how humor in your life defuses stress. The essay continues with information about how humor provokes many *other* good results. Choose the author's next sentence from the two below:

1. Teamwork can also be fostered by humor.
2. Humor can also foster teamwork.

Remember that the idea you want to emphasize belongs at the end of the sentence. The emphasis here is on an additional, positive result of humor—teamwork. Sentence 2 is the better choice in this case.

PRACTICE

I **Directions:** Rewrite the following sentences, putting the more important idea at the end of each sentence.

1. Adults are 55 percent of the 500,000 annual visitors.
2. The Harvest Festival starts its national tour when fall leaves begin to change color and temperatures begin to cool.
3. Today's visitor to Alaska can see it more comfortably from the deck of a luxury cruise ship, while the early gold seekers endured great hardships.
4. Before the supplies run out, the assistant manager should replace them.
5. Almost everyone agrees that imagination can be developed as a skill, although few people agree upon the method of accomplishment.

Strong Sentences Eliminate Unnecessary Words

You want your reader to quickly understand your writing. One way to do this is to use only as many words as necessary—not one extra. In Chapter 15, you learned to eliminate word and phrase repetitions.

Example: The ~~*ancient*~~ *old* wall was typical of the best of New England Walls.

The wall is either ancient or old, but not both.

Example: *Because there were latecomers*, the concert was interrupted.

You can strengthen this sentence by changing the italicized part to one word followed by the action word *interrupted.*

Latecomers interrupted the concert.

Example: *So that we can* meet our production schedule, we'll need your engineering plans by February 1.

Strengthen this sentence, by using the word *To* in place of the italicized words.

To meet our production schedule, we'll need your engineering plans by February 1.

Example: Buy a suit *that is useful* for any occasion.

Simplify the sentence by eliminating unnecessary words.

Buy a suit useful for any occasion.

PRACTICE
II **Directions:** Trim away any unnecessary words in these sentences.

1. Our town council was looking for a new member who had experience.
(Hint: Change the form and placement of the word *experience*.)
2. Because there were many people who wanted to be heard, the meeting was made to run late.
3. The telephone company installed an extra phone, which was installed mainly for Dad.
4. So that we'll arrive at the meeting on time, we'll need to study the departure schedule.
(Hint: Start the sentence with *To*.)
5. Because there were updrafts, the flight was bumpy.

Strong Sentences Use Action Words

Whenever possible, use action words instead of the *linking word and action word* combination. Action words add vigor and interest to your writing and also help you to eliminate unnecessary words. Action words help you find the "lost" or buried subject.

Example: The medical plan *was offered* by the company.

How can you make this a stronger sentence, using *offered* as the action word? What is the subject of this sentence?

The company *offered* a medical plan.

Using the action word *offered* shortens and strengthens the sentence. Using the subject *the company* clarifies the meaning.

Look at another example:

For the newly arrived students, a tour of the school *was given*.

Change this to a stronger sentence.

The school *gave* a tour for the newly arrived students.

PRACTICE III

Directions: In the following sentences, change linking word and action word combinations to action words.

1. More than three garments at a time in the dressing room cannot be allowed. (Hint: Change *cannot be allowed* to *cannot allow*; then ask yourself, "Who cannot allow?" in order to find the subject of the new sentence.)
2. Thousands of these requests are received by people.
3. The inspector's number was placed in the coat pocket by us.
4. It is believed by nutritionists that cutting down on fat is the healthful thing to do.
5. A topic sentence is something most paragraphs have.

Strong Sentences Are Balanced

One way to make it easier for your reader to follow your ideas is to write balanced sentences. For a complete discussion of balanced sentences, turn back to Chapter 12, page 138. Following is a reminder of what makes a sentence *unbalanced:*

> Robert Todd Lincoln *practiced law* in Chicago, *presided as president* of the Pullman Company, and *he was a director* of various banks.

A balanced sentence is one in which *related actions, descriptions, or ideas are presented in the same form.* Which activity mentioned in the sentence about Lincoln is not in the same form? The last one is incorrect. The sentence should read:

> Robert Todd Lincoln *practiced law* in Chicago, *presided as president* of the Pullman Company, and *served as a director* of various banks.

In Chapter 12, also review the section on Coordinated Thoughts, page 145. Coordination of ideas is another test of an effective, balanced sentence.

INCORRECT: Jenna *not only played* tennis well, *but she also was* a low-handicap golfer.

CORRECT: Jenna *not only played* tennis well, *but also was* a low-handicap golfer.

Not only played is coordinate with but also was.

PRACTICE IV

Directions: Rewrite each sentence so that related ideas are expressed in the same form.

1. It is not only important to know your rights under the law, but you should think about your responsibilities.
2. To find an apartment, you can check your newspaper advertisements or ask your friends for leads, and there are always rental agencies which you can call.
3. Once you find an apartment you like, inspect it carefully, examine the plumbing and electricity, and you should check with other residents about the general living conditions.
4. When you buy a car, don't be misled by the advertised, artificially low interest rates, and then there are the other cost-shifting techniques.
5. Either look for a car dealer's legitimate low-interest factory rate, and sometimes you'll have to compare the rates offered by other lenders.

Well-Developed Paragraphs

The Topic Sentence

A paragraph is a group of sentences about one topic. To give the reader a clear idea of what it is about, the paragraph contains a *topic sentence.* Although topic sentences can appear, for variety and emphasis, in other parts of the paragraph, they are most frequently the first sentence in the paragraph. There are good reasons for that placement. First, it is the easiest way for the writer to develop the topic. Second, it gives the reader the most important idea immediately. Placed first, the topic sentence prepares the reader for what is to come.

Example:

> Decide to concentrate on the most important task first. From your list of 10 things to do on Monday, choose the most important and place it at the top of your list. Next to it, put a red star, the number 1, or the letter "A" to emphasize that this comes first. Once you decide what's most important, don't get stuck on minor tasks.

Were you able to locate the topic sentence in the sample paragraph? Yes, the first sentence presents the main idea and prepares the reader for what is to come. The paragraph develops by giving two examples of how to concentrate on major tasks.

PRACTICE V

Directions: Underline the topic sentence in each paragraph. Then restate the topic in your own words, following the hints that were given earlier in this chapter for composing strong, concise sentences.

1. Life today is full of pressures, and that is the reason why people try to offset these same pressures both with pleasurable activities and relaxation. While some devote their leisure time to physical exercise in the form of sports or fitness programs, others become involved in handicrafts, reading, or even restoring automobiles. Still other individuals see the value in planned relaxation, such as meditation or yoga.

Topic:

2. In the data it indicates that the damage to the crops is not limited to just one geographical area. Six states, as well as British Columbia, are involved. The greatest amount of damage, however, is distributed among Georgia, North Carolina, and Tennessee.

Topic:

3. Backache, which is one of the commonest of ailments, occurs partly as a result of our upright posture, partly because there are degenerative changes that occur in the spine, and partly from improper posture and muscle use. To begin with, our upright posture places the considerable weight of the upper body on the lower spine. Then from middle age on, arthritic and degenerative changes occur in the discs. Finally, slouch-

ing with abdominal muscles relaxed or picking up heavy objects by bending over with knees locked can stress the spine and cause pain.

Topic:

The Paragraph Plan

There are a number of ways to develop a paragraph. The way you word your topic sentence and the type of details included in the paragraph will depend upon the development plan you have chosen. A well-developed paragraph provides enough information to explain the topic, with every idea directly related to the topic sentence.

Some Methods of Paragraph Development

- *Defend the opinion* stated in the topic sentence.
- *Give examples or details* that explain the topic sentence.
- *Describe chronologically* [in time order] what the topic sentence states.
- *Define a word or explain a process* stated in the topic sentence.
- *Compare and contrast* two items stated in the topic sentence.
- *Link* the topic sentence to an earlier topic or one to come.

PRACTICE VI

Directions: Using the preceding list, label each paragraph according to its plan.

1. I feel that book censorship in the schools is a foolish and wasteful practice. For one thing, students can easily find these forbidden books elsewhere. Also, by censoring certain literature, we are depriving readers of an opportunity to broaden their thinking about the controversial contents of these books. We should not forget that qualified teachers not only instruct about literary styles, but also present the social attitudes of the times, together with the author's intent, thus helping the student to understand a book's controversial nature.
2. After World War II, Jacques-Ives Cousteau turned his atten-

tion to research on devices for underwater exploration. In 1943, with Émil Gagnan, Cousteau received great acclaim for his invention of the Aqualung, an underwater breathing apparatus. The Aqualung, which allows divers to spend prolonged periods underwater, is used in exploration, salvage operations, nautical archaeology, and recreational diving. Later, in 1959, with Jean Mollard, Cousteau invented the Diving Saucer, a highly maneuverable submarine in which several observers can film the ocean's depth.

3. The characteristics that help a plant survive in a particular environment are called adaptations. For example, in the desert environment, the widespread root system of the barrow cactus allows the plant to gather water after an infrequent rainstorm. Furthermore, the fleshy stem of the cactus is well adapted to store a large amount of water.

4. Used in the following way, a card system will keep your notes organized and prevent your retracing steps. Use at least two cards for each publication. On the first card, record the title, author, publisher, page number, catalog number, and date of publication for each book or periodical. Be sure to give each card a cross-reference number. Then, on your second (third, fourth, etc.) card, along with your research, write the cross-reference number from your title card.

5. Different people choose to make their purchases in a variety of stores and in different atmospheres. Perhaps you choose to do most of your buying in a particular store that has both a relaxed, comfortable atmosphere and personnel readily available to provide product information and a high degree of service and input. On the other hand, for others, that degree of service and input is the least important and, indeed, may be bothersome. Perhaps they, unlike you, like to shop in different stores and prefer to be left alone to read labels, browse, and make solitary decisions.

6. On the other hand, this same technology that provides an information and entertainment boon to the home viewer presents an ongoing problem for the producers and copyright owners. Questions arise. How will copyright owners be reimbursed for providing free programs? Is our existing copyright law obsolete since the private viewer has the ability to take

information that was meant to be shown only once? The old solutions to copyright infringement don't seem to apply.

Successful Essays

Although this part of the chapter is modeled after the essay portion (Part II) of the GED Writing Skills test, it offers useful instruction for any of your writing needs.

Four steps are involved in the creation of a successful essay:

1. *Think* about the topic or question.
2. *Plan* the essay. List one-, two-, or three-word notes or thoughts about the topic as they occur to you, or, preferably, use the clustering and mapping techniques described in the following pages. Remember not to edit your thoughts as you jot them down—let your ideas flow. Final steps in the planning process will be to organize your notes in logical order and to plan logical paragraph divisions.
3. *Write* the essay. Follow your notes to ensure that you stay on the topic.
4. *Revise* the essay.

The GED Writing Skills test allows 45 minutes to plan, write, and revise a 200-word essay; therefore, you have to apportion your time accordingly. A suggested schedule follows. This decision, of course, must be a personal one: You may need less than 20 minutes for writing and more time for planning. You will have an opportunity to find out later in this chapter when you are asked to compose essays.

1.	Read the test instructions and the topic. Underline key words and decide on your point of view.	4 minutes
2.	Plan the essay.	9 minutes
3.	Write the essay.	20 minutes
4.	Revise the essay.	12 minutes
	Total	45 minutes

Thinking

Reading the essay question carefully is essential to determining what the topic is and what you're asked to do. If you write on an unassigned topic, your essay will receive a failing grade. The essay question will ask you either to state an opinion and support it or to explain a process or situation. Since there are no right or wrong answers and the topics require no specialized knowledge, you simply establish your opinion or state your explanation as effectively as you can.

Begin by reading the question to understand the topic and to decide what you are asked to do. Underlining the key words in the question will help you.

PRACTICE VII **Directions:** Look at the sample essay topic that follows. Underline the key words that reveal the topic, as well as the words that tell you what to do. After you have finished underlining, take a moment to write the topic sentence. This sentence, placed in the introductory paragraph, sets the topic for the entire essay. Each paragraph thereafter must relate to this main topic.

Sample essay topic

Many people become involved in extracurricular activities such as music, sports, and politics. In working towards the goals of the group, such as performing well at a concert, winning a game, or organizing a rally, participants often experience personal growth.

In what ways can participation in these activities facilitate personal development? Write a composition of about 200 words explaining your answer. Provide reasons and examples to support your view.

Topic sentence:

Planning

Next, start your plan. Make notes (brainstorm) on the topic, listing—in any order or form—ideas that pop into your head. One-, two-, or three-word notes will do if they're meaningful to you. If you keep your proposed topic sentence in front of you as you brainstorm, you'll be more likely to stick to the subject. Listed below are three methods of preparing notes: horizontal listing; vertical listing; clustering and mapping. The first two methods are shown here in preliminary form. The third (clustering and mapping) is shown as it evolves to a more complete form.

Proposed Topic Sentence: Working with others to reach a goal develops personal skills.

1. Horizontal listing of notes

   Organization of time, communication skills, listening, healthful office environment, interpersonal skills, organize people, accept tasks, leadership ability, dealing with personalities.

2. Vertical listing of notes

   4. Organization of time. Enough time? Can I manage everything?
   3. Skills in dealing with personalities
   2. Leadership ability
   1. Communication skills
   1a. Listening, 1b speaking, etc.
   2. Learn to accept tasks
   4. Ability to organize people/equipment/paperwork, etc.

   ~~Healthful office environment.~~

   Check your notes to decide on a logical order of presentation. To keep your thoughts in order, assign each idea a number (see example under *vertical listing*). As you do this, it will become clear whether some ideas are unrelated. If so, cross them out. Note, too, where one idea is introduced, supported with detail, and concluded, and where a second idea begins. You're looking for the natural paragraph division in which only one main idea occupies a paragraph.

3. Clustering and mapping.

   Clustering: Draw a circle in the center of your paper. Write your proposed topic sentence in the circle. Now let your ideas flow. Put each idea on a separate spoke anywhere around the circle. Don't judge each thought; just write it.

The feature of the clustering procedure is that, as you put ideas on paper, you are concerned only with creating or thinking, not with correcting yourself as you proceed. (In this case, you decide *after* finishing the clustering exercise that, although a healthful office environment is an important issue, it is not related to the topic sentence. Therefore, you cross out the phrase.) In addition, clustering offers no opportunity to be stymied by having to think and create in numbered order as you do with an outline. Ordering ideas comes later. Consequently, you are able to generate ideas quickly, and with the application of a second step—mapping—you put your ideas into a usable form.

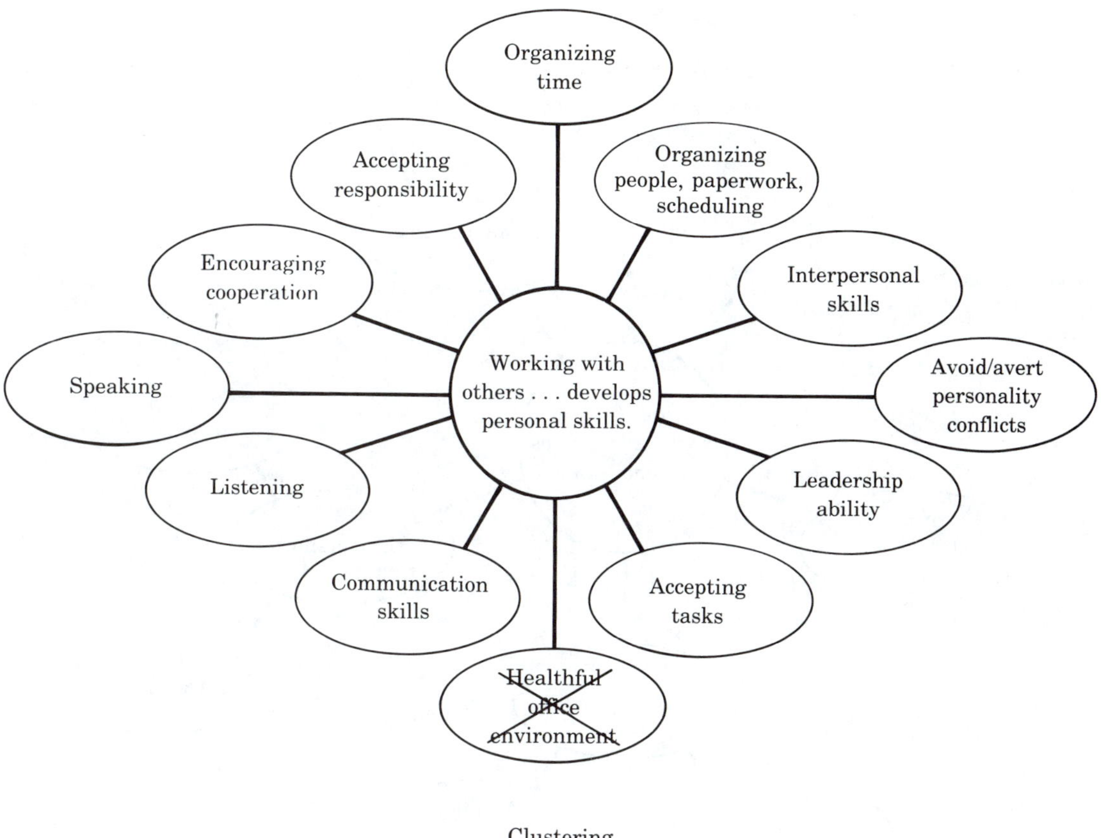

Clustering

Mapping: Several things occur to you as you map your ideas:

(1) You decide that, for you, *communication* is the most important skill in working with others. You assign the number (1) to that idea. You also see that *listening* and *speaking* are both part of communication.

(2) You decide that learning to accept assigned tasks is a corollary to accepting responsibility, and that both are part of *leadership* skills. All three items should be assigned a (2).

(3) You decide that encouraging cooperation and avoiding personality conflicts are *interpersonal skills*. You assign a (3) to those ideas.

(4) You notice that *organization* appears twice. You assign the number (4) to both circles because they are related ideas. Both will appear in one paragraph.

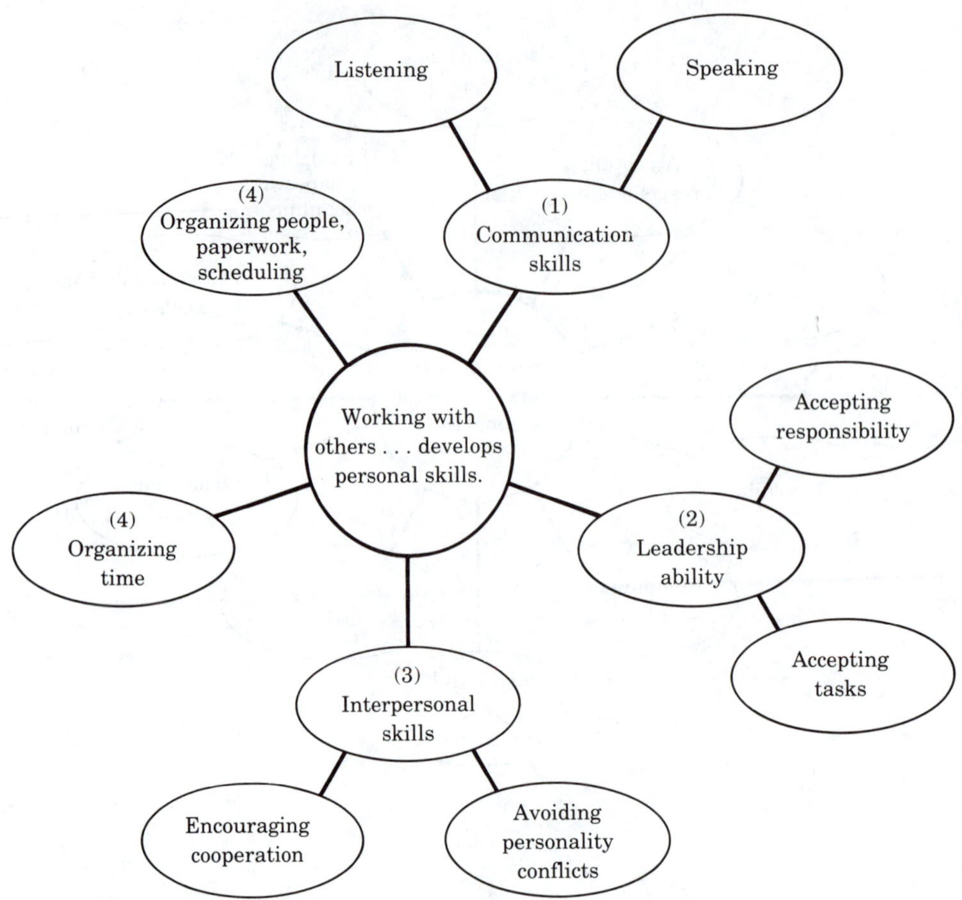

Mapping/Organizing Ideas

Now you can organize your final map, the one from which you will write your essay. By reviewing the decisions you just made in your preliminary map, you determine what main points the essay will cover: (1) communication skills, (2) leadership skills, (3) interpersonal skills, and (4) organizational skills. Each main point should be mentioned in your introductory paragraph. Furthermore, on the final map, each main idea should be shown on a spoke leading to examples supporting that idea. Note that, because of the introductory paragraph, the topic *communication skills* becomes paragraph (2).

A conclusion, the last paragraph, restating your position, brings the essay to an end. Note: Once you have become accustomed to planning this way, it takes only a few minutes to map your thinking.

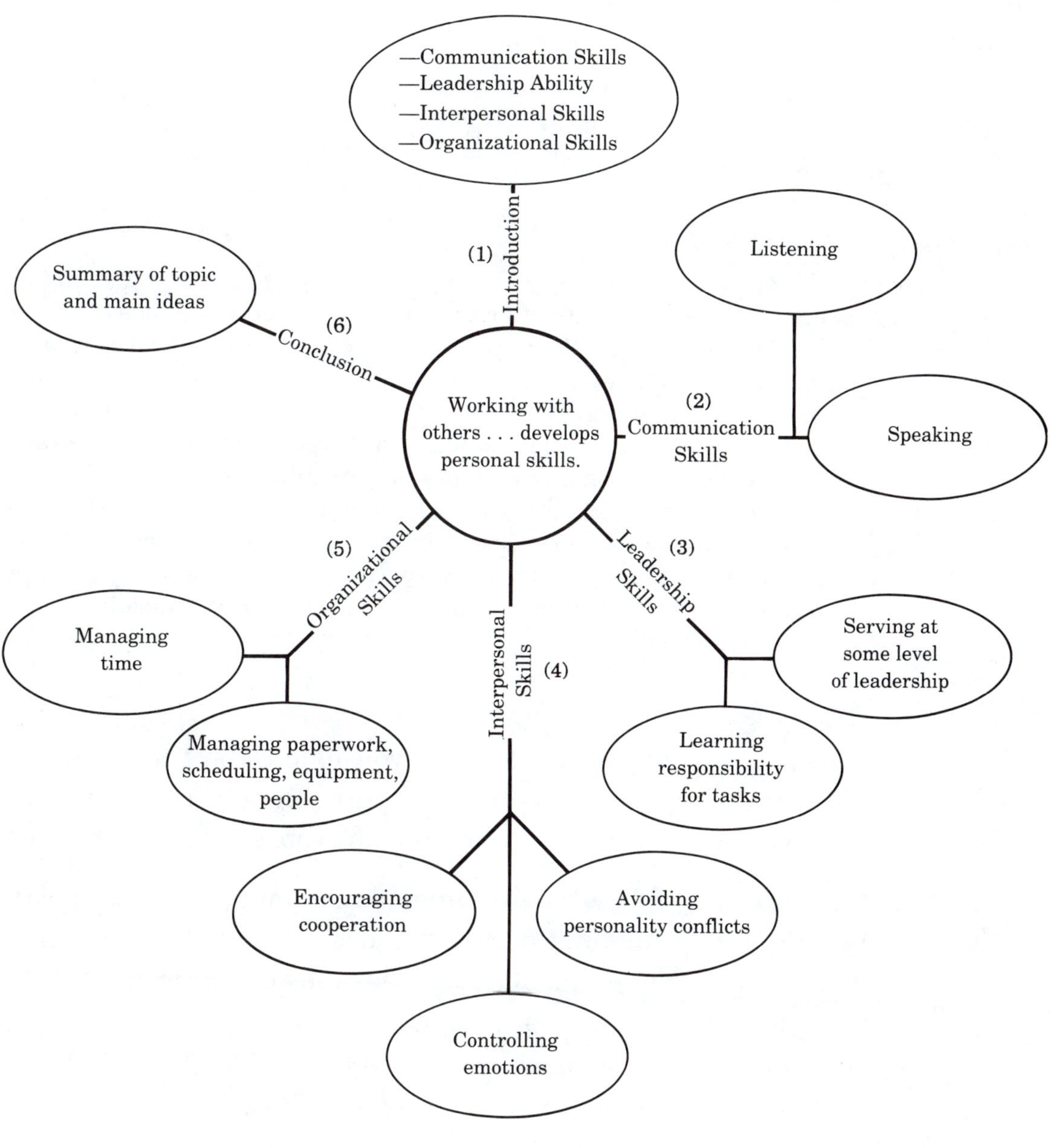

Final Map

Writing

After you have completed your final map (or outline), you are ready to begin writing your essay. Start with the topic sentence you composed for your essay assignment. Then look back at your final map or outline to see what ideas will support your topic sentence, and mention these in the introductory paragraph. In the next three or four paragraphs, for each supporting idea add details, explanations, examples. In your final paragraph, restate the main idea and your conclusion(s), using different words.

The order of your finished essay should follow this scheme:

First paragraph: Introduction

Paragraphs 2-4 (or more): Supporting details

Final Paragraph: Conclusion

PRACTICE VIII

Directions: Following the suggestions just given for writing an essay, take 20 minutes to compose a 200-word essay based on the final map on page 309. Begin with the topic sentence you composed for Practice VII (or use the sample one in the Answer Key on page 325). Then check the final map for supporting ideas (communication, leadership, interpersonal, and organizational skills), and include these in the introductory paragraph. In paragraph 2, write a topic sentence indicating the importance of communication skills in working with others. Continue with explanatory details. Write paragraphs 3, 4, and 5 in this way. In the final paragraph, restate, in new words, the essay's main point and your conclusion.

Revising

Don't forget step 4, revising your essay. If you follow the time schedule outlined earlier in this chapter, you will have approximately 12 minutes for revising and proofreading what you have written. Ask yourself these questions:

1. PLAN: Does your essay follow your original plan or map? Perhaps you did follow your plan or map but now find that the ideas could be arranged more effectively. Then move those misplaced paragraphs or sentences.
2. SUPPORT IDEAS: Are your ideas well supported? You may need to expand on an idea and add evidence to your argument. On the other hand, if you've gone beyond the subject matter in defending a point, you may need to shorten that paragraph or delete an entire section.
3. ACCOMPLISH YOUR PURPOSE: Have you accomplished your purpose? Did you demonstrate the main idea? Does your essay do what the test question asks—that is, does it present an opinion or an issue or explain something?
4. START OUT WITH THE CENTRAL POINT: Is there an opening paragraph? Does it contain the main idea of the essay?

5. SUPPORT THE CENTRAL POINT: Do the following paragraphs develop your point of view with supporting details?
6. RESTATE THE CENTRAL POINT: Does the final paragraph, in different words, restate and explain your central point of view.
7. CHECK FOR SENTENCE ERRORS: Are there sentence errors? Correct any run-on sentences and sentence fragments.
8. FOLLOW THE RULES OF AGREEMENT: Are action and linking words used correctly, according to the rules of time and number? Are there errors in pronoun usage?
9. CHOOSE THE MOST PRECISE WORDS: Have you chosen the correct, the most precise words? Is your meaning clear?
10. CHECK SPELLING, PUNCTUATION, AND CAPITALIZATION: Are the mechanics in order? Minor errors such as these can detract from the quality of your essay.

Now, review the entire essay to be sure that any changes you made did not create new problems.

PRACTICE IX

Directions: Read the topic below and review the essay which follows. As you do, keep in mind the four steps to writing a successful essay (Thinking, Planning, Writing, Revising) that you read about earlier in this chapter. Then, on a separate sheet of paper, rewrite the essay, making all necessary corrections. Watch for errors in grammar, word usage, sentence structure, and mechanics. Mapping the ideas in the essay will help you organize it for rewriting. After you have finished, compare your revision and map with the sample essay and map in the Answer Key.

Essay Topic:

Applying for a job can be an anxiety-producing event.

Describe a time when you applied for a job. Are your memories pleasant or unpleasant? Use examples and specifics.

Essay:

I have a stack of ads that I cut out, glued to index cards, and in response to which I have called or sent my resume. Usually, the eye-catching ads that offer the most highest starting salaries involves sales work. That's not, however, something I enjoy doing. As I learned in High School.

One job I really wanted was manager trainee in a bookstore. Part of the interview entailed a 30-page questionnaire. Question topics included corruption and drug abuse; employee theft; possible criminal record of applicant; and, my personal favorite, "Do you have any bad habits"? I had to say no. Sometimes, I wonder if having bad habits would have gotten me the job.

I am currently looking for a job, and finding more gray hairs then prospects. The classified's have become first on my reading list. After six weeks, I can tell at a glance which ads are new and which are *still* around. For instance, an ad for a Brazilian band was in for only two weeks. I almost regretted exchanging my drumsticks for a pen.

The job search, although a bit stressful, is not all bad. I am gaining a better understanding of me and my goals. My interviewing skills are improving. The cover letters I write now are more effective than it was when my job search began. All this, *and* I'm catching up on the "soaps"!

I had a job interview last week for an entry-level position at a publishing company. It went well, as far as I know. The personnel representative who I spoke with seemed impressed with myself and my resume. With the result that the resume and I was sent upstairs to speak with a higher-up. I am keeping my fingers crossed.

PRACTICE

X **Directions:** For each of the following topics, write a practice essay of about 200 words using the skills you have just learned. Try to observe the 45-minute time limit to plan, write, and revise your essay.

Topic 1:

With more and more women returning to the work force, day care has become an important issue.

Write an opinion essay for or against required day care. Should businesses be required to provide day care for employees with young children? Who should pay? the business? the parent(s)? the government? Choose a position and support it with specific details.

Topic 2:

Many suburban businesses are suffering because employees are not available. Cities, however, still have high unemployment rates. One solution to this joint problem would be mass transportation between cities and suburbs.

Write an opinion essay on this topic. Can such transportation feasibly be provided? What form should it take? Who should pay? the government? the employee? the employer? Support your opinion with specific details.

More Writing Skills: Letters and Memoranda

Writing takes many forms: letters, memos, reports, notes, lists, and books, to name just a few. Depending on your intention, the form you choose will determine the structure of your writing. We discuss letters and memos in the following pages.

Letters

In the age of audiovisual miracles, letter writing has become a forgotten art. When phones were not available to exchange news or greetings, letters were common. Because people wrote often, they wrote well.

We still need letters on occasion in our personal lives: thank you notes, condolence notes, letters to distant friends or relatives, and greetings of all kinds. Letter writing is also helpful when we want to request information, complain about a product, let our congressmen know our views, or apply for a job.

Another type of letter that has not been eliminated by the telephone is the business letter. Anyone who works for a business, large or small, should be able to write a clear business letter. While modern office technology may somewhat reduce the need for letters, it won't eliminate it. Although computer software—spellchecks and grammar-checks—override human error, the machines continue to be only as good as their operators.

This chapter will not attempt to deal with all the skills necessary to write a perfect letter. Elements such as grammar, spelling, and punctuation, covered earlier, play an important role. This chapter provides you with models and helpful hints for form and style.

Headings

Headings consist of your address, the date, the name and address of the recipient, and the salutation or greeting. Business letters include each of these elements (see Sample Business Letter on page 317). However, when writing to a friend or relative, your address and the recipient's address need not be included. The sample letters later in the chapter will show you the correct formats to use for both informal letters and business letters.

Part of the heading is the salutation or greeting—the "Dear [Somebody]." Changes in language usage and business itself have made "Dear [Somebody]" increasingly complicated. Once upon a time, if you were addressing an unknown group, the term "Gentlemen:" was appropriate. Today, those gentlemen include women who would not take kindly to that greeting. Often, business people sign letters that give no clue to the signator's gender. For example: "T. Warren" or "Terry Smith." "Ladies and Gentlemen:," "Dear T. Warren:," or "Dear XYZ Company:" could replace more conventional salutations. Some sample salutations follow:

FRIENDLY SALUTATIONS	FORMAL SALUTATIONS
Dear Aunt Sue,	Gentlemen:
Dear Rosa,	Dear Sir:
Dearest William,	Dear Sirs:
	Dear Mr. Wright:
	Dear Ms. Smith:
	Dear Dr. Schwarz:
	Dear Director of Personnel:
	Dear Salespeople:
	Ladies and Gentlemen:
	Dear T. Warren:
	Dear XYZ Company:

Introduction, Body, Conclusion

Since your opening paragraph is like a first meeting with your reader, the impression you make is a lasting one. The reader expects to have your purpose revealed. Whether it is to complain, compliment, or inform, it should be clear immediately.

Throughout the letter, say what you want to say as clearly and as briefly as possible. Your letter may be long, but it should not ramble. Every sentence should be a necessary one.

The traditional interviewer-reporter questions help keep a letter clear and concise. Note which questions apply to your letter: *who, what, when, where, why*. If you answer these questions, you will probably give all the necessary information for situations ranging from a party invitation to a complaint about a broken radio.

Just as your first impression is a lasting one, so is your final one. Make sure your reader knows what you expect. If you plan a follow-up phone call, say so and say when. If you want a written or telephone response, ask for it. If you began the letter by thanking the person, reinforce your appreciation in the final paragraph.

Closings

Closings range from "Love," to "Very truly yours," depending upon the purpose and audience of your letter. The closing should be in the same style as the salutation. A letter would not begin "Dear Sir:" and end with "Love."

FRIENDLY CLOSINGS	FORMAL CLOSINGS
Sincerely,	Very truly yours,
Warmly,	Yours very truly,
With Love,	Yours truly,
Love,	Sincerely yours,
Fondly,	Yours sincerely,
Warmest regards,	Sincerely,
(Any other nice thought	Respectfully yours,
you may want to use)	Very respectfully yours,
	Yours respectfully,

Business Letter Format

Sender's Address:

This is obviously not necessary on printed stationery. If your letter will be on plain paper, place your address in the upper right-hand corner or upper left.

Date:

Spell out the month in a business letter. Date can be right or left, but it must be aligned with the recipient's address and closing. In this age of personal computers many people keep their letters "flush left." Everything lines up with the left margin.

Recipient's Address:

On the left-hand side of the page, include the name (and title or position if you know it) of the person to whom you are writing. Then, put the name of the company or organization and, finally, the complete address of the organization.

Salutation:

See page 314 for examples of formal salutations.

Introduction:

One short paragraph states the subject or purpose of the letter. Make your purpose clear immediately.

Body:

One, two, three or more paragraphs contain the relevant details. Each paragraph should expand on one main point.

Conclusion:

The conclusion should give direction. One short paragraph finishes the letter with a summary, a recommendation, an instruction, or a thank you.

Closing:

See page 315 for formal closings.

Name and Signature:

Business form dictates typing your name and title beneath your signature. If your title is on your letterhead, do not repeat it. If you are hand writing a business letter as a consumer, print your name beneath your signature. You want the response addressed to you correctly. Name and signature should be aligned with the date and closing.

Sample Personal Letter

July 15, 1988

Dear Aunt Polly,

Thank you so much for the leather-bound dictionary. It was a perfect graduation gift. I will treasure it always.

My family and I were sorry you couldn't come to Arizona for the graduation and party. We all missed you very much. I'm enclosing some photos for you.

Love,
David

Sample Business Letter

ABC Corporation

---

231 West 53 Street, New York, New York 10022

July 10, 1995

Ms. Cary Jeffers
66 Columbus Avenue
Tarrytown, New York 10571

Dear Ms. Jeffers:

Thank you for your resume and letter (dated June 25, 1995), asking about employment opportunities at the ABC Corporation. Because we receive so many unsolicited requests each year, we must limit interviews to those with relevant work experience. While your resume indicates a strong manufacturing background, you have no experience with our specialized product.

Thank you for considering ABC Corporation. We wish you every success in your employment search.

Very truly yours,

David Green

David Green
Personnel Director
DG/sl

Sample Complaint Letter

106 Goodtree Drive
Columbus, Ohio 43201
March 10, 1995

Mr. William Wellington, President
Cool-It, Inc.
738 Second Avenue
New York, New York 10017

Dear Mr. Wellington:

On February 23, 1995, while a local Cool-It, Inc., representative was servicing my air-conditioner, the tank of freon exploded in my basement. The tank was located next to my clothes dryer, so this explosion caused damage to my dryer as well as some clothing that was in the dryer at the time. This event led to an expensive dryer service call and the need to replace a complete load of laundry. I would appreciate full reimbursement for the items listed on the attached bills.

The serviceman who repaired the dryer suggested that the malfunction was mostly caused by the freon. The spilled freon permanently froze the dryer thermostat, preventing the dryer from cooling down. A full load of towels and underwear that were in the dryer at the time became excessively dried out to the point of disintegration. In fact, when I removed the laundry from the dryer, the laundry fell apart in my hands. Prior to the explosion, the load of laundry was fine and the dryer worked perfectly.

I've always had an excellent relationship with your company and look forward to your continuing service. Your representative, by the way, was courteous and thorough in his job of repairing the air-conditioning system. I look forward to your payment within a reasonable amount of time.

Thank you.

Sincerely,
Mary Edwards
Mary Edwards

PRACTICE XI **Directions:** Read the following facts and write a letter of complaint from Tom Williams based on those facts. You can include your opinion or attitude toward the problem in the letter.

Tom Williams bought a clock radio at Warren's Department Store on May 15, 1995. Tom could not get the alarm to work properly from the start. He brought the clock radio back to the store on May 19, 1995, and was told he would have to mail the item to the manufacturer for repair. Tom lives at 1419 Maple Street, Dayton, Ohio 82050. The clock radio was made by the Wake-Up Corporation located at 2042 Main Street, Chicago, Illinois 60791.

PRACTICE XII **Directions:** Rewrite Matthew Manager's letter: Remember to write simply and clearly.

February 10, 1995

Ms. Suzanne Jones
1 Willow Way
Edison, New Jersey 08817

Dear Ms. Jones:

I wish to thank you for choosing to inform me about the incident which occurred at MarketRite last Friday. It is important to us in management to know what is going on when salespeople help—or don't help—as the case may be customers.

John Rich is usually a generally friendly person. He has been under very extreme personal pressure even though that should not enter into it. I have taken the liberty of speaking with John and am assured that what happened to you won't happen again at least from him.

Please be kind enough to accept the enclosed herewith gift certificate as a small token of our regret.

Thank you for shopping at MarketRite.

Sincerely,

Matthew Manager

Matthew Manager
Vice President
Customer Relations

Memoranda

A memorandum is commonly used for interoffice communications, such as sharing information, setting procedures, or asking questions within a company or organization. Every business has its preferred style for memos, but the tips that follow can be applied in most situations. Treat a memo as you would any other kind of writing. Plan ahead, and then construct clear and concise sentences that convey your intentions. Either write a brief outline or jot down phrases that will help you organize your thinking. Stick to the subject at hand. State your purpose first, then give all the necessary facts. Tell what you want done or request information. If you are informing the reader, do so simply and clearly, keeping your tone friendly and positive. A memo need not be an edict. Simply answer the question, "What do I want to accomplish?" Again, make sure that what you say is accurate because memos, when filed, become records.

Format for Memos

Although a memo is very much like a letter in purpose, its format is different. It is not signed at the bottom the way a letter would be. Instead, the sender initials the memo next to his or her name at the top. Sometimes, for security reasons, companies require full signatures on memos.

Note the structure of sample memo 1 on page 321. The opening gets right to the point. Helms recalls that he and Sperry have agreed that there is a potential problem. The memo proposes a solution. For emphasis, the solution is set off—highlighted—in its own paragraph. Other ways to visually emphasize ideas include using numbers, letters, headings, or bullets (black dots) at the left-hand margin. The final two sentences tell the reader what to do.

Note also that job titles appear next to the names. These titles can be omitted in very informal memos. However, memos that will be filed for future reference should have the titles included.

Sample memo 2 is a very informal one between two co-workers. No last names appear in the heading, and without these names, the memo would be almost useless as a record. Mary gets to the point immediately, however, noting co-responsibility for coordinating the company's calendar and letting Pat know the times during the week that she will be available. Mary then tells Pat what to do—that is, to decide on a convenient time to work together.

Sample Memo 1

MEMORANDUM

TO: Janice Sperry, Vice President, Marketing
FROM: Rob Helms, Purchasing Agent
DATE: July 10, 1995
SUBJECT: Purchase Agreement #47

When we spoke last Thursday, we agreed that the above purchase agreement #47 was vague and could cause problems with the completed job. I propose the following changes:

1. Delete lines 4–7.
2. Insert the following in place of lines 2–7: "The seller is under no obligation to accept returned merchandise 90 days after delivery."

Let me know by the 15th if you agree with these changes or have another suggestion. Thank you.

RH:cd

Sample Memo 2

MEMO

TO: Pat
FROM: Mary
DATE: November 3, 1994
SUBJECT: Company Calendar

You and I are responsible for coordinating the company calendar. I'm available any morning next week. Please let me know the day and time convenient for you.

Now read sample memo 3. Does it meet all the requirements of a well-written memo? Yes. This short memo gets the job done. The subject is clearly stated in the SUBJECT line. In the first sentence, the reader learns the new due date and what has to be done. Sentences 2 and 3 show the writer's concern for Bill Greenway's well-being. There is nothing wrong with a personal touch. One improvement would be to include the job titles and/or department names.

Sample Memo 3

FROM THE DESK OF JOHN SMITH:

TO: Bill Greenway
DATE: December 10, 1994
SUBJECT: Monthly Report

You should be pleased to know that your December monthly report will not be due until January 7, 1995. This extension should make your vacation a little more relaxing. Enjoy the holidays.

Long Memos

Sometimes you will need to write a longer memo. For example, you may want to provide background information related to the subject, as well as give current information. Read sample memo 4 on page 323 and note how the need dictates form. In this memo, the introduction explains the background of Dr. Taylor's idea. The first part of the memo tells what the writer intends to do. The memo then asks Martin Atkins, the reader, to do three things: read, select, and estimate. The memo concludes with a due date. It is effective and should result in Dr. Taylor's getting what he wants.

Disciplinary Memos

If you find it necessary to write a disciplinary memo, bear in mind that a disciplinary memo must:

- document inappropriate or unacceptable behavior
- focus on the serious effect of such behavior
- establish guidelines for future behavior
- state consequences of continued inappropriate behavior
- schedule a follow up review of progress

Sample Memo 4

MEMO

TO:	Martin Atkins, Director of Rehabilitation Services
FROM:	Bruce Taylor, M.D., Hospital Administrator
DATE:	June 10, 1994
SUBJECT:	Development of a hortitherapy program for patients

At the recent Hospital Directors' Round Table, Dr. Seymour Watson of the New England Hortitherapy Council gave a speech on the positive results achieved with hospitalized patients who had been taking care of plants. He further explained the long-term benefits of hortitherapy, especially its continued use after the patient's discharge.

Dr. Watson gave me some guidelines on raising funds for such a project. I plan to survey the board to see how much money could be made available for our own hortitherapy program.

I've attached Dr. Watson's studies, "The Use of Hortitherapy in Geriatric Settings," "Hortitherapy in a Psychiatric Setting," and "Outpatient Programs in Hortitherapy." Please study these and decide which approach we could use at Sunnycrest.

After you decide which patients would benefit most from the program, estimate what personnel and supplies would cost for 20 patients. I'll need your cost estimates by July 16, 1994, so that I can review them before presenting my report to the Board of Directors on July 30.

BT:sz

PRACTICE XIII

Directions: Rewrite the memo below to conform with the guidelines for a disciplinary memo.

Memo

TO:	Edna Employee
FROM:	Sandy Supervisor
DATE:	March 25, 1995

We talked today about your being late a lot lately. This is not the way we do things around here. It makes it look like you don't care about your job, and other people complain about it.

The next time you're late it could be serious.

PRACTICE XIV

Directions: Write an appropriate memo for each situation below.

1. From a supervisor in the order department to the inventory control manager, noting a shortage in a recent shipment to a key client.
2. From a supervisor, who plans to be away, to an employee designated to cover that supervisor's duties during that time.

ANSWER KEY

Chapter 21

Writing Skills: Essays

Practice I *Page 296.*

1. Fifty-five percent of the 500,000 annual visitors are adults.
2. When fall leaves begin to change color and temperatures begin to cool, the Harvest Festival starts its national tour.
3. While the early gold seekers endured great hardship, today's visitor to Alaska can see it more comfortably from the deck of a luxury cruise ship.
4. The assistant manager should replace the supplies before they run out.
5. Although few people agree upon the method of accomplishment, almost everyone agrees that imagination can be developed as a skill.

Practice II *Page 298.*

Answers may vary.

1. Our town council was looking for a new, experienced member.
2. Because there were many people who wanted to be heard, the meeting ran late.
3. The telephone company installed an extra phone, mainly for Dad.
4. To arrive at the meeting on time, we'll need to study the departure schedule.
5. Updrafts made the flight bumpy.

Practice III *Page 299.*

1. We [or the store] cannot allow more than three garments at a time in the dressing room.
2. People receive thousands of these requests.
3. We placed the inspector's number in the coat pocket.
4. Nutritionists believe that cutting down on fat is the healthful thing to do.
5. Most paragraphs have a topic sentence.

Practice IV *Page 300.*

Answers may vary.

1. It is important to know not only your rights under the law, but also your responsibilities.
2. To find an apartment, you can check the newspaper advertisements, ask your friends for leads, or call rental agencies.
3. Once you find an apartment you like, inspect it carefully, examine the plumbing and electricity, and check with other residents about the general living conditions.
4. When you buy a car, don't be misled by the advertised, artificially low interest rates or the other cost-shifting techniques.
5. Either look for a car dealer's legitimate low-interest factory rate, or compare the rates offered by other lenders.

Practice V *Page 301.*

1. *Topic:* To defuse the many pressures of modern life, people participate in a variety of leisure activities and planned relaxation.

2. *Topic:* The data indicate that the crop damage is not limited to one geographical area.
3. *Topic:* Backache, one of the most common ailments, results from three things: our upright posture, degenerative changes in the spine, and improper posture and muscle use.

Practice VI *Page 302.*

1. Defends the opinion stated in the topic sentence.
2. Describes chronologically what the topic sentence states.
3. Explains a process stated in the topic sentence.
4. Gives details that explain the topic sentence.
5. Contrasts the items stated in the topic sentence.
6. Links the topic sentence to an earlier topic.

Practice VII *Page 305.*

Suggested underlining:

Many people become involved in extracurricular activities such as music, sports, and politics. In working towards the goals of the group, such as performing well at a concert, winning a game, or organizing a rally, participants often experience personal growth.

In what ways can participation in these activities facilitate personal development? Write a composition of about 200 words explaining your answer. Provide reasons and examples to support your view.

Sample topic sentence: Working closely with others to achieve a common goal often facilitates personal development in several areas. (Answers will vary.)

Practice VIII *Page 310.*

Answers will vary.

Sample essay:

Working closely with others to achieve a common goal often facilitates personal development in several areas. Various skills are required for successful group interactions: the art of communication; leadership ability; skill in interpersonal relationships; and organizational skills.

Effective listening and communication skills are important factors in working well with others. In a group situation, participants learn how to communicate effectively, a two-way street that entails not only expressing one's thoughts, but also listening to understand.

In organizations, there are frequently various levels of leadership opportunities that members may choose to accept. For example, a drama club may have—in addition to the executive officers—board members, committee chairmen, and a stage or business manager. Every member, however, learns responsibility for performing certain tasks.

Interpersonal skills play a vital role in the successful operation of a group. Cooperation promotes efficiency and good will, as does learning to control emotions and to avoid or avert personality conflicts.

Developing organizational skills is another benefit of working with others. Active participants learn to manage their time, balancing practice, performances, or meetings with school or work commitments. They can also learn to improve other organizational skills by assuming responsibility for paperwork, scheduling, equipment, or management of a subgroup.

Therefore, if you want to experience personal growth in a variety of ways while at the same time having fun, join a group of your choice, be an active participant, and enjoy!

Practice IX *Page 311.*

Answers will vary.

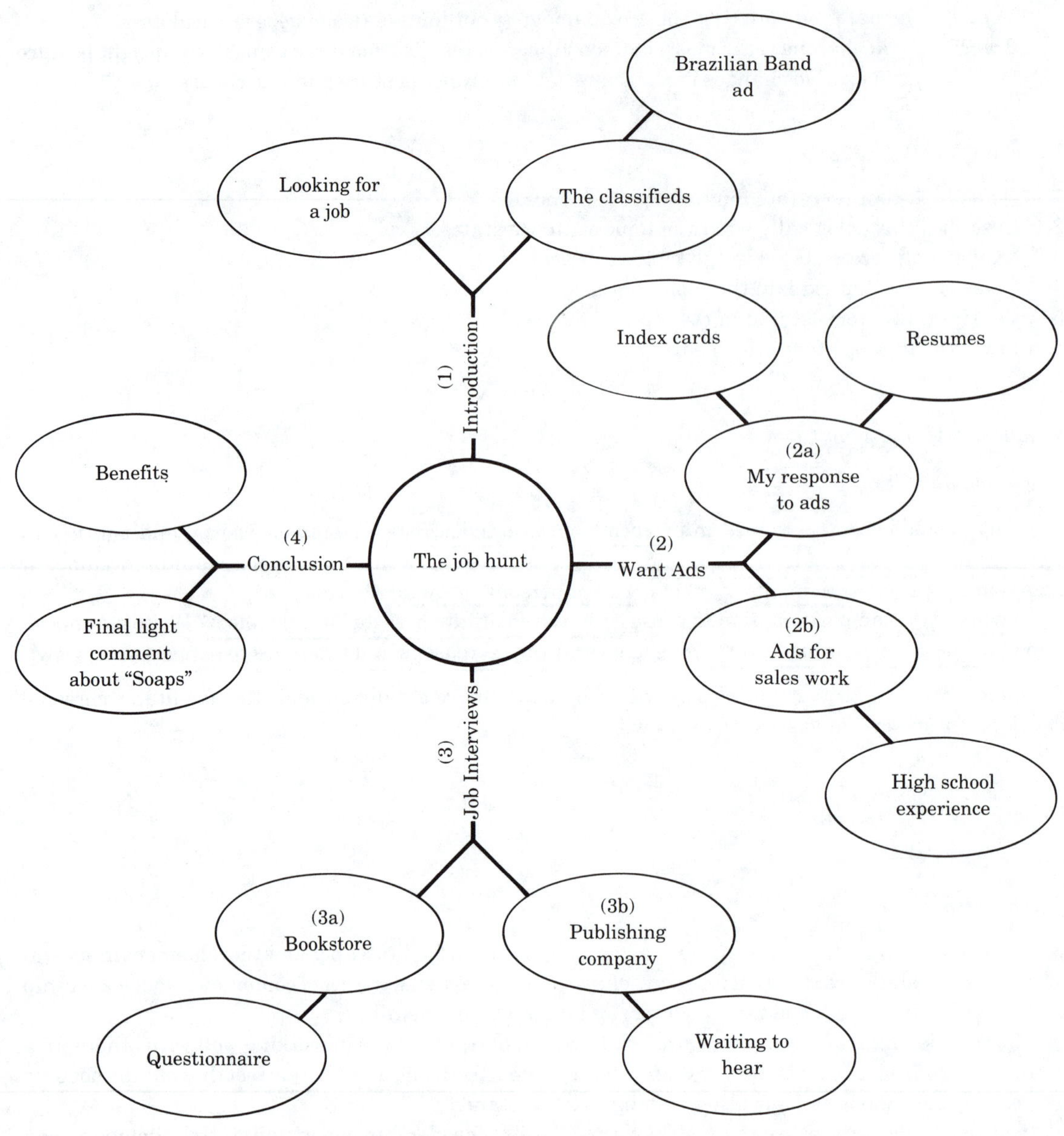

Sample Map:

Sample essay:

I am currently looking for a job and finding more gray hairs *than* prospects. The *classifieds* have become first on my reading list. After six weeks, I can tell at a glance which ads are new and which are *still* around. For instance, an ad for a Brazilian band was in for only two weeks. I almost regretted exchanging my drumsticks for a pen.

I have a stack of ads that I cut *out and glued to index cards. I have responded to each by calling or sending* my resume.

Usually, the eye-catching ads that offer the *highest* starting salaries *involve* sales work. That's not, however, something I enjoy doing, as I learned in *h*igh *s*chool. I was not an effective salesperson of chocolate bunnies for the Italian Club or peanut chewies for the band. [This last sentence adds an example for the previous statement.]

One job I really wanted was manager trainee in a bookstore. Part of the interview entailed a 30-page questionnaire. Question topics included corruption and drug abuse; employee theft; possible criminal record of applicant; and, my personal favorite, "Do you have any bad habits?" I had to say no. Sometimes, I wonder if having bad habits would have gotten me the job.

I had *an interview* last week for an entry-level position at a publishing company. It went well, as far as I know. The personnel representative *whom* I spoke with seemed impressed with *me* and my resume. *As a* result, the resume and I *were* sent upstairs to speak with a higher-up. I am keeping my fingers crossed.

The job search, although a bit stressful, is not all bad. I am gaining a better understanding of *myself* and my goals. My interviewing skills are improving. The cover letters I write now are more effective than *they were* when my job search began. All this, *and* I'm catching up on the "soaps"!

Practice X *Page 312.*
Answers will vary.

Sample essays:

Topic 1: Today, day care is no longer a luxury; it is a necessity. Two-wage-earner and single-parent families are common in our modern economy. Yet, there is a shortage of available, affordable day care. The solution must be a joint effort by government, business, and families participating in the program.

Many families require two wage earners just to provide the basic needs. Other families need two wage earners to reach beyond the basic needs in order to provide better-quality homes, education, and social needs. Many single parents must provide both child care and dollar support. For all these families, day care is a requirement.

The major issues facing those in need of day-care services are availability and affordability. Businesses should either provide on-site programs for a reasonable fee or encourage the establishment of day-care centers conveniently located for their workers. These off-site centers could be subsidized by a partnership of business, government, and the families using the service.

In our modern economy, where both parents work or a single parent heads the family, day care has, indeed, become a necessity. To solve the problems of availability and affordability requires a cooperative effort by business, family, and government.

Topic 2: The dual problems of lack of employees to fill jobs in the suburbs and high unemployment in the cities could be alleviated by providing mass transportation between city and suburb. Suburban businesses could work together with government to establish a transit system affordable to the average worker. Business, workers, and the government would all benefit.

The current plight of the business community has two faces. One is a suburb with new office buildings, restaurants, industrial parks, and shopping malls—and no workers to fill available positions. The other is a city being vacated by business and industry and plagued by unemployment. Each has problems. The suburb has businesses nearly failing or even closing because they lack help. The city has people eager to work but unable to, because they lack local employment or transportation to a suburban job.

Suburban businesses can help themselves and their neighbors by working with government to establish a transit system between city and suburb. The form it can take—bus or rail line—will depend on the unique situation of each city and its suburb. Each employer within an area could contribute a set amount, to be supplemented with local, state and/or federal funds. Workers would pay a minimal but reasonable transportation fee.

A mass transit system between city and suburb would benefit everyone concerned. Suburban businesses would remain open; the urban unemployed would find work; and the role of government as service and financial provider to the unemployed would decrease.

Practice XI

1419 Maple Street
Dayton, Ohio 82050
May 20, 1995

Service Manager
Wake-Up Corporation
2042 Main Street
Chicago, Illinois 60791

Dear Service Manager:

I bought the enclosed clock radio at Warren's Department Store in Dayton, Ohio, on May 15, 1995. The alarm did not work properly from the start.

On May 19, I brought the clock radio back to Warren's to exchange it for a new model or to have it repaired. The salesman would not accept the clock radio. He insisted that I return it to you. This is a great inconvenience. I never even used this appliance.

Please send me a new clock radio immediately. I also would encourage you to work out a fairer arrangement with your distributors. I know I would never buy a Wake-Up product again because of the inconvenience.

Very truly yours,

Tom Williams

Tom Williams

Practice XII

February 10, 1995

Ms. Suzanne Jones
1 Willow Way
Edison, New Jersey 08817

Dear Ms. Jones:

Thank you for informing me about the unfortunate experience you had at MarketRite last Friday. You clearly understand the importance of sharing such information with management. We do want to make our shopping environment pleasant.

The treatment you received was inexcusable. John Rich surprised and embarrassed himself by yelling at you. Although that behavior was not typical, it never should have occurred at all. Of course, I have spoken with John and extend his personal apology.

Please accept the enclosed gift certificate and my apology. You are our valued customer. When you are in MarketRite again, please ask for me. I would like to thank you personally for helping us improve our service.

Sincerely,

Matthew Manager

Matthew Manager
Vice President
Customer Relations

MM:er
enc.

22.
Practice Examination

This sample examination follows the format of the Writing Skills parts of the Tests of General Educational Development and aims to give the test-taker practice in the type and level of questions found in the official test. The questions encompass all of the concepts presented in *Grammar—in Plain English,* Chapters 1-21:

- Usage
- Punctuation
- Effective Expression
- Capitalization
- Spelling

An Answer Key is provided at the end of this chapter.

WRITING SKILLS TEST, PART I

Directions*

55 Items

The Writing Skills Test is intended to measure your ability to use clear and effective English. It is a test of English as it should be written, not as it might be spoken. This test includes both multiple-choice questions and an essay. These directions apply only to the multiple-choice section; a separate set of directions is given for the essay.

The multiple-choice section consists of paragraphs with numbered sentences. Some of the sentences contain errors in sentence structure, usage, or mechanics (spelling, punctuation, and capitalization). After reading the numbered sentences, answer the multiple-choice questions that follow. Some questions refer to sentences that are correct as written. The best answer for these questions is the one which leaves the sentence as originally written. The best answer for some questions is the one which produces a sentence that is con-

*These directions are reprinted from *The Official Teacher's Guide to the Tests of General Educational Development* with permission from the American Council on Education.

sistent with the verb tense and point of view used throughout the paragraph.

You should spend no more than 75 minutes on the multiple-choice questions and 45 minutes on your essay. Work carefully, but do not spend too much time on any one question. You may begin working on the essay part of this test as soon as you complete the multiple-choice section.

To record your answers, mark one numbered space beside the number that corresponds to the question in the test.

FOR EXAMPLE:

Sentence 1: **We were all honored to meet governor Phillips.**

What correction should be made to this sentence?

① ② ❸ ④ ⑤

(1) insert a comma after honored
(2) change the spelling of honored to honered
(3) change governor to Governor
(4) replace were with was
(5) no correction is necessary

In this example, the word "governor" should be capitalized; therefore, answer space 3 would be marked.

Directions: Choose the one best answer to each item.

Items 1 to 6 refer to the following paragraphs.

(1) One of the most commonly heard New Year's resolutions is, "this year I'm going on a diet." (2) As a matter of fact, from studies, we know that millions of people go on diets each year, unfortunately, 95 percent of the dieters regain the weight they've lost. (3) It's no wonder that experts in diet and health care have devoted many studies to finding diets that work.

(4) One of the interesting conclusions that some experts have reached is that families that diet together have a greater chance of success. (5) Logically, if everyone in a household is watching calories, there's likely to be much less junk food brought into the house. (6) And what about creative, healthful menus? (7) Chances are that someone in the family will have a new and better idea just when they need it. (8) One family diet program, for example, tags foods as they enter the house: red for high-fat, high-calorie foods such as candy, ice cream,

and chips, yellow for medium-calorie foods such as poultry, bread, and low-fat dairy products; green for the low-calorie foods that can be eaten at any time, such as vegetables, some fruits, and unbuttered popcorn. (9) The colors are a constant reminder of a low-fat, low-calorie diet. (10) Finally, remember this. (11) The idea that children grow leaner as they grow taller is a myth. (12) Their participation now in a healthful eating plan may prevent them from dieting later.

1. Sentence 1: **One of the most commonly heard New Year's resolutions is, "this year I'm going on a diet."**

   What correction should be made to this sentence?

   ① ② ③ ④ ⑤

   (1) remove One of
   (2) change commonly to common
   (3) change New Year's to new year's
   (4) replace the comma after is with a semicolon
   (5) change this to This

2. Sentence 2: **As a matter of fact, from studies, we know that millions of people go on diets each year, unfortunately, 95 percent of the dieters regain the weight they've lost.**

   Which of the following is the best way to write the underlined portion of this sentence? If you think the original is the best way, choose option (1).

   ① ② ③ ④ ⑤

   (1) year, unfortunately,
   (2) year, unfortunately.
   (3) year, unfortunately
   (4) year; unfortunately,
   (5) year unfortunately.

3. Sentence 7: **Chances are that someone in the family will have a new and better idea just when they need it.**

   Which of the following is the best way to write the underlined portion of this sentence? If you think the original is the best way, choose option (1).

(1) they need it. ① ② ③ ④ ⑤
(2) one will be needed.
(3) one is needed.
(4) they needed it.
(5) they will need it.

4. Sentence 8: **One family diet program, for example, tags foods as they enter the house: red for high-fat, high-calorie foods such as candy, ice cream, and chips, yellow for medium-calorie foods such as poultry, bread, and low-fat dairy products; green for the low-calorie foods that can be eaten at any time, such as vegetables, some fruits, and unbuttered popcorn.**

What correction should be made to this sentence?

(1) remove the comma after program ① ② ③ ④ ⑤
(2) change tags to tag
(3) replace the comma after chips with a semicolon
(4) replace the semicolon after products with a comma
(5) no correction is necessary

5. Sentences 10 and 11: **Finally, remember this. The idea that children grow leaner as they grow taller is a myth.**

Which of the following is the best way to write the underlined portion of these sentences? If you think the original is the best way, choose option (1).

(1) remember this. The idea ① ② ③ ④ ⑤
(2) remember this also, the idea
(3) remember this, the idea
(4) remember. That this idea
(5) remember this. That the idea

6. Sentence 12: **Their participation now in a healthful eating plan may prevent them from dieting later.**

What correction should be made to this sentence?

(1) replace Their with There ① ② ③ ④ ⑤
(2) replace now with at this time
(3) change healthful to healthy
(4) insert a semicolon after plan
(5) no correction is necessary

Items 7 to 13 refer to the following paragraphs.

(1) Spending money is easier to do than ever before. (2) Because of computer technology. (3) Industry and Wall Street exchanged vast amounts of money in different markets around the world just by pressing buttons on a computer terminal. (4) Shoppers still use checks and credit cards to complete there purchases. (5) Banks and stores, however, are intent upon making the act of spending money even easier and faster.

(6) Everyday finances and purchases will become more computerized in the future. (7) That's with the use of the new EFT (Electronic Fund Transfer) card and the computer. (8) A banks computers will transfer money from your account directly to the store's bank account. (9) With this system, you, the customer, won't need cash, check, or credit card. (10) Banks like electronic transfer and so do stores because it makes their bookkeeping simpler.

7. Sentences 1 and 2: **Spending money is easier to do than ever before. Because of computer technology.**

Which of the following is the best way to write the underlined portion of these sentences? If you think the original is the best way, choose option (1).

(1) before. Because ① ② ③ ④ ⑤
(2) before: because
(3) before; because
(4) before because
(5) before, it's because

8. Sentence 3: **Industry and Wall Street exchanged vast amounts of money in different markets around the world just by pressing buttons on a computer terminal.**

What correction should be made to this sentence?

(1) change Wall Street to Wall street ① ② ③ ④ ⑤
(2) change exchanged to exchange
(3) replace vast amounts with a lot
(4) insert a variety of after in
(5) insert a comma after world

9. Sentence 4: **Shoppers still use checks and credit cards to complete there purchases.**

What correction should be made to this sentence?

(1) replace Shoppers with A shopper ① ② ③ ④ ⑤
(2) insert they after Shoppers
(3) insert in order after cards
(4) replace there with their
(5) change purchases to purchase

10. Sentence 5: **Banks and stores, however, are intent upon making the act of spending money even easier and faster.**

What correction should be made to this sentence?

(1) remove the comma after however ① ② ③ ④ ⑤
(2) change are to were
(3) insert more after even
(4) change faster to fastest
(5) no correction is necessary

11. Sentences 6 and 7: **Everyday finances and purchases will become more computerized in the future. That's with the use of the new EFT (Electronic Fund Transfer) card and the computer.**

The most effective combination of sentences 6 and 7 would include which of the following groups of words?

(1) future—that's with the use of ① ② ③ ④ ⑤
(2) future, that's with the use of
(3) future, because that's with the use of
(4) future with the use of
(5) future because of the use of

12. Sentence 8: **A banks computers will transfer money from your account directly to the store's bank account.**

What correction should be made to this sentence?

(1) change banks to bank's ① ② ③ ④ ⑤
(2) insert a comma after your account
(3) insert bank after your
(4) change directly to direct
(5) change store's to stores

13. Sentence 10: **Banks like electronic transfer and so do stores because it makes their bookkeeping simpler.**

If you rewrote sentence 10 beginning with

Both banks and stores like electronic transfer

the next words should be

(1) because they simplify ① ② ③ ④ ⑤
(2) because the bank simplifies
(3) because it simplifies
(4) because you simplify
(5) because it simplified

Items 14 to 19 refer to the following paragraphs.

(1) Many things can and do go wrong within families and that is why so much has been written about the unhappy ones. (2) On the other hand, what do we know about happy families? (3) It is only in the recent past that psychologists and other family therapists were studying the characteristics that happy families have in common. (4) The following are just a few of them.

(5) Happy families spend time together in a pleasant way. (6) Whether they are doing yard work together making dinner or going to a movie, the key word is "pleasant." (7) Pleasant times built up reserves of good feelings so that when troubled times arrive, family members have good feelings to remember. (8) Otherwise, family life means only family problems.

(9) Not surprisingly, happy families spend a lot of time talking to each other. (10) They also yell and fight. (11) The important thing is that they get conflicts out in the open; they share feelings in a straightforward way.

(12) Giving praise and knowing how to receive it are important skills in the happy family. (13) Family members learn to see positive things in others, and then they will learn to say what they see. (14) Families that recognize good qualities—and show it—give each other the warmth and support they need.

14. Sentence 1: **Many things can and do go wrong within families and that is why so much has been written about the unhappy ones.**

What correction should be made to this sentence?

(1) remove and do after can ① ② ③ ④ ⑤
(2) change families to family's
(3) insert a comma after families
(4) change has been to is
(5) replace about with on

15. Sentence 3: **It is only in the recent past that psychologists and other family therapists were studying the characteristics that happy families have in common.**

What correction should be made to this sentence?

(1) insert a comma after past ① ② ③ ④ ⑤
(2) replace that with when
(3) change were to have been
(4) change studying to studied
(5) no correction is necessary

16. Sentence 6: **Whether they are doing yard work together making dinner or going to a movie, the key word is "pleasant."**

What correction should be made to this sentence?

(1) replace Whether with Weather ① ② ③ ④ ⑤
(2) replace they with you
(3) change are doing to have done
(4) insert commas after together and dinner
(5) remove the comma after movie

17. Sentence 7: **Pleasant times built up reserves of good feelings so that when troubled times arrive, family members have good feelings to remember.**

What correction should be made to this sentence?

(1) insert have after times ① ② ③ ④ ⑤
(2) change built to build
(3) replace of good feelings with of well feelings
(4) insert a comma before so
(5) replace the comma after arrive with a semicolon

18. Sentence 11: **The important thing is that they get conflicts out in the open; they share feelings in a straightforward way.**

If you rewrote sentence 10 beginning with

By sharing feelings in a straightforward way

the next words should be

(1) conflicts are gotten out ① ② ③ ④ ⑤
(2) they get conflicts out
(3) they will be getting conflicts out
(4) conflicts get out
(5) they may be getting conflicts out

19. Sentence 13: **Family members learn to see positive things in others, and then they will learn to say what they see.**

Which of the following is the best way to write the underlined portion of this sentence? If you think the original is the best way, choose option (1).

(1) , and then they will learn to say ① ② ③ ④ ⑤
(2) and to say
(3) and then they'll learn to say
(4) , and then they can learn to say
(5) and if they learn to say

Items 20 to 26 refer to the following paragraphs.

(1) It's no longer unusual for both parents in a family to work. (2) Which means that children need care during work hours. (3) Parents are concerned not only with finding affordable day care, but they have to know what makes one center better than another. (4) The best way to make a choice is to visit a few centers and asking questions is a must. (5) It is suggested that parents make an appointment before they visit a center, and then someone will be free to show them around.

(6) An important question to ask is if the center was licensed. (7) If it is, the center follows rules set by the state for the safety and well-being of the children. (8) Other questions can be answered by what is visible in the day care center. (9) The most important is whether or not the children seems happy, busy at tasks and play. (10) The room should be pleasing to look at, bright and colorful, with the children's work in view.

20. Sentences 1 and 2: **It's no longer unusual for both parents in a family to work. Which means that children need care during work hours.**

Which of the following is the best way to write the underlined portion of these sentences? If you think the original is the best way, choose option (1).

(1) It's no longer unusual for both parents in a family to work. Which means ① ② ③ ④ ⑤
(2) It's no longer unusual for both parents in a family to work; which means
(3) The fact that it's no longer unusual for both parents in a family to work means
(4) It's no longer unusual for both parents in a family to work. And this means
(5) It's no longer unusual for both parents in a family to work: Which means

21. Sentence 3: **Parents are concerned not only with finding affordable day care, but they have to know what makes one center better than another.**

Which of the following is the best way to write the underlined portion of this sentence? If you think the original is the best way, choose option (1).

(1) but they have to know ① ② ③ ④ ⑤
(2) but if you know
(3) and they have to know
(4) but—they have to know
(5) but also with knowing

22. Sentence 4: **The best way to make a choice is to visit a few centers and asking questions is a must.**

Which of the following is the best way to write the underlined portion of this sentence? If you think the original is the best way, choose option (1).

(1) and asking questions is a must. ① ② ③ ④ ⑤
(2) and ask questions.
(3) and asking good questions is a must.
(4) and then asking questions.
(5) and asking questions is a must!

23. Sentence 5: **It is suggested that parents make an appointment before they visit a center, and then someone will be free to show them around.**

If you rewrote sentence 5 beginning with

If parents make an appointment before they visit a center,

the next words should be

(1) then someone will be ① ② ③ ④ ⑤
(2) and then someone will be
(3) parents will be
(4) and anyone can
(5) no one will be

24. Sentence 6: **An important question to ask is if the center was licensed.**

What correction should be made to this sentence?

(1) remove to ask ① ② ③ ④ ⑤
(2) insert a comma after question
(3) nsert quotation marks before if and after licensed
(4) change was to is
(5) change was to were

25. Sentence 7: **If it is, the center follows rules set by the state for the safety and well-being of the children.**

What correction should be made to this sentence?

(1) remove the comma after is ① ② ③ ④ ⑤
(2) change follows to will be following
(3) insert a comma after safety
(4) remove the hyphen from well-being
(5) no correction is necessary

26. Sentence 9: **The most important is whether or not the children seems happy, busy at tasks and play.**

What correction should be made to this sentence?

(1) replace whether with weather ① ② ③ ④ ⑤
(2) change seems to seem
(3) remove the comma after happy
(4) change busy to busier
(5) insert a comma after tasks

Items 27 to 33 refer to the following paragraphs.

(1) How many times have you been told that to much fat, cholesterol, sugar, or salt can cause serious health problems? (2) It is a subject often discussed and written about. (3) People are beginning to believe that to protect their health you have to know what packaged foods contain.

(4) Public health experts agree that we need as much information as possible from labels. (5) After all, more than half of the thousands of food products sold are processed. (6) They need to know what's in food.

(7) Labels list ingredients in order of amounts. (8) The ingredient present in the largest amount are listed first. (9) On a cereal label, for example, if sugar is listed first. (10) Yet, that probably isn't the whole story. (11) Sugars have different names and were listed separately as sucrose, dextrose, or inert sugar. (12) Other sweeteners are honey, molasses, corn syrup, and corn sweetener. (13) When you add up all the sweeteners, you have a lot more than you thought.

27. Sentence 1: **How many times have you been told that to much fat, cholesterol, sugar, or salt can cause serious health problems?**

What correction should be made to this sentence?

(1) insert a comma after <u>times</u> ① ② ③ ④ ⑤
(2) replace <u>been told</u> with <u>heard</u>
(3) replace <u>to</u> with <u>too</u>
(4) remove the comma after <u>sugar</u>
(5) remove <u>can</u>

28. Sentence 3: **People are beginning to believe that to protect their health you have to know what packaged foods contain.**

What correction should be made to this sentence?

(1) change <u>are</u> to <u>were</u> ① ② ③ ④ ⑤
(2) change the spelling of <u>believe</u> to <u>beleive</u>
(3) replace <u>their</u> with <u>they're</u>
(4) replace <u>you</u> with <u>they</u>
(5) change <u>contain</u> to <u>contains</u>

29. Sentence 4: **Public health experts agree that we need as much information as possible from labels.**

What correction should be made to this sentence?

(1) change <u>health</u> to <u>Health</u> ① ② ③ ④ ⑤
(2) insert a comma after <u>agree</u>
(3) replace <u>as much</u> with <u>more</u>
(4) insert a comma after <u>possible</u>
(5) no correction is necessary

30. Sentence 6: **They need to know what's in food.**

What correction should be made to this sentence?

(1) replace They with Consumers ① ② ③ ④ ⑤
(2) change need to needs
(3) replace know with no
(4) change what's to what is
(5) no correction is necessary

31. Sentence 8: **The ingredient present in the largest amount are listed first.**

Which of the following is the best way to write the underlined portion of this sentence? If you think the original is the best way, choose option (1).

(1) amount are listed ① ② ③ ④ ⑤
(2) amounts is listed
(3) amount is listed
(4) amounts is listing
(5) amount have been listed

32. Sentence 9: **On a cereal label, for example, if sugar is listed first.**

Which of the following is the best way to write the underlined portion of this sentence? If you think the original is the best way, choose option (1).

(1) if sugar is ① ② ③ ④ ⑤
(2) when sugar is
(3) sometimes if sugar is
(4) because sugar is
(5) sugar may be

33. Sentence 11: **Sugars have different names and were listed separately as sucrose, dextrose, or inert sugar.**

What correction should be made to this sentence?

(1) change have to has ① ② ③ ④ ⑤
(2) change were to are
(3) change separately to separate
(4) insert a comma after separately
(5) replace or with and

Items 34 to 40 refer to the following paragraphs.

(1) A look at America's History tells us that we haven't always used renewable resources wisely. (2) In the 1620's, America's forests was huge. (3) One story tells about an imaginary squirrel. (4) Supposedly, it traveled through the treetops from the Atlantic ocean to the Mississippi River and never once had to touch the ground.

(5) What happened to the forests, our supposedly renewable resource? (6) It has taken only three hundred years for people to destroy one third of those forests. (7) How did this happen? (8) Settlers moved across the country as they did, they became accustomed to using natural resources. (9) They didn't establish the habit of helping resources to renew or improve. (10) Now at least we have begun to learn some important facts about conservation. (11) With care we can conserve forests, farmland, and surface water. (12) These can even be improved.

34. Sentence 1: **A look at America's History tells us that we haven't always used renewable resources wisely.**

What correction should be made to this sentence?

(1) remove the apostrophe from America's ① ② ③ ④ ⑤
(2) change History to history
(3) change tells to tell
(4) replace that with when
(5) change haven't always to always haven't

35. Sentence 2: **In the 1620's, America's forests was huge.**

What correction should be made to this sentence?

(1) remove the apostrophe from America's ① ② ③ ④ ⑤
(2) replace the comma after 1620's with a colon
(3) change America's forests to the forests of America
(4) change forests to forests'
(5) change was to were

36. Sentence 4: **Supposedly, it traveled through the treetops from the Atlantic ocean to the Mississippi River and never once had to touch the ground.**

What correction should be made to this sentence?

(1) insert the squirrel after Supposedly, ① ② ③ ④ ⑤
(2) replace the comma after Supposedly with a dash
(3) change Atlantic to atlantic
(4) change ocean to Ocean
(5) insert a semicolon after River

37. Sentence 6: **It has taken only three hundred years for people to destroy one third of those forests.**

If you rewrote sentence 6 beginning with

In only three hundred years

the next words should be

(1) it has taken ① ② ③ ④ ⑤
(2) only three hundred people
(3) people have taken
(4) people can destroy
(5) people have destroyed

38. Sentence 8: **Settlers moved across the <u>country as they</u> did, they became accustomed to using natural resources.**

Which of the following is the best way to write the underlined portion of this sentence? If you think the original is the best way, choose option (1).

(1) country as they ① ② ③ ④ ⑤
(2) country—as they
(3) country. Because they
(4) country, as they
(5) country. As they

39. Sentence 10: **Now at least we have begun to learn some important facts about conservation.**

What correction should be made to this sentence?

(1) insert commas before and after <u>at least</u> ① ② ③ ④ ⑤
(2) change <u>begun</u> to <u>began</u>
(3) replace <u>learn</u> with <u>teach</u>
(4) change <u>facts</u> to <u>fact</u>
(5) no correction is necessary

40. Sentences 11 and 12: **With care we can conserve forests, farmland, and surface water. These can even be improved.**

The most effective combination of sentences 11 and 12 would include which of the following groups of words?

(1) water; and even improve them. ① ② ③ ④ ⑤
(2) water while these can even improve.
(3) water and can even improve them.
(4) water. While these can even improve.
(5) water. they can even be improved.

Items 41 to 48 refer to the following paragraphs.

(1) Did your landlord refuse to return your $250 security deposit but you left the apartment in its original condition? (2) Has your electrician gone off on vacation with your $75, leaving you in the dark? (3) Don't give up. (4) You don't have to incur a lawyer's fee to get your money back. (5) In your local district, use the Small Claims Court to pursue your grievance instead.

(6) Whether you had an oral or written contract—up to $1,000—your money may be recovered. (7) Although it may not be able to get the plumber to finish the work, it can order a refund. (8) Filing a claim is not expensive it will cost you under $10. (9) The plaintiff will receive a date to appear in court by certified mail. (10) You may either bring a witness with you, or have one summoned by the judge for another small fee. (11) As for your electrician, either he will appear willingly in court, or the court ordered a sheriff to escort him there.

41. Sentence 1: **Did your landlord refuse to return your $250 security deposit but you left the apartment in its original condition?**

Which of the following is the best way to write the underlined portion of this sentence? If you think the original is the best way, choose option (1).

(1) but ① ② ③ ④ ⑤
(2) even though
(3) when
(4) while
(5) perhaps

42. Sentence 2: **Has your electrician gone off on vacation with your $75, leaving you in the dark?**

What correction should be made to this sentence?

(1) change gone to went ① ② ③ ④ ⑤
(2) replace your with you're
(3) replace the comma after $75 with a semicolon
(4) change $75 to $seventy five
(5) no correction is necessary

43. Sentence 5: **In your local district, use the Small Claims Court to pursue your grievance instead.**

If you rewrote sentence 5 beginning with

Instead, you can use the Small Claims Court

the next words should be

(1) in your local district to ① ② ③ ④ ⑤
(2) to pursue your grievance in
(3) to pursue your local district
(4) and which is in your local district
(5) in which you will be able to pursue

44. Sentence 7: **Although it may not be able to get the plumber to finish the work, it can order a refund.**

What correction should be made to this sentence?

(1) replace Although with When ① ② ③ ④ ⑤
(2) insert a comma after Although
(3) replace it may with the court may
(4) change the spelling of plumber to plummer
(5) replace order with demand

45. Sentence 8: **Filing a claim is not expensive it will cost you under $10.**

Which of the following is the best way to write the underlined portion of this sentence? If you think the original is the best way, choose option (1).

(1) expensive it ① ② ③ ④ ⑤
(2) expensive, it
(3) expensive, and it
(4) expensive; it
(5) change the spelling of Filing to Fileing

46. Sentence 9: **The plaintiff will receive a date to appear in court by certified mail.**

What correction should be made to this sentence?

(1) change the spelling of plaintiff to plaintif ① ② ③ ④ ⑤
(2) change will receive to received
(3) replace date with time
(4) change court to Court
(5) remove by certified mail and place it after receive

47. Sentence 10: **You may either bring a witness with you, or have one summoned by the judge for another small fee.**

What correction should be made to this sentence?

(1) replace the comma with a period ① ② ③ ④ ⑤
(2) change either bring to bring either
(3) replace one summoned by the judge with the judge summon one
(4) change judge to Judge
(5) no correction is necessary

48. Sentence 11: **As for your electrician, either he will appear willingly in court, or the court ordered a sheriff to escort him there.**

What correction should be made to this sentence?

(1) change either he will to he will either ① ② ③ ④ ⑤
(2) change he after either to him
(3) replace the comma after electrician with a colon
(4) change willingly to willing
(5) change ordered to will order

Items 49 to 55 refer to the following paragraphs.

(1) When you're looking for a job, you enlist all your friends and family for ideas and contacts. (2) Sometimes, though, after doing that and after checking the newspaper ads. (3) You may still want to use an employment service.

(4) Two kinds of services exist to help you: public and private. (5) Partially supported by the federal government, most states run a cooperative placement service free of charge. (6) Here, all of the job applicants is tested, interviewed, and matched with job listings. (7) The alternatives to public employment services are the private ones that charge fees to companies and individuals.

(8) Private employment agencies serve their client companies by maintaining a list of available jobs for which they interview and screen candidates. (9) For jobseekers, the agency provides counseling, helps with resumes, gives information about the job, schedules interviews with the employer, and will search for a position that suits the applicant's needs.

(10) If you work with a private agency, be sure you understand the conditions of a contract before you sign them. (11) Most importantly, understand what "Fee paid by the employer" does and does not mean. (12) It should mean that if you fulfill your promise by accepting and keeping the job, the employer will pay it. (13) Find out if you were obligated to pay the fee if, for example, you're forced to leave the job by illness or a move. (14) Finally, what if you're offered a job that is not listed with the agency? (15) Before you accept the job you should clarify the fee obligation with the employer and the agency.

49. Sentences 2 and 3: **Sometimes, though, after doing that and after checking the newspaper ads. You may still want to use an employment service.**

Which is the best way to write the underlined portion of these sentences? If you think the original is the best way, choose option (1).

(1) ads. You ① ② ③ ④ ⑤
(2) ads. And then you
(3) ads; you
(4) ads, you
(5) ads you

50. Sentence 6: **Here, all of the job applicants is tested, interviewed, and matched with job listings.**

What correction should be made to this sentence?

(1) remove the comma after Here ① ② ③ ④ ⑤
(2) change is to are
(3) remove the comma after interviewed
(4) change the spelling of applicants to aplicants
(5) insert a comma after matched

51. Sentence 10: **If you work with a private agency, be sure you understand the conditions of a contract before you sign them.**

What correction should be made to this sentence?

(1) replace If with Since ① ② ③ ④ ⑤
(2) remove the comma after agency
(3) change conditions to condition
(4) replace you sign with one signs
(5) replace them with it

52. Sentence 12: **It should mean that if you fulfill your promise by accepting and keeping the job, the employer will pay it.**

What correction should be made to this sentence?

(1) replace It should with The job should ① ② ③ ④ ⑤
(2) change the spelling of fulfill to fullfil
(3) change keeping to keep
(4) replace the comma after job with a semicolon
(5) replace pay it with pay the agency fee

53. Sentence 13: **Find out if you were obligated to pay the fee if, for example, you're forced to leave the job because of illness or a move.**

What correction should be made to this sentence?

(1) change were to are ① ② ③ ④ ⑤
(2) remove the commas after if and example
(3) replace you're with your
(4) change forced to being forced
(5) insert out of town after move

54. Sentence 14: **Finally, what if you're offered a job that is not listed with the agency?**

What correction should be made to this sentence?

(1) remove the comma after Finally ① ② ③ ④ ⑤
(2) change the spelling of offered to offerred
(3) insert a comma after job
(4) change that is not to that isn't
(5) no correction is necessary

55. Sentence 15: **Before you accept the job you should clarify the fee obligation with the employer and the agency.**

What correction should be made to this sentence?

(1) replace Before with When ① ② ③ ④ ⑤
(2) replace you accept with one accepts
(3) insert a comma after job
(4) insert a semicolon after job
(5) change clarify to have clarified

WRITING SKILLS TEST, PART II

Directions*

This part of the Writing Skills Test is intended to determine how well you write. You are asked to write an essay that explains something or presents an opinion on an issue. In preparing your essay, you should take the following steps:

1. Read carefully the directions and the essay topic given below.
2. Plan your essay carefully before you write.
3. Use scratch paper to make any notes.
4. Write your essay on the lined pages of the separate answer sheet.
5. Read carefully what you have written and make any changes that will improve your essay.
6. Check your paragraphs, sentence structure, spelling, punctuation, capitalization, and usage, and make any necessary corrections.

You will have 45 minutes to write on the topic below.

America's youth has always been a major concern of the American people. Opinions on the youth of our nation differ widely. Some people have a high regard for America's young. Others wonder "what the youth of America is coming to."

In an essay of about 200 words, present your views on America's youth today. Your evaluation may include positive or negative arguments or both. Support your views with appropriate reasons and examples.

END OF EXAMINATION

* These directions are reprinted from *The Official Teacher's Guide to the Tests of General Educational Development* with permission from the American Council on Education.

ANSWER KEY

Practice Test

1. (5)
2. (4)
3. (3)
4. (3)
5. (1)
6. (5)
7. (4)
8. (2)
9. (4)
10. (5)
11. (4)
12. (1)
13. (3)
14. (3)
15. (3)
16. (4)
17. (2)
18. (2)
19. (2)
20. (3)
21. (5)
22. (2)
23. (1)
24. (4)
25. (5)
26. (2)
27. (3)
28. (4)
29. (5)
30. (1)
31. (3)
32. (5)
33. (2)
34. (2)
35. (5)
36. (4)
37. (5)
38. (5)
39. (1)
40. (3)
41. (2)
42. (5)
43. (1)
44. (3)
45. (4)
46. (5)
47. (3)
48. (5)
49. (4)
50. (2)
51. (5)
52. (5)
53. (1)
54. (5)
55. (3)

Guide to Grammatical Terms

The grammatical terms in this guide that have counterparts throughout the book are simply defined. Those that are newly introduced in this glossary include examples.

Adjective: A word that describes a noun or pronoun. *Adjectives* are descriptive words explained in Chapters 3 and 4.

Adverb: A word that describes a verb, an adjective, or another adverb. *Adverbs* are also explained as descriptive words in Chapters 3 and 4.

Antecedent: The noun or pronoun to which a pronoun refers. The antecedent may appear earlier in the sentence or in a preceding sentence.

Uniforms should not be given to employees until *they* have been pressed. (Who or what should be pressed?)

A common grammatical problem is that of using pronouns without clear antecedents. *They* does not have a clear antecedent. Although *they* refers to *uniforms,* it is closer to *employees.* Pronouns should be as close as possible to their antecedents.

She told the receptionist her phone was not working. (Whose phone?)

Compound Sentence: Two or more independent clauses (subject + verb) joined by a semicolon or a comma + and.

The new policy offers no additional services, and it costs twice as much.

Complex Sentence: One independent clause (subject + verb) + one or more dependent clauses (clauses that cannot stand alone as sentences).

If I have time, I will finish the report today

The new policy offers no additional services and costs twice as much.

Conjunction: A word that connects words or phrases. Common conjunctions: and, but, so.

Iris works at the bookstore and she attends computer classes.

Conjunctive Adjective: A word that connects the main clauses of a compound sentence (see definition).

I missed my train; *therefore,* I was late for work.

Demonstrative Pronoun/Adjective: *This*, *that*, *these*, and *those* are demonstrative pronouns/adjectives. Use determines correct label. *This* and *that* are singular, and *these* and *those* are plural. *This* and *those* refer to persons and things closer. *That* and *these* refer to things farther. Demonstratives can be used in place of nouns (pronouns) or to describe nouns (adjectives).

Dangling Modifier: A modifier that does not make sense in the sentence. It just *dangles.*

After writing the proposal, the computer shut down before Sam could correct his errors. (The computer did not write the proposal.)

Direct Object: A noun or pronoun that receives action.

Juan threw the ball. (*Ball* is the direct object.)

Indirect Object: A noun or pronoun that indirectly receives the action.

Juan threw the ball to me. (*Me* is the indirect object.)

Intransitive Verb: "Passive voice" verbs—the subject receives the action. It does not perform the action.

The ball was thrown to first base. (*Ball* receives the action; it was thrown.)

Linking Verb: See *State of Being Verb.*

Noun: Person, place, or thing

Objective Complement: See *Predicate Noun* and *Predicate Adjective*. A word or phrase that follows a linking verb and either is the same as the subject, describes the subject, or tells more about the linking verb. Linking verbs are described in Chapter 7, *Linking Words.*

Predicate Adjective: Adjective that follows a linking verb (see definition). It describes the subject. Linking verbs are described in Chapter 7,

Linking Words. The words in italics below are predicate adjectives.

The eggs smell *rotten.*

Harry seems *tired.*

Maury is *tall.*

Predicate adjectives can also be used to tell more about the linking verb as they describe the subject.

The thunderstorm became *severe.*

Predicate Noun: Noun that follows a linking verb (see definition). The linking verb acts like an equal sign: the predicate noun is the same person, place, or thing as subject, and defines it. Linking verbs are described in Chapter 7, *Linking Words.*

Mary is the *district manager.*

Preposition: A small word that relates nouns or pronouns to other words. Prepositions begin descriptive phrases and are explained in Chapter 5.

Pronoun: A word that takes the place of a noun. Pronouns are explained in Chapter 10.

Simple Sentence: One independent clause (subject + verb; subject + verb + object)

My plan won't work.

State of Being Verb: Verbs that don't act, but *are.* Linking verbs are described in Chapter 7, *Linking Words.* Some linking verbs: *appear, be, seem, smell.*

Subject: The person or thing acting in the sentence. In Chapter 1, we refer to *subjects* as *performers.*

Transitive Verb: Verb that shows action; the subject acts. These are "active voice" verbs and they always take a direct object.

The boy *hits* the ball.

Verb: The action in the sentence. In Chapter 1, we refer to *verbs* as *actions.*